Understanding Creative Users of ICTs

The disjuncture between the design intent of the developers of ICTs and the needs of the users has often led to surprising use of new technologies, as users have refused to become mere agents of the designers. Individual users have adopted their own uses of ICTs based on the complex webs of relations and meanings in which they function as social actors. Instead of adjusting these webs to new ICTs, they have fit the ICTs into their pre-existing social webs, often resulting in imaginative and creative uses of new technologies, not envisaged by the original designers.

The contributions in this volume provide studies of such integrations of ICTs into the lives of human users, and demonstrate that such uses should not be regarded as 'faulty' or 'mistaken', merely because they 'fail' to meet the expectations of the original designers of the ICTs. Instead, human users should be given precedence over ICTs, and the creative uses of 'universal' technologies by individual users should be emphasised and studied, so as to move towards a better understanding and appreciation of the integration of ICTs into human lives.

This book was originally published as a special issue of *The Information Society.*

David Kurt Herold taught and researched in China for over nine years, before joining the Hong Kong Polytechnic University as Lecturer for Sociology. His research focuses on the use of ICTs by humans, online and offline China, encounters between Chinese and non-Chinese online, and online education.

Harmeet Sawhney studied engineering, business, mass communication, and telecommunications policy and worked in marketing and advertising before joining the faculty of the Department of Telecommunications, Indiana University, Bloomington. His research interests focus on how telecommunications networks are envisioned and created.

Leopoldina Fortunati studied letters and philosophy before embracing sociology. She taught at several Italian universities before joining the Faculty of Education and the Department of Human Sciences, University of Udine, Italy. Her research interests focus on cultural processes and social phenomena, and in particular on the practices of use of communication and information technologies.

Understanding Creative Users of ICTs

Users as Social Actors

Edited by
David Kurt Herold, Harmeet Sawhney and Leopoldina Fortunati

Routledge
Taylor & Francis Group
LONDON AND NEW YORK

First published 2012
by Routledge
2 Park Square, Milton Park, Abingdon, Oxon, OX14 4RN

Simultaneously published in the USA and Canada
by Routledge
711 Third Avenue, New York, NY 10017

Routledge is an imprint of the Taylor & Francis Group, an informa business

This book is a reproduction of *The Information Society*, vol. 26, issue 4. The Publisher requests to those authors who may be citing this book to state, also, the bibliographical details of the special issue on which the book was based.

British Library Cataloguing in Publication Data
A catalogue record for this book is available from the British Library

ISBN13: 978-0-415-69747-7

Typeset in Times New Roman
by Taylor & Francis Books

Disclaimer
The publisher would like to make readers aware that the chapters in this book are referred to as articles as they had been in the special issue. The publisher accepts responsibility for any inconsistencies that may have arisen in the course of preparing this volume for print.

Contents

Introduction

David Kurt Herold, Harmeet Sawhney and Leopoldina Fortunati

Developmental discourses on the introduction, diffusion, or domestication of new technology emphasise the affordances new technologies and their attendant devices offer, and their influence on the lives of users of new technologies. While neither linear nor deterministic, such discourses still convey the idea that new technologies are responsible for changes to the lives of their users, and that users welcome or dislike these changes. However, as the studies collected here demonstrate, users of different forms of ICT devices often focus less on the various affordances of new technologies and are more concerned with their integration into the users' pre-existing life-styles and attendant habits and usages. The users' life-styles and their socio-economic context to a large extent determine how a specific technological device is employed and given meaning.

In the course of this integration, ICT users frequently employ new technologies in 'wrong' ways or they 'redesign' technology, i.e. they come to usage decisions not envisaged by the original designers of the new technology (Goggin & Newell 2007, 159). These usage decisions lead to 'new' or 'different' ways of utilising devices, and create new habits in the lives of the users, until the new device is fully 'domesticated' (see the study by Quandt and von Pape in this volume), or as Andy Clark puts it in quasi-poetic language (Clark 2003, 197):

> Our brains and bodies couple to new tools, yielding new extended thinking systems. These new thinking systems create new waves of designer environments, in which yet further kinds of extended thinking systems emerge.

This 'misuse' or 'expression of user creativity' is often the consequence of a 'can do, will do' mindset among ICT developers, who ignore the (potential) needs of end users. Developers push technological boundaries, explore new technologies, and attempt to bring the most 'powerful' feature-sets to market, regardless of possible usage decisions, or as Leslie Haddon (2005, 2) put it: 'Technology developers tend to be pragmatic, their everyday life concern is to build something that did not exist before and that can be said to work.' Be it that ever faster computers have to be developed, or increasingly sophisticated car engines, or flight computers smarter and with faster reaction time than the human pilots, or full HD-video in hand-held video cameras (Thorpe, Nagumo, & Ike 1998, 164).

Within these discourses the perceived 'needs' of targeted end-users are largely unimportant. Science, engineering, etc. are seen as 'the art of the possible', not an answer to user requests. This ultimately very modernist discourse seems to continue to permeate much of the debates on the introduction and use of ICT devices, despite abundant proof of the more post-modern adoption of proffered simulations in the form of lifestyle choices by ICT users (Tobias 2007). Even social scientists seem more concerned with the inclusion of users in 'a democratic process' (Haddon 2005, 2) that leads to inclusive developmental decisions, than in fitting technology into the lives of users. The emphasis is on improving users' lives through an increased and increasingly capable use of technology, and not on providing tools to help users do what they want to do (Akiyoshi & Ono 2008, 292).

The logic of the discourse demands the continued and continuing development of better, faster, smarter, etc. devices, as well as compliant and adaptive human beings, otherwise whole segments of society will find themselves 'excluded'. Governments all over Europe emphasize the affordances technology offers societies to become more 'inclusive', and attempt to find ways to help 'excluded' population groups to adapt to this brave new world. People who can't keep up (with development), are labeled technologically incompetent, or 'less competent' – although it might be more appropriate to question the design choices made by the creators of such exclusionary devices, instead of blaming humans for not being able to keep up with ICTs.

The 'information society' people live in, seems to demand the subordination of human practices to the needs of the machines and ICTs they use, where 'we' humans 'accommodate ourselves to the requirements of new technologies' (Postman 1993, 70). Humans are transformed from being 'possessive individuals' to being 'possessed individuals' whose needs are mere posits for the developers of technology (Kroker 2001, 6). Instead of machines being taught how to fit into the lives of humans, humans are expected to learn how to manipulate ever more complex technological products and to integrate them into their lives (Ling 2008, 336) 'as emerging technologies shift the balance of power between human and machine' (Dinello 2005, 5).

The agency or creativity of users is restricted to finding uses for new ICT gadgets, or to the integration of such gadgets into their lives (Brown, Venkatesh & Bala 2006, 207). However, this limitation and its underlying assumptions constitute a denial of the many forms of resistance against ICTs and the information society by people who refuse to allow machines to control their lives, or who prefer to use them differently (Lamb & Kling 2003, 198). The imperative embedded in these discourses demands the willing submission of human users to new ICT devices, so as to become or remain valuable members of the modern 'information society'. Students who do not know how to use a computer to access the internet, to collate different sources from it, and to edit their sources together with a personal argument in word-processing software are no longer 'fit' to succeed in the labour market and thus become full members of society. The 'proper' use of ICTs has become a measure of an individual's membership in *human* society – more so than even a student's *interpersonal* skills.

The discussion of users and their relationship to ICTs are surprisingly one-dimensional in their unquestioning acceptance of the necessity of technology, as Randy Rutsky (1999, 2) pointed out in his discussion of the underlying presuppositions of technological discourses (see also Cassidy 1998, IX). Even the discourses on user creativity are ultimately too positive about technology and its impact on human lives (see e.g. the chapters in Haddon *et al.* 2005; or Heath & Bell 2006, 252). While this introduction is not be understood as a 'call-to-arms' against ICTs or machines in general, a more thorough approach to ICTs and their meaning and function within *human* society (McCarthy & Wright 2004, 183), rather than the exclusive study of the *Information* Society and how humans fit into it, might be advisable (compare Jones 2006, 1–2; to the enthusiam of Prensky 2001). Roberta Lamb and Rob Kling also argued for such a change of approach, pleading for the

> 'systematic research of complex, highly contextualized ICT use [...], rather than encouraging the study of isolated aspects of ICT use in decontextualized settings' (2003, 219); because 'social actors are not primarily users of ICTs. They often have conflicting and ambiguous requirements about the activities they perform, and the socially legitimate ways in which to perform their work as attorneys, biotechnology research teams, inspectors, plant representatives, real estate brokers, pension fund investors, students, or teachers' (2003, 218).

Involving end-users in design processes

Since the early 1980s, attempts have been made to include users in design processes, both out of a growing conviction of the importance of users, as well as for financial reasons. The attempts have served to help deconstruct and better to understand the process involved in the design of technology. Operators and manufacturers were forced to rethink their internal organisations and technology design processes following market failures of innovative product designs and an increase in competition among ICT producers (Fortunati 2007). In particular in the area of widely used consumer devices, e.g. the mobile phone, users began to expect a greater variety of choices both in the functionality, as well as in the design of each class of devices that reflected the identity and self-understanding of the users. They demanded devices that complemented their lifestyle choices, forcing manufacturers and telecom operators to adjust and diversify their product offerings based on their requirements, thus democratising the design of mobile phones (Fortunati 2006).

The manufacturing re-think was paralleled by a growth of academic studies on the possibilities of 'participatory design', which argued for the creation of user-centric models of design. An inclusion of the end-user in the design process had the goal of changing its focus from the innovation and creativity of professional designers to the needs of the users of ICTs. Although participatory design has been studied for the past thirty years, though, it has proved difficult to implement outside of small-scale and strictly controlled applications.

In one example, Buchmüller, *et al.* (2011) describe a highly successful attempt to construct and implement a more participatory model for design processes, but come to the conclusion that any inclusive design process requires both flexibility, as well as a personal investment by all involved. User choices are not static, and so any truly participatory design has to be adaptable over time, as the design has to change with the preferences of its users, which requires a commitment to a continuous design process by the users, and the realisation and acceptance thereof that no design is ever 'finished' (Maceli & Atwood 2011).

In their study of participatory design in Information Systems Development Bødker, Kensing and Simonsen (2011) came to a similar conclusion and argued that any inclusive design practices require the careful consideration of '*how* to engage *which* users in *what* type of design activities' (2001, 116; emphasis in original). Participatory design projects require additional 'meta-method' projects that function as adaptive 'control' of the design processes, and that are subject to structural, ideological, and other strictures, e.g. the abilities or knowledge of users, budget considerations (time and money), purpose of design projects, etc. (see also Bolmsten 2011, for the need to develop end-user capabilities).

While participatory design might include the actual intended users of specific ICTs, e.g. company employees, the strictures enforced by the 'meta-method' require the involvement of not only the users, but also the 'customers' who finance the design project and often define the 'frame' within which participatory design is allowed to happen, e.g. company managers (Bødker *et al.* 2011, 121–28). Additionally, the *intended* users involved in the design process might not be the same as the *actual* users of the 'finished product', as all design processes 'need to predict the context of use because use time occurs after design time' (Maceli & Atwood 2011, 77).

Marco Cantamessa (2011) suggested that while the diffusion of knowledge about design and design processes made participatory approaches to design unavoidable, the context of actual design projects within industrial environments limited their effectiveness. Instead of user-centric participatory design, he suggested that the design 'artifacts' should be seen as the focus points of design processes, and that 'participation' of users, stakeholders, or customers was restricted to evaluations of their usage decisions by designers and producers of the 'artifacts', e.g. through market research, which could be fed back into the design process with the goal of adapting 'artifacts' to users. Participatory design thus would be limited in 'the real world' to the creation of feedback mechanisms and usage evaluations, but not be 'true' empowerment of end-users in the design process.

Participatory design radically changes the definition of the profession of 'designer'. As a result, truly participatory projects require not only a willingness to engage users in the design process, but also a renegotiation of e.g. the employment contracts and job descriptions for those who expect to be paid for their work as 'designers'.

> 'The participatory design process becomes a social negotiation among partners, and the designer's responsibility in this process is to faithfully translate, collaborate, and respond to the concerns of the other stakeholders.'
>
> 'These propositions are radical because they fundamentally challenge conceptions of design as a profession and of what it means to be a designer.' (Carroll & Rosson 2007, 244 and 243).

Successful implementation of participatory design approaches into ICT development requires the careful embedding of the process and its entire context into 'communities of design' in which technical skills, e.g. knowledge of design theory, do not lead to empowerment through professionalism, but are employed to facilitate the design processes within the community. Additionally, participatory design has to 'demonstrate that PD can deliver ICT designs that appeal both to users and to those who pay' (Kyng 2010a, 50).

Morten Kyng (2010a, 2010b) argued convincingly that one of the biggest challenges for participatory design is to get away from 'ideals' to the development of practicable design processes, which can be implemented in real-life situations, involving all the stakeholders. He concluded that unless participatory design is cost- and time-effective in production, and appealing to *paying* customers it will not be employed, whether in the design of new ICTs, or of university courses (Kyng 2010b, 99).

Although the ideals of participatory design are very appealing, and promise to lead to a move away from a focus on ICTs to more user-centric models of technology use, their 'successful' implementation or widespread adoption remains in doubt. As this volume demonstrates, users still feel ignored by designers of ICTs, and still have to 'redesign' technological 'artefacts' to meet their needs.

Usage disjunctures

Each of the studies collected here presents research of a less than perfect integration of ICTs into the lives of human actors. Each of the disjunctures discussed offers a perspective on the lack of integration of technology into human society by elaborating on the responses of human actors to the adoption of specific ICTs into their lives. Each of them offers an illustration for Albert Borgmann's contention that the introduction of technological devices into the lives of humans always cause ruptures, and that 'a timesaving device creates a hole in traditional practices no less than does a device that devours time' (1992, 112).

The discussions offer very different approaches to a variety of topics. The common thread running through them is the observation that the adoption of a form of ICT does not always produce the anticipated results, but can lead to problems and individual adaptations. The introductions of ICTs into the lives of individuals do not follow predictable patterns, nor are they without their specific challenges. Individual users are social actors, interacting with other individuals and groups often within institutionalised settings. New ICTs do not suddenly improve the lives of individuals upon their introduction, but disrupt and change complex social webs, often with unexpected or even undesired consequences (Wilding 2009).

In their perspective piece on the online interactions between audiences and the producers of newspapers, Leopoldina Fortunati and Mauro Sarrica argue for the adoption of a socio-technical approach to study the ways in which technology is employed and how the usages of technology are shaped by factors independent of technology. They demonstrate how editors and journalists of online versions of newspapers are employing the affordances of ICTs in the transmission of news and the elicitation of feedback from their audience, without integrating these uses of ICTs into a new socio-technical system. The adoption of ICTs does not follow a strategic plan for the incorporation of new possibilities into the relationship between editors, journalists, and audiences, but seems to happen ad-hoc as new technologies are developed and become fashionable. Online news sites allow for more input and feedback by the audiences than ever before, which is however underutilised as the necessary mechanisms are not in place to cope with this audience input. Neither journalists nor audiences are involved in decisions about ICTs as editors increasingly base their decisions on the availability of technology instead of its suitability within the existing framework of the newspaper.

Helen Kennedy, Simon Evans, and Siobhan Thomas also discuss the problems that emerge from the lack of consideration of end users among designers and creators of ICT affordances. In an effort to improve the usability of websites for people with intellectual disabilities (ID), they conducted a project to familiarise web designers with the needs of these users, which demonstrated that the design of web pages depended not on the actual intended users, but rather on the skills, attitudes, and preferences of designers, and the decision makers they work for. While the web designers reacted positively to their opportunity of learning about design requirements of people with ID, the design process of web pages, and the lack of interest or knowledge about potential users among the stakeholders in the design process made the integration of user demands into web page design very difficult. Their data and their conclusions suggest that the creators of web pages in particular, and possibly ICTs in general have not developed strategies to include users in the design process of new ICTs (or even web sites), as the aesthetics and skill levels of the stakeholders, as well as the affordances of the ICTs are deemed sufficient parameters for the design process.

Helen Grace shows how the mobile phone camera has become a tool of empowerment for non-professional photographers, despite not being used to create a photographic record. The phone camera has become an expression of creativity, of beauty, and of self-expression within the moment of taking a picture. Using the evocative example of camera phone use at a Bjork concert, she demonstrates how pictures are taken not to preserve the memory of an event or to share one's perceptions with others, but as an expression of one's presence in the moment. The mobile phone camera flash has become the new 'lighter' at concerts. Moments become real through the photographic 'Here I am' of the mobile phone camera. The camera has turned into an experiential tool that allows its user to claim the experience of specific times and spaces instead of merely recording a memory, or creating a digital work of art for the appreciation of others.

In her study on mobile phone cameras, Dong-Hoo Lee focuses on the ceding of emotional control over an individual's responses to places to the mobile phone and its uploaded pictures. She points to the discrepancy between the expansion of the photographic repertoire of individual amateur photographers through easy-to-handle compact digital cameras and the increased use of sub-standard mobile phone cameras. She argues that with mobile phone cameras the ordinary has become a part of the individual's photographic memory and is shared with the world as such. Photos taken with mobile phones have become a new way of representing a sense of spaces that contributes to the definition and reputation of spaces through the sharing of photos online. They provide voyeuristic closeness while allowing the user to keep the reflective distance necessary to evaluate spaces and to assign values to different spaces online.

Petter Nielsen and Annita Fjuk, in their research on the mobile Internet (MI) before the Apple's iOS and Google's Android OS changed MI, demonstrated that the reasons for the slow adoption of MI by users could be found in the lack of integration of MI into the users' life styles. According to their data MI was only used as a stop-gap measure when access to a PC was either impossible or inconvenient, as the affordances MI provided its users were few, and the perceived costs high. Their final challenge to the mobile phone industry that 'growth in usage may come from actively helping the users accessing existing services, rather than solely developing new innovative services' sounds almost prophetic, in the iPhone, iPad, Android world of 2011, in which Apple's CEO Steve Jobs has proclaimed that we have reached the 'post-PC World', while predicting that mobile devices (and MI) will soon make PCs obsolete, as users will be able to do on them everything they used to use a PC for. Same services, plus different ones.

Carsten Sørensen argues that as a result of ubiquitous encounters between humans and different types of ICTs, individual users of ICTs have shaped (or cultivated) their interactions with ICTs to suit their own individual needs and preferences. Users of interactive software, with its constant demands on the attention of the user, are not merely using all the affordances technology provides, but instead accepting or rejecting the assistance of ICTs in their own ways. While the individual users are typically constantly adapting their ways of interacting with others to changing needs, four different shapes of interactive settings have emerged that are employed by users to automate their regulation and control. Individual users delegate differing amounts of control over their interactions with ICTs and through ICTs with others to the ICTs themselves. Although some users prefer not to delegate the management of their interactions to ICTs, most users choose to allow ICTs to either employ simple filters for instances of ICT communications, or to recognise and classify communications based on pre-defined relationship data, or even to filter entire relationships based on user-defined parameters. In short, human responses to ICT affordances present themselves as a graded acceptance of an ICT's supremacy over an individual's life and interactions with others.

Work habits and the focus of an individual's attention have become a part of the individual's interaction with ICTs rather than the opposite, with humans fighting a rear-guard action to minimize the interruptive quality of ICTs while maximising their productivity. The ubiquitous interactions of humans with ICTs discussed by Christian Licoppe have created the sense of constant availability of individual users, and its concomitant sense of the permissibility of ICT-based interruptions. The general undesirability and discomfort of interruptions have prompted the provision of individually customizable and adaptive notification systems and patterns to minimise the disruptive effect of such interruptions. The customisation provisions of individual notification systems have grown to such an extent that individual users have now become 'pragmatic amateurs' skilled at interpreting the different meanings of a variety of nuances of ICT notifications. ICT notifications and their disruptive qualities have been integrated into the flow of ICT usage to minimize their disruption of the flow while providing enough information about the content of the notification to allow the user to make a choice on whether or not and when to access this content.

The users of ICT notification systems can be presented as actors with choices over their interactions with the ICTs they employ, just as users of digital cameras alongside mobile phone cameras can be portrayed as highly capable photographers with a variety of situation-specific tools. The underlying subtext is still that only the full use of ICTs and their affordances are evidence of the skills of the user, while anything less demonstrates a lack of skills. The 'default position' in human-ICT interactions is the knowledgeable application of ICTs according to its design specifications by the human user, who becomes the agent of the designers, but loses his/her status as a free actor.

Thorsten Quandt and Thilo von Pape in their research also addressed the issue of how ICTs are integrated into a user's pre-existing environment, and they argue that researchers might find it useful to employ the metaphor of a 'domestication' of ICTs to conceptualise this process. They argue that different ICTs are used in different spaces, with different symbolic and social connotations, and that these connotations often determine usage patterns beyond the designs of their creators. They argue that users of ICTs do not adopt a new device in an empty space, but that instead, each new device has to be integrated into a household by the user, in which the new device has to 'compete' for the attention of the user with other ICT devices. The actual use of a device is negotiated between the affordances of its designers, the techno-spatial realities of a user's household, and the user's socio-cultural context. ICT devices are therefore not used merely according to the designs of their creators in predictable or 'designable' usage patterns, but highly individualised and contextualised by each user.

In his study of mobile phone usage among low-income families in Chile, Sebastian Ureta makes similar observations by pointing out that low-income households utilise their mobile phones not as mobile communication devices, but rather as landline substitutions. While mobile phones offer cheap, ubiquitous, and mobile communication affordances, the economic restraints of these households have meant an integration of this new device into their household as an unmovable, shared communication device. The socio-economic context of the users thus dictates their choices in the utilisation of their ICTs. The device is 'domesticated' or adapted to their context, but does not transform the lives of the users. ICTs are not 'neutral' technological devices that provide their built-in affordances to all users equally. Instead, the usage patterns and symbolic meanings of ICTs are determined by the pre-existing conditions of the socio-economic and spatial context of individual users.

While the studies collected here represent very different views on the usage of ICTs by individual human actors, a critical attitude towards the integration of the users into different ICT contexts emerges in each one of them. Instead of focussing on the 'wrong' or 'creative' use of new ICTs by individual users, an approach studying the 'context-free' or 'unnecessary' development of ICT gadgets based on profit-driven market research might prove more beneficial. Humans should not be made to fit into a technological environment. ICTs should be designed to fit into human lives – whether through another look at 'participatory design' approaches, or through a more thorough deconstruction of the discourses surrounding the adoption of ICTs.

References

Akiyoshi, M., and H. Ono. 2008. The Diffusion of Mobile Internet in Japan. *The Information Society,* 24(5):292–303.

Bødker, K., F. Kensing, and J. Simonsen. 2011. Participatory Design in Information Systems Development. In *Reframing Humans in Information Systems Development*, ed. H. Isomäki and S. Pekkola, Vol. 201, 115-134. London: Springer.

Bolmsten, J. 2011. Infrastructuring with a Focus on Developing End-Users Capabilities. In *End-User Development*, ed. M. Costabile, Y. Dittrich, G. Fischer, and A. Piccinno, Vol. 6654, 375–78. Berlin and Heidelberg: Springer.

Borgmann, A. 1992. *Crossing the postmodern divide.* Chicago and London: Chicago University Press.

Brown, S., V. Venkatesh, and H. Bala. 2006. Household Technology Use: Integrating Household Life Cycle and the Model of Adoption of Technology in Households. *The Information Society*, 22(4):205–18.

Buchmüller, S., G. Joost, N. Bessing, and S. Stein. 2011. Bridging the gender and generation gap by ICT applying a participatory design process. *Personal and Ubiquitous Computing*, 1-16.

Cantamessa, M. 2011. Design … but of What? In *The Future of Design Methodology*, ed. H. Birkhofer, 229–37. London: Springer.

Carroll, J. M., and M. B. Rosson. 2007. Participatory design in community informatics. *Design Studies,* 28(3):243–61.

Cassidy, E. J. 1998. Preface: Virtual Futures. In *Virtual Futures: Cyberotics, technology and post-human pragmatism*, ed. J. B. Dixon & E. J. Cassidy, IX–XII. London and New York: Routledge.

Clark, A. 2003. *Natural-Born Cyborgs: Minds, Technologies, and the Future of Human Intelligence.* Oxford and New York: Oxford University Press.

Dinello, D. 2005. *Technophobia!: Science fiction visions of posthuman technology.* Austin, TX: University of Texas Press.

Fortunati, L. 2006. User Design and the Democratization of the Mobile Phone. *First Monday. Special Issue 7*, http://firstmonday.org/htbin/cgiwrap/bin/ojs/index.php/fm/article/view/1615/1530.

Fortunati, L. 2007. Understanding Mobile Phone Design. In *The Social Construction and Usage of Communication Technologies. Asian and European Experiences*, ed. R. Pertierra, 20–47. Diliman, Quezon City: University of the Philippines Press.

Goggin, G., and C. Newell. 2007. The Business of Digital Disability. *The Information Society,* 23(3):159–68.

Haddon, L. 2005. Introduction. In *Everyday Innovators: Researching the Role of Users in Shaping ICT's*, ed. L. Haddon, E. Mante, B. Sapio, K.-H. Kommonen, L. Fortunati and A. Kant, 1–16. Dordrecht: Springer.

Haddon, L., E. Mante, B. Sapio, K.-H. Kommonen, L. Fortunati, and A. Kant, ed. 2005. *Everyday innovators: Researching the role of users in shaping ICT's.* Dordrecht: Springer.

Heath, P., and N. Bell. 2006. The Changing World of Home Technology: A Microsoft Case Study. *The Information Society*, 22(4):251–59.

Jones, S. E. 2006. *Against technology: From the Luddites to Neo-Luddism*. London and New York: Routledge.

Kroker, A. 2001. *The possessed individual: Technology and the French postmodern*. Montreal: CTheory.

Kyng, M. 2010a. Bridging the gap between politics and techniques: On the next practices of participatory design. *Scandinavian Journal of Information Systems,* 22(1):49–68.

Kyng, M. 2010b. On the multifaceted future of participatory design: A response to the responses. *Scandinavian Journal of Information Systems*, 22(1):93–102.

Lamb, R., and R. Kling. 2003. Reconceptualizing Users as Social Actors in Information Systems Research. *Management Information Systems Quarterly*, 27(2):197–236.

Ling, R. 2008. Should We Be Concerned That the Elderly Don't Text? *The Information Society*, 24(5):334–41.

Maceli, M., and M. Atwood. 2011. From Human Crafters to Human Factors to Human Actors and Back Again: Bridging the Design Time – Use Time Divide. In *End-User Development*, ed. M. Costabile, Y. Dittrich, G. Fischer and A. Piccinno, Vol. 6654, 76–91, Berlin / Heidelberg: Springer.

McCarthy, J., and P. Wright. 2004. *Technology as experience*. Cambridge, MA and London: MIT Press.

Postman, N. 1993. *Technopoly: The surrender of culture to technology*. New York: Vintage Books.

Prensky, M. 2001. Digital natives, digital immigrants. *On the Horizon*, 9(5):1–6.

Rutsky, R. L. 1999. *High techne: Art and technology from the machine aesthetic to the posthuman*. Minneapolis and London: University of Minnesota Press.

Thorpe, L. J., F. Nagumo, and K. Ike. 1998. The HDTV camcorder and the march to marketplace reality. *SMPTE Journal-Society of Motion Picture and Television Engineers*, 107(3):164–77.

Tobias, J. 2007. Accessibility and Product Ecosystems. *The Information Society*, 23(3):183–86.

Wilding, R. 2009. Refugee youth, social inclusion, and ICTs: can good intentions go bad? *Journal of Information, Communication and Ethics in Society*, 7(2/3):159–74.

The Future of the Press: Insights from the Sociotechnical Approach

Leopoldina Fortunati

Department of Economics, Society, and Territory, University of Udine, Udine, Italy

Mauro Sarrica

Department of Communication and Social Research, University of Rome 'Sapienza', Rome, Italy

In Europe and the United States, the decline of newspapers started long before the advent of the Internet. However, the spread of the Internet has accelerated this decline. But is the future of newspapers really endangered? To answer this question, the authors propose that a reflection on the insights the sociotechnical system perspective, drawn from organizational studies, can offer for media research. The authors first analyze four of the main principles of the sociotechnical perspective: open systems, dynamic stability, optimization of technical and social functions, and control of boundaries. They then employ these analytical tools to examine the power relationships between journalists, the publishers, editors, and the audiences. The sociotechnical approach proves to be an interesting approach for the interpretation of the changes occurring in the journalism and for the elaboration of future solutions and management strategies.

THE FUTURE OF THE PRESS

The future of press is a heated and debated issue (Meyer 2004; Bell 2007) and it is also the focus of this position paper. Newspapers sales are stagnant or even declining in European and North American countries (Engel 2003). According to the Newspapers Association of America, the number of employees in this industry decreased 18 percent between 1990 and 2004.[1] However, the health of this industry is not totally negative. The increase in the number of free presses, which do not charge customers, and online Web sites has enlarged newspapers penetration even in industrialized areas (World Association of Newspapers 2008). Globally, sales of newspapers increased 2.6 percent in 2007, and if we also take into account the free press, the growth goes up to 3.7 percent.[2] The pattern varies across regions. In the post-Communist countries, official newspapers collapsed after 1989, but new outlets saw a veritable boom (Sparks and Reading 1994; Sparks 2008). In main Asian countries, the picture is even more positive, thanks to the sharp increase in the distribution of national newspapers (Erni and Chua 2005). China with 107 million newspaper copies, India with 99 million, and Japan with 68 million represent the largest markets in the world (World Association of Newspapers 2008).

Beyond newspaper sales, newspapers have to also grapple with the changing role of newspapers and news professionals (journalists, editors, etc.) in society, especially in European and North American countries. In this case, there is a preoccupation with the analysis of the effects of the Internet on journalism (Sabadin 2007). This approach, however, is exposed to the risks of technological determinism, which stresses the impact of new technologies and thereby makes it difficult to understand the internal institutional dynamics within the media industries. As Jo Bardoel and Mark Deuze argued (2001, 11), "We should be cautious not to mix up technological possibilities with social realities; technology does not determine what will happen here, but it will take a patient process of 'social shaping' that determines what will be the impact of the new communications technologies, especially in the private sphere." Furthermore, the assumption that journalism is a liberal profession[3] distorts our understanding of how deeply outsourcing and the use of user-generated content (often produced by young people) have changed journalism and made it a precarious professional with little job security. Recently, few studies try to interpret this transformation looking at press as one of the industrial sectors characterized by immaterial labor (Deuze and Fortunati forthcoming). In sum, the impact metaphor and the static view of journalism as a liberal profession limit the scope of research and contribute to the widely shared belief that the press is in danger of disappearing.

The need for more analytical depth prompts us to ask: What theoretical instruments can we adopt to understand the origin of this crisis? Do perspectives developed in other fields of studies offer the opportunity to improve not only our interpretation of the current scenario but also of the future dynamics of the print press and our capacity to single out constructive solutions?

We propose that insights from the sociotechnical system perspective, drawn from organizational studies, can enhance our analytical power. We use this framework to focus on the power relationships between journalists, the publishers, editors, and the audiences.

JOURNALISM AS A SOCIOTECHNICAL SYSTEM

The sociotechnical perspective is based on the observation that in all the industrial sectors, a technical system and a social system are always present and simultaneously operating: The global result of the system activity depends on their interrelation. This notion was introduced in the late 1960s to counteract the rather simplistic technological determinism in mainstream organization theory. The term was coined by the Tavistock Institute of Human Relations in Britain, whose researchers argued that "technology merely constrains human action, rather than rigidly determining behavioral outcomes. Conscious choice can build good human relations into the technical workflow. Indeed, for any productive problem there is typically a range of technologically equivalent solutions, with different implications for human relations" (Scott and Marshall 2005, 627).

This perspective looks at organizations (but also at larger entities such as entire industrial sectors) as systems of related parts. Their elements interact with each other and with the external environment to achieve a specific purpose. Systems are open; that is, they receive input from the environment, they transform it into their goals, and they use feedback information to calibrate their output. At the same time, organizations are dynamic: "When changes in environment or organizational practices make current resources inadequate, the organizations attempt to return to a steady state, which may mirror or significantly differ from the state of equilibrium" (Furnham 1997, 74).

The sociotechnical approach was mainly developed for managers with the aim of increasing their appreciation for the importance of consultation, innovation, flexibility, and open-mindedness in the design of work-flow processes. In the course of time, the general analysis of sociotechnical systems has reached, as Luciano Gallino argued (1993), a high degree of elaboration and formalization (Emery 1969, 1980; Thrist, Higgin, Murray and Pollock 1963; Taylor 1986), becoming foundational framework for sociology and psychology of organizations.

Here we briefly sketch four main principles that are at the foundations of the sociotechnical approach (Gallino 1993) and use them to analyze the changes occurring in journalism. Our main hypothesis is that the press as sociotechnical system has suffered because of a specific difficulty in reconciling economic, technical, and social efficiency, as we see in the following points drawn from Gallino (1993):

1. Media as *open systems*. The idea that any system continuously exchanges inputs and outputs with the external environment lies at the core of the sociotechnical approach. Inputs, outputs, and feedbacks influence the relationship between elements of the system as well as its relationships with the external environment. In our case, we may wonder whether journalists were open to the novelties brought by technological innovation, and, vice versa, whether journalists themselves were able to influence the development of new technologies. The journalists' perception of services and functions provided by the Internet offers some interesting insights.

   First, with regard to the relationship between elements of the system (i.e., publishers, editors and journalists), the journalists tend to believe that the implementation of the Internet in newsrooms was led by top-down decisions, largely carried out without appropriate co-management of the process with workers. The consequence of these decisions and behaviors was that journalists were not able to implement the new technology in a creative way, and in many cases, this created an implicit resistance against it (Agostini 2004). Recent data (Fortunati et al. 2009; Sarrica et al. in press) show a substantial acceptance of the Internet by journalists, but some resistance remains, as it is perceived as being less important for traditional (i.e. investigative) journalism tasks.

   Two, with regard to the relationship with the external environment, the Internet could provide a great amount of feedback to news industries. However, this feedback is mainly used by managers to monitor the success of online journals (in terms of number of users and time spent online) and not to improve the content. According to research carried out with a convenience sample of journalists of the most read Italian newspapers, professionals do not receive information about the readership and about the opinions expressed in online forums of their own outlet (Fortunati, Sarrica, and de Luca 2007; Fortunati 2009). These data suggest that the press may suffer from a lack of internal and external interaction.

2. Systems' *dynamic stability*. Theory postulates that a sociotechnical system is able to pass to superior degrees of heterogeneity and complexity, continuing to operate with efficacy and maintaining a relatively satisfactory internal ambience. The journalism sector is far from displaying dynamic stability. The rapid pace of technological change has increasingly challenged press's stability to the point that there is much talk about the death of print newspapers and economic inefficiency of online versions.
   Adopting a multilevel perspective, Frank Geels and Johan Schot (2007) identified four transition pathways: transformation, reconfiguration, technological substitution, and dealignment and realignment. These four shifts depend on the interaction between sociotechnical regimes, niche innovations (where radical innovations take place), and sociotechnical landscape (the exogenous societal context). In our case, as we shall see in the next section, we may wonder if journalism is facing a *reconfiguration* pathway or a *technological substitution*. In both cases, radical innovations (e.g. blogs, twitter) are initially developed in niches but their interaction with the established systems might lead to totally different outcomes. In *reconfiguration* "they have symbiotic relations with the regime, they can be easily adopted as add-on or component replacement. These adoptions are driven by economic considerations: (improve performance, solve small problems), leaving most regime rules unchanged" (Geels and Schot 2007, 411). In *technological substitution*, instead, a sudden change in the landscape gives the niche players new opportunities to enter the market, regime actors try to defend themselves from the technological advanced niches players, but the economic improvement and the fit to the new landscape offered by new technologies often lead to the downfall of incumbent firms.
3. Systems should seek the *optimization of their technical and social functions*. The sociotechnical approach stresses that methods of management that optimize only a few of the systemic functions (e.g., those aimed to optimize the technical-economic performance) result in modest outcome, since those functions that have been ignored or undervalued interfere with those that were the focus of pseudo-optimization. Journalism is a good example of the effects of incomplete optimization on the quality of newspapers and on the professional milieu.
   With regard to newspapers, great amounts of economic resources were saved through the introduction of information and communication technologies in newsroom and in the new production processes (even if this created a great deal of discomfort for journalists). From our perspective, managers took advantage of technological innovations to restructure the sector, but they often decide only from a techno-economic point of view (i.e., using the technology to reduce costs). This seems especially attractive when the focus is on efficient use of content across multiple media platforms. If technological and economical perspective (essentially seen as possibility of costs cutting and increase of profits) will dominate and the sociological and cultural dimensions will be considered marginal, the quality of newspaper will suffer. With regard to this risk, European journalists are somehow ambivalent: They do not think that the Internet threatens the quality of journalism per se, but they acknowledge that online journalism is more exposed to unreliable information, and especially professionals from southern countries are critical about the risks for journalists of becoming "information packers" (Fortunati et al. 2009).
   Underestimation of social and cultural aspects threatens also the professional milieu. The interaction between technological advances and societal changes is destructuring the professional fabric of journalism. Media companies resort to outsourcing that makes several categories of jobs precarious (Deuze and Fortunati forthcoming). The consequence is that journalism is invaded by a large number of nonprofessionals, customers often become content providers, there is a big confusion of role matches, and the production of outcomes is modest. With regard to the difficulty of accepting the online journalism activities as a real profession, in a recent study (Sarrica et al. forthcoming) only one tenth of the 239 interviewed European Union (EU) journalists considered themselves online journalists, whereas a quarter declared a double identity (print and online journalists). Moreover, self-defined professional roles differed across countries, showing the importance of the societal context: A lower percentage of professionals considered themselves "online journalists" in southern countries than in northern EU countries, indicating the persistence of a more "traditional" journalistic environment.
4. The fourth notion, *control of boundaries*, is crucial for the performance of sociotechnical system. This element regards the managerial activity at every level and postulates that sociotechnical systems are able

to realize and regulate transformations autonomously, on condition that the necessary resources are supplied with continuity. The activity of managers should thus assure to the system the regular influx of resources. To effectively do this, managers should locate and control the boundaries of the systems, in order to remove bottlenecks and elements that may disturb the influx of resources. At the end of the production cycle, and without interfering with the internal activity of microsystems, managers should check that the output of the system is the one agreed with the work team. The organizational model of assembly islands, which is one of the most widely employed applications of the sociotechnical thinking, is based on this concept. In this model, the sharing of information and knowledge is particularly relevant: Managers should locate boundaries so that workers can receive useful information and feedback from the organization and can share them with colleagues. The ultimate goal is that every team becomes autonomous in its task and, at the same time, contributes to the goals of the organization.

Can the newsroom be approached in that way? Our impression is that the organization of work in newsrooms is still old-fashioned. Let us see why.

First, as we previously noted, our research in Italy showed that publishers do not widely share the feedback provided by readers on the media website (Fortunati, Sarrica, and de Luca 2007; Fortunati 2009). That is, there are some boundaries that stop the inflow of this relevant resource for journalists and that limit their autonomous interaction with readers. Second, both with Italian and EU convenience samples, journalists show very fragmented knowledge about the initiatives their media organizations set up. For example, they hardly know when their outlet published the online version, whether it provides files in .pdf format, or whether it has Web radio. Sociotechnical research suggests that understanding of the whole productive strategy would foster the motivation to work and generate a sense of belonging to the media organization. Third, the precarious nature of employment in journalism increases dependence rather than the autonomy of employees. On the one hand, this increasing power differential gives the publishers a free hand to impose controls. On the other hand, there is self-censorship on the part of journalists, and that affects the quality of work and undermines job satisfaction.

In sum, the sociotechnical systems theoretical framework seems promising for the study of journalism. It analyzes both social and technical phenomena, individuals and machines, and answers to the call for a greater attention on the two-way path of technization of society and socialization of technology (Ropohl 1982; Bijker, Hughes and Pinch 1987; Bijker and Law 1992; Kling, Rosenbaum, and Sawyer 2005).

What can we learn from the analysis of journalism as a sociotechnical system?

One, we may investigate whether and how old organizational notions are still at work: whether social and cultural aspects are underevaluated, and whether technical advancements are implemented only for their capacity to improve the cost-benefit ratio. Probably this limitation is present in the management of many enterprises, because the value of human and cultural factors and of related processes is difficult to measure, whereas editors and publishers must present concrete data in the shareholders. Nevertheless, the underevaluation of social, cultural, and communicative aspects of the system becomes more dramatic in a field like journalism, whose products are cultural.

Two, we may investigate how societal change and technological improvements interact with the media system. The multilevel perspective (Geels and Schot 2007) offers interesting insights and allows development of hypotheses on the stability of the system, on its radical change in the near future, and on its capacity to evolve by maintaining the same basic structure.

Three, the sociotechnical approach directs attention to interaction between the different elements and to the dynamic and stability in the reciprocal relationships. This is the focus of the next section.

INTERACTION BETWEEN PUBLISHERS, EDITORS, JOURNALISTS, AND AUDIENCES

The sociotechnical perspective also allows consideration of the press as a system characterized by power relationships, which reflects the relative influence of the main players according to the positions they held. This analysis could offer valuable insights for the future of the press. In this section we therefore look at the different actors involved and the changes they are bringing to the press system.

Vigorous confrontation and negotiation is currently underway among three main actors: publishers (and their *longa manus* executive editors), journalists, and audiences. On the one hand, publishers and journalists are involved in a continuous negotiation on the organization of work in newsrooms; on the control over the information content and on the recognition of the immaterial work produced by journalists through adequate financial compensation, freedom, and social status. On the other hand, there are negotiation between professionals (publishers/journalists) and audiences and concerns about the cost and quality of information and the influence that readers have (or may have) on the contents of newspapers.

Editors

Editors' point of view on the future of the press is well-known. According to the Newsrooms Barometer survey (World Editors Forum 2008; sample consisting of 700 editor-in-chiefs and managing editors, all of whom were senior news executives), the percentage of editors who believe that the online platform will be the most used modality to read news is increasing (44 percent vs. 41 percent of the previous year), while the percentage of those who cite print newspapers is decreasing (31 percent vs. 35 percent of the previous year). Only 12 percent of editors indicate "mobile phones" as the future. In accordance with this vision, more than half of editors believe that news in the future will be free and that some editorial functions will be outsourced. But only 45 percent of editors think that the quality of journalism will improve. These opinions mirror publishers' difficulties in defining a successful (in terms of quality of the product and of economic advantage) business model of their increasingly multiform activity. Today they consider themselves producers of information platforms (Küng, Picard, and Towse 2008); however, the majority of them still continue to put the print newspaper at the center and all the other modalities (online publishing and multimedia production) at the periphery. Moreover, the pretense of offering online readers value, by assuring them with the credibility of a great brand, should be considered critically. As we saw, this attitude reflects an attempt of *reconfiguration*: modifying the system to add the technological novelties into it, but leaving regime rules unchanged (e.g., professionals provide credible information, written information is more credible than multimedia). This thinking has shaped how news executives have sought to exploit the opportunities offered by the Internet (Quinn 2005). Research actually shows that some online versions of traditional newspapers remain points of reference for Internet users (Hindman 2008). The "credibility" of strong publishing groups, however, was built in a structural situation of readers' relative impotence; today, the access to the Net allows readers to express frustrations, dissatisfactions, and resistance that were excluded in the unidirectional world of traditional mass media. This shift might change power relationships among the social actors involved and modify even the concept of credibility of important brands. Moreover, we cannot exclude the possibility that further development of online opportunities (e.g., Twitter) will bring a more radical technological substitution.

Readers

The readers are producing an implicit theorization about the future of the press, initiating a powerful practice, which will have considerable consequences for this field. Readers bought computers and access to the Internet, thus becoming the owners of these technologies. This enables users to break out of their traditional subordination and to change their relationship with information, culture, and education. Today the readers are e-actors (Fortunati et al. 2010; Gebhardt, Greif, Lasen, and Lobet-Maris 2010): a social figure that subsumes the roles of consumers, producers, designers, and stakeholders. E-actors are overturning the power relationship with publishing groups, which were the traditional mediators of information, culture, and entertainment (Haas 2005). Former simple users have transformed themselves into competitors (O'Sullivan and Heinonen 2008). They are unusual competitors as they do not have the economic power of the traditional publishing groups and as they have different interests, aims, and perspectives (Gillmor 2004).

Readers are building another autonomous road to information, which has the characteristics of gratuitousness of free press and also most of those features that traditionally were considered indispensable for a good journalism, primarily the direct checking of facts. We-journalism, citizen journalism, and participatory journalism are some of the labels applied to this kind of "grass-roots" journalism, and in the last decade (Bowman and Willis 2003), several studies showed that online news credibility is increasing among both Internet users (Johnson and Kaye 1998) and journalists (Pew Research Center 2004; Cassidy 2007).

Furthermore, readers as e-actors supply immaterial and cooperative labor, from which publishing groups may draw information and ideas without paying. Lev Manovich (2001) captured this condition of Internet users as nonpaid workers since the late 1990s. As several studies report, most journalists regularly use work blogs, news sites, and other Internet technologies (see, e.g., Middleberg/Ross Media Survey 2002). Other surveys show that 64 percent of journalists among an international sample use news from the Internet in their articles (EURO RSCG Magnet and Columbia University Survey of the Media 2005), and that the number of journalists who use the Internet as a tool for newsgathering has increased (Garrison 2003).

Journalists

Journalists can count on a glorious past narrative; however, that narrative is not sufficient to guarantee a future. Journalists are now facing the relationship with publishers in a self-defensive manner (Agostini 2004). The latter, in fact, have been able to use the Internet to reduce the contractual power of journalists, who were once one of the most powerful and best paid professional groups. The reduction of journalists' social power has meant that their independence and autonomy from political and economical groups has been reduced, too. Italy is an example (Censis 2005a),[4] but journalists' social role does not seem to differ much across different countries (Weaver and Wilhoit 1986, 1996; Weaver et al. 2003, 2006; Splichal and Sparks 1994; Deuze 2005). In regard to their relationship with readers, the latter has not considered journalists independent from political power for a long time. It is clear to audiences (see again the case of Italy; Censis 2005b) that information is increasingly becoming an instrument of "conditioned" and limited freedom and is an instrument of power, in particular of economic power (Curran 2002; Deuze 2007). It is also clear to audiences that non-information passes through journalists: Costs of fake and of omitted news are high, and we can only imagine the dimension of silences and omissions that opaquely accomplish the will of the powers that be.

From these premises we can interpret data we collected on journalists' perceptions of the future of the press and on the consequences of the use of the Internet in newsrooms. A survey we carried out with a convenience sample of journalists working in eleven European countries (Fortunati et al. 2009; Sarrica et al. forthcoming) indicates that journalists mainly appreciate the practical opportunities offered by Internet for their job (e.g., search and retrieval functions). However, they "hesitate, as argued by O' Sullivan and Heinonen (2008), to abandon the conventions of traditional journalism, both at organizational and at professional level" (Fortunati et al. 2009, 953). As we already noted, journalists are somehow resistant to editorial multimedia strategies. Moreover, they still tend to prefer unidirectional communications with readers (from professional to audience), and they are ambivalent about online information: They use it, yet they are suspicious of its reliability. On the whole, it seems that journalists are facing the changes of the system with a passive attitude: They try to take advantage of some of the novelties for their everyday tasks without fully considering the wider changes occurring in their profession. Last but not least, the societal context interacts with journalists' perceptions of their future: Relevant differences emerge between countries, mainly between southern and northern ones in Europe, where the latter are more keen to recognize the usefulness of the Internet and the former more resistant and doubtful.

In conclusion, we can say that publishers took the offensive to maintain the structure of the system, audiences are getting empowered, and journalists' social role seems to be decreasing. Within this context, each actor tries to attract technological developments into its influence sphere so as to use them to enhance their relative power. Seen this way, the question of the future of the press gets out of the narrow horizons of technocentric thinking and becomes a social question that involves power conflicts, information as social need, and changes in the relationship between producers and consumers of information.

DIFFERENT APPLIED STRATEGIES

Some publishers are convinced that a solution to the problems of the print press is to move newspapers online and to ask audiences to pay a fee. This fee will be low in the beginning to attract audiences but will create the habit of paying for reading the newspapers online. Later, the fee will increase when the audience for the online newspaper is assured.

This vision is based on economic considerations: The number of print copies sold is decreasing, so consumers are offered the possibility of buying online the same commodity for less. This approach considers print newspapers already dead and tries to elaborate a solution that preserves the same structure of the sociotechnical system, just transposing it on the Internet. In this case the Internet is conceptualized as an instrument of publishing and distributing news. Newspapers distribution earlier moved from the early twentieth century newspapers boys to supermarkets. The Internet is a new, cheaper medium for delivering newspapers, as it moves the costs of distribution onto the shoulders of readers: Users have to pay for the personal computer (maintenance), the electricity, the software, the paper, the ink, the cost of access to the Internet, and so on.

But this approach has several limitations: as it seeks to impose a particular kind of system that in many ways goes against the grain of the Internet. Many questions, such as the following, remain unanswered: (a) Will users accept paying for content, and who will control that content so that the same information will not be copied and shared free online? (b) Research show that people access online newspapers from the workplace or universities. In effect, entrepreneurs now pay for the time their employees spend online, for how long will they accept paying these costs? Will they take charge of the printing costs saved by news companies? (c) Online readers are mainly interested in short articles, and there are many other opportunities to hear or to read short news stories (e.g., accessing Web sites of press agencies). Will readers use the Internet to read longer articles? Comments and interpretations need to be read in a very comfortable situation: in an armchair rather than at the desk. Will the readers choose to print longer articles and to read them afterward?

In sum, the solution preferred by the newspaper industry tries to keep the whole system as it is, without introducing true innovation. The power structure remains untouched, communication is unidirectional (from professional to audience), and the Internet is used only to reduce costs (and to pass them implicitly to readers).

A second view focuses on technological convergence and multimedia platforms. Media organizations passed from being specialized and dedicated to only one medium to organizations in which the concentration of diverse media allows for economies of scale that enable better resistance to market fluctuations. However, this process assumes that the work can be optimized, producing contents for different platforms. For example, the articles for a newspaper could also facilitate content for a Web site or inspire a television program. This is a very problematic operation from a cultural point of view: If we agree with Marshell McLuhan (1964) that the medium is the message, separating the message from the medium is an operation that does not necessarily preserve the quality of the content produced. As noted since the works of Roman Jakobson (2002), the difficulties of the recodification process have to be carefully considered. Also, this vision is very technocratic and is quite indifferent toward considering the changes brought to the sociotechnical system by audience and the effects on the professional role of journalists.

A third view—a technology-driven one—sees the solution in a proper exploitation of the multimedia capabilities offered by the Internet. This vision is endorsed by publishers and journalists. The basic idea here is to provide online users elaborated articles that include video and interactive conversation between audiences and politicians, celebrities, artists, writers, culture representatives, and so on. This view sees in the technological innovation the cure for the crisis and seeks to resolve it through more sophisticated products. Although research on online newspapers shows that videos, for example, are not necessarily more important than text headers in the choices made by readers (Vahlberg et al. 2008), multimedia supporters continue to pursue this goal. They are convinced that the future journalist will be a multimedia journalist, a journalist able to produce for every platform and in multiple languages. This vision has inspired the strategy, applied in several newspapers, of merging print and online newsrooms to optimize the human resources. Interchange between the staffs seems the mantra that accompanies this kind of restructuring of the organizations. It is accompanied by the hope that the new, younger journalists will be more available to become at the same time photographers, directors, audio technicians, and so on.

The focus of this approach is on new languages and innovations, and it thus seems nearer to the technological substitution process than the other two strategies. However, if it will not carefully take into consideration the new role of audiences, it risks reproducing an older model—the television—rather than the Internet.

FINAL REMARKS

All three approaches privilege the economic and technical efficiency relative to social and cultural considerations, which are completely marginalized. This thinking reflects the long-standing illusion that the solution to our problems lie in technology.

The sociotechnical perspective, on the contrary, offers alternative insights and asks for a reflection on the long term configuration of the system that publishers and editors want to achieve. As we saw in the first section, four main points should be addressed to recover a proactive role in the sociotechnical evolution of the press:

- If mass media aim to be open systems, journalists and editors should define how they want to influence the development of new technologies (e.g., do they prefer powerful processors or more portable supports?). In this way, they could fully contribute to the development of future technologies and thus achieve a slow, reciprocal adaptation, rather than dealing with sudden changes imposed by technological advanced niches.
- The dynamic stability of the system requires analytical consideration of the different variables and of their interaction with the exogenous societal context. What kind of transition do the editors envisage? Are they trying to transform the system or are they preparing a veritable technological substitution? What role do journalists and readers want to play in the ongoing transitions? The sociotechnical analysis suggests considering these questions more explicitly and relating them to the different societal contexts.
- External boundaries should be reshaped so that journalists can fully benefit from the information and feedbacks provided by other e-actors (readers, bloggers, etc.) without being overwhelmed. At the same time, internal boundaries need to be reconsidered in order to improve the internal satisfaction of workers.
- Finally, technical and social function should be optimized together. In this regard, the marginalization of journalists and audiences implicit in the three strategies examined in the last section poses serious problems. Journalists and readers, instead, should be involved in the evolution of the system as these are essential elements: the first as workers and the second as e-actors.

If purely economic or technical strategies continue to be pursued, in our opinion, the results will be modest. Sociotechnical analysis rather suggests development of approaches that take care of the new role of audiences and journalists and aspire to really serve (also) their interests and aspirations. This may lead to the development of a new conception of newspapers, in which workers contribute with their specific, and acknowledged, professionalism to multidisciplinary teams; contents are shaped by the active presence of audiences; and press rooms are designed to include the ever-evolving opportunities provided by the Internet and by the next technologies.

NOTES

1. See http://www.naa.org/search.aspx?search=decrease%20of%20employees

2. This increase has recently shown a relative decrease in several industrialized countries.

3. According to the Directive on Recognition of Professional Qualifications (2005/36/EC), "liberal professions" are "those practised on the basis of relevant professional qualifications in a personal, responsible and professionally independent capacity by those providing intellectual and conceptual services in the interest of the client and the public." Here we suggest that outsourcing and the use of user-generated contents (often produced by young people) deeply changed journalism into a precarious and dependent job.

4. The three main criticisms of Italian respondents were as follows: (1) Journalists want to impose their personal point of view when describing facts, so they are biased; (2) they are obsequious toward powerful persons; and (3) it is increasingly more difficult to understand what they write.

REFERENCES

Agostini, A. 2004. *Giornalismi. Media e giornalisti in Italia* [Journalisms: Media and journalists in Italy]. Bologna: Il Mulino.

Bardoel, J., and M. Deuze. 2001. Network journalism: Converging competences of media professional and professionalism. *Australian Journalism Review* 23:91–103. https://scholarworks.iu.edu/dspace/bitstream/handle/2022/3201/BardoelDeuze+NetworkJournalism+2001.pdf?sequence=1 (accessed September 4, 2009).

Bell, E. 2007. End of the offline? *British Journalism Review* 18:47–52.

Bijker, W. E., T. P. Hughes, and T. Pinch.1987. *The social construction of technical systems. News directions in the sociology and history of technology*. Cambridge, MA: MIT Press.

Bijiker, W. E., and J. Law. 1992. *Shaping technology/Building society. Studies in sociotechnical change*. Cambridge, MA: MIT Press.

Bowman, S., and C. Willis. 2003. *We Media. How audiences are shaping the future of news and information*. http://www.hypergene.net/wemedia/download/we_media.pdf (accessed September 4, 2009).

Cassidy, W. P. 2007. Online news credibility: An examination of the perceptions of newspaper journalists. *Journal of Computer-Mediated Communication* 12:478–98.

CENSIS. 2005a. *Cinque anni di evoluzione e rivoluzione nell'uso dei media, 5° Rapporto Censis/Ucsi sulla comunicazione in Italia.* [Five years of evolution and revolution in the use of media]. Rome: Censis. http://www.censis.it/277/372/5357/5657/5665/5671/content.asp (accessed September 4, 2009).

———. 2005b. *I giornalisti e la libertà di stampa* [Journalists and the freedom of the press]. Rome: Censis. http://www.odg.it/download/CENSIS_X_ORDINE.pdf (accessed June 4, 2008).

Curran, J. 2002. *Media and power.* London: Routledge.

Deuze, M. 2005. What is journalism? Professional identity and ideology of journalists reconsidered. *Journalism Theory Practice & Criticism* 6:443–65.

Deuze, M. 2007. *Media work*. Cambridge: Polity.

Deuze, M., and L. Fortunati. Forthcoming. Journalism without journalists. In *News online: Transformations and continuities*, ed. G. Meikle and G. Redden. Basingstoke: Palgrave Macmillan.

Emery, F. E., ed. 1969. *Systems thinking: Selected readings*. Harmondsworth: Penguin.

———. 1980. Designing socio-technical systems for "greenfield" sites. *Journal of Occupational Behaviour* 1:19–27.

Engel, M. 2003. The country where newspaper journalism is dying. *British Journalism Review* 14(1):17–22.

Erni, J. N., and K. S. Chua, eds. 2005. *Asian media studies: Politics of subjectivities*. Malden, MA: Blackwell.

EURO RSCG Magnet and Columbia University Survey of the Media. 2005. *Rebuilding trust: Can credibility be rebuilt in the newsroom and in the boardroom?* http://magnet.mediaroom.com/file.php/binaries/31/RebuildingTrust.pdf (accessed May 31, 2006).

Fortunati, L. 2009. Interactivity and e-Participation. *Communication, Politics & Culture* 42(4):65–86.

Fortunati, L., J. Gebhardt, J. Vincent, A. Petrovčič, and O. Vershinskaya, eds. 2010. *Interacting with broadband society.* Berlin: Peter Lang.

Fortunati, L., M. Sarrica, A. Balcytiete, H. Harro-Loit, P. Macgregor, N. Roussou, R. Salaverría, J. O'Sullivan, and F. de Luca. 2009. The influence of the Internet on European journalism. *Journal of Computer Mediated Communication* 14:928–63.

Fortunati, L., M. Sarrica, and F. de Luca. 2007. L'interattività in redazione. Un'indagine in Italia. *Problemi dell'informazione* 1: 91–116.

Furnham, A. 1997. *The psychology of behaviour at work: The individual in the organization.* Hove, England: Psychology Press.

Gallino, L. 1993. *Dizionario di sociologia* [Dictionary of sociology]. Torino: UTET.

Garrison, B. 2003. How newspaper reporters use the Web to gather news. *Newspaper Research Journal* 24:62–75.

Gebhardt, J., H. Greif, A. Lasen, and C. Lobet-Maris, eds. 2010. *Experiencing broadband society*. Berlin: Lang.

Geels, F. W., and J. Schot. 2007. Typology of sociotechnical transition pathways. *Research Policy* 36:399–417.

Gillmor, D. 2004. *We the media: Grassroots journalism by the people, for the people*. http://www.authorama.com/we-the-media-1.html (accessed September 4, 2009).

Haas, T. 2005. From "public journalism" to the "public's journalism"? Rhetoric and reality in the discourse on Weblogs. *Journalism Studies* 6:387–96.

Hindman, M. 2008. *The myth of digital democracy*. Princeton, NJ: Princeton University Press.

Jakobson, R. 2002. *Saggi di linguistica generale* [Essays of general linguistics]. Milano: Feltrinelli.

Johnson, T. J., and B. K. Kaye. 1998. Cruising is believing? Comparing Internet and traditional sources on media credibility measures. *Journalism & Mass Communication Quarterly* 75(2): 325–40.

Kling, R., H. Rosenbaum, and S. Sawyer. 2005. *Understanding and communicating social informatics: A framework for studying and teaching the human contexts of information and communications technologies*. Medford, NJ: Information Today.

Küng, L., R. G. Picard, and R. Towse, eds. 2008. *The Internet and the mass media*. London: Sage.

Manovich, L. 2001. *The language of new media*. Cambridge, MA: MIT Press.

McLuhan, M. 1964. *Understanding media.* New York: McGraw-Hill.

Meyer, P. 2004. *The vanishing newspaper. saving journalism in the information age*. Collumbia: University of Missouri Press.

Middleberg/Ross Media Survey. 2002. *The eighth annual media survey: Change and its impact on communication.* http://web.archive.org/web/20040407135726/www.middleberg.com/toolsforsuccess/fulloverview_2002.cfm (accessed September 4, 2009).

O'Sullivan, J., and A. Heinonen. 2008. Old values, new media. Journalism role perception in a changing world. *Journalism Practice* 2(3):357–71.

Pew Research Center. 2004. *How journalists see journalists in 2004*. http://people-press.org/reports/pdf/214.pdf (accessed September 4, 2009).

Quinn, S. 2005. Convergence's fundamental question. *Journalism Studies* 6(1):29–38.

Ropohl, G. 1982. Some methodological aspects of modelling sociotechnical systems. In *Structure and dynamics of socioeconomic systems: Cybernetics in organization and management, engineering systems methodology*, ed. R. Trappl, F. de Paula Hanika, and R. Tomlinson, vol. 10, 525–36. Washington, DC: Hemisphere.

Sabadin, V. 2007. *L'ultima copia del "New York Times": il futuro dei giornali di carta* [The last copy of The New York Times: the future of print newspapers]. Rome: Donzelli.

Sarrica, M., L. Fortunati, J. O'Sullivan, A. Balcytiene, P. Macgregor, V. Nuust, N. Roussou, K. Meso, X. Pereira, and F. de Luca. Forthcoming. The early stages of the integration of the Internet in EU Newsrooms. *European Journal of Communication*.

Scott, J., and G. Marshall. 2005. *Dictionary of sociology*. Oxford: Oxford University Press.

Sparks, C., and A. Reading. 1994. Understanding media change in East Central Europe. *Media, Culture & Society* 16:243–70.

Sparks, C. 2008. Media systems in transition: Poland, Russia, China. *Chinese Journal of Communication* 1:7–24.

Splichal, S., and C. Sparks. 1994. *Journalists for the 21st century: Tendencies of professionalization among first-year students in 22 countries*. Norwood, NJ: Ablex.

Taylor, J. C. 1986. Long-term sociotechnical systems change in a computer operations department. *Journal of Applied Behavioral Sciences* 22:303–13.

Thrist, E. L., G. W. Higgin, H. Murray, and A. B. Pollock. 1963. *Organizational choice* London: Tavistock.

Vahlberg, V., E. Shearer, L. Peer, V. Williams, and B. Figueroa. 2008. From "too much" to "just right." Media Management Center, Northwestern University. http://www.mediamanagementcenter.org/research/youthelection.pdf (accessed September 4, 2009).

World Association of Newspapers. 2008. World press trends: Newspapers are a growth business. http://www.wan-press.org/article17377.html (accessed September 4, 2009).

World Editors Forum. 2008. Trends in newsrooms, fourth annual report. http://www.trends-in-newsrooms.org/home.php (accessed September 4, 2009).

Weaver, D. H., R. A. Beam, B. J. Brownlee, P. S. Voakes, and G. C. Wilhoit. 2003. The face and mind of the American journalist. http://poynter.org/content/content_view.asp?id=28235 (accessed September 4, 2009).

Weaver, D. H., R. A. Beam, B. J. Brownlee, P. S. Voakes, and G. C. Wilhoit. 2006. *The American journalist in the 21st century: U.S. news people at the dawn of a new millennium*. Mahwah, NJ: Erlbaum.

Weaver, D. H., and G. C. Wilhoit. 1986. *The American journalist: A portrait of US news people and their work*. Bloomington: Indiana University Press.

Weaver, D. H., and G. C. Wilhoit. 1996. *The American journalist in the 1990s: U.S. news people at the end of an era*. Mahwah, NJ: Erlbaum.

Can the Web Be Made Accessible for People with Intellectual Disabilities?

Helen Kennedy

Institute of Communication Studies, University of Leeds, Leeds, United Kingdom

Simon Evans

Cognable, Skelmersdale, United Kingdom

Siobhan Thomas

Department of Arts and Media, London Southbank University, London, United Kingdom

This article presents the findings of a research project that aimed to contribute to the social inclusion of people with intellectual disabilities (ID) in the World Wide Web (the Web). The Inclusive New Media Design (INMD) project brought together thirty-one Web designers and developers with twenty-nine people with intellectual disabilities to explore the best practice for building Web sites accessible to the ID community. Specifically, the project took accessibility techniques identified in ID accessibility research, and investigated what would (or would not) make it possible for Web professionals to implement them. This article suggests some tentative answers to the question of whether a fully accessible Web can be built, one that includes people with ID. While the article outlines simple steps that can be taken to facilitate accessibility for people at the mild end of the ID spectrum, it also highlights a number of barriers that exist to implementing ID accessibility guidance, most notably the power holders and decision makers with whom Web designers work, who may not share the designers' commitment to accessibility.

"The power of the Web is in its universality. Access by everyone regardless of disability is an essential aspect" (Berners-Lee n.d.). These words by World Wide Web (WWW; the Web) inventor Tim Berners-Lee mark the birth of ever-increasing awareness (among governments, legislative bodies, and Web producers and consumers) of the need for the WWW to be accessible to all of the world's citizens. Efforts to ensure "access by everyone regardless of disability," most notably in the form of the World Wide Web Consortium's Web Accessibility Initiative (WAI: http://www.w3.org/WAI), aim to achieve this inclusion. Guidance developed by the WAI plays a crucial role in promoting accessible practices: Authoring Tools Accessibility Guidelines (ATAG) for producers of Web design software; User Agent Accessibility Guidelines (UAAG) for the manufacturers of Web browsers and the assistive technologies that people with disabilities use to access the Web, such as screen readers; and Web Content Accessibility Guidelines (WCAG; http://www.w3.org/TR/WCAG) for Web designers and other people involved in the production of Web sites.

Unfortunately, the accessibility needs of people with intellectual disabilities (ID) have historically been poorly understood, and therefore overlooked, by such efforts. Web accessibility experts who have been involved in producing the various iterations of the WCAG documents have generally had expertise in the fields of sensory and physical disability. Specialist ID accessibility knowledge has therefore been absent from WCAG working groups. The invisibility of people with intellectual disabilities in many areas of life, the complexity of the conditions that constitute intellectual disabilities, the diversity of intellectual disabilities, the overlap of intellectual disabilities with other similar conditions such as cognitive and learning disability, and the subsequent general confusion surrounding intellectual disability all serve to compound the marginalization of people with intellectual disabilities in Web accessibility initiatives (and elsewhere).

The absence of intellectual disability from WCAG guidance notwithstanding, the WAI has been responsible, at least in part, for accessibility becoming an everyday practice for many Web designers (see Kennedy 2010 for further discussion of the centrality of accessibility in the work of Web designers). In this context—of a parallel commitment to accessibility among Web professionals and an absence of ID accessibility guidance—it becomes necessary to ask whether the Web can be made accessible for people with intellectual disabilities. This question was at the heart of Inclusive New Media Design (INMD), a research project that aimed to contribute to the social inclusion of people with intellectual disabilities in the WWW by exploring the best ways to encourage Web designers and developers to build Web sites accessible to this community of disabled Web users. The project brought together thirty-one Web professionals (designers, developers, information architects, and others) with twenty-nine people with intellectual disabilities in a series of accessibility training workshops. This article presents the findings of INMD and some tentative answers to the question of whether a fully accessible Web can be built, one that includes people with ID among its audiences. It proposes that a number of barriers exist to implementing ID accessibility guidance, such as the power holders and decision makers with whom Web designers work, who may not share the designers' commitment to accessibility. Furthermore, for people at the profound end of the ID spectrum, whose accessibility needs are potentially more intrusive for Web audiences who are not perceived to share these needs, even greater barriers to inclusion exist. But before presenting our findings, we first locate our research in the context of debate about Web accessibility and intellectual disability.

INTELLECTUAL DISABILITY: THE MISSING LINK IN THE ACCESSIBILITY CHAIN

Until recently, disability was absent from humanities and social science scholarship, which had successfully resurrected other social identities—race, gender, sexuality—from the margins (Mitchell and Snyder 1997). The emergent field of disability studies represents a successful attempt to fill this gap (e.g., Davis 2006). Disability studies scholars and disability rights activists have argued convincingly that the historical, medical model of disability—which sees disability as an individual problem to be fixed by medical intervention—should be replaced by a social one (Goggin and Newell 2003). That is, we should acknowledge that disability is constructed by a society's choices and practices, not predetermined or biological, and that a different set of choices would be *enabling*, not *disabling*.

Such a shift away from medical models can be witnessed in changing understandings of what constitutes intellectual disability. Historically, intellectual disability was defined through intelligent quotient (IQ) scores—0–70 points for people with ID, compared with a general population range of 100 $\pm$ 15 points, according to the World Health Organization (WHO). But IQ does not reveal much about an individual's practical capabilities and support requirements, so current approaches focus on an individual's adaptive behavior, life skills, and social and physical abilities. These behaviors, skills, and abilities are usually considered in terms of a spectrum of severity, including mild, moderate, severe, and profound. This range includes productive individuals living independently, requiring only minimal and irregular support as adults (mild to moderate) and others requiring 24-7 lifelong care and support for all aspects of their daily life and personal needs (severe to profound). People with mild intellectual difficulties might learn slowly in school; they usually have problems reading or writing, but they may still be able to work. They usually have good social relationships and are able to contribute to society with a little help and support. People with moderate intellectual disabilities need support to live productive and independent lives as adults. Many people with moderate intellectual disabilities are able to achieve independence through supported living and employment schemes. In contrast, people with severe intellectual disabilities need considerable help and support with daily living, even as adults. They will often have limited communication and will have no literacy or numeracy skills. A smaller number of adults have profound intellectual disabilities and need intense support in all aspects of their lives. They almost always have additional physical and sensory disabilities. People with profound intellectual disabilities may indicate their mood and immediate needs to people who know them well, but do not understand or communicate using conventional language (for more discussion, see Emerson et al. 2001).

In accessibility guidance and discourse the term "cognitive disability" is often assumed to include ID. Furthermore, adding to the confusion, the term "learning disability" is used to refer to the ID population by influential UK organizations such as Mencap and governmental departments, whereas for most of the world and within the majority of accessibility-related publications, "learning disability" refers to specific scholastic disabilities such as dyslexia or dyscalculia. While the terms overlap, they are also distinct: Cognitive disability can be acquired at any age, whereas learning disabilities are lifelong; cognitive disability usually refers to a specific condition, whereas intellectual disability is often characterized by a complex of cognitive impairments. The current version of WCAG (2.0) uses the term "cognitive, language and learning accessibility issues" to refer to the broad group that would include people with learning/scholastic disabilities like dyslexia, as well as people at the mild end of the ID spectrum with some conventional communication and literacy (http://www.w3.org/TR/WCAG). However, the needs of severe and profound ID users demand far greater technical and authoring adaptations than are provided for in the WCAG guidance. For instance, even at the highest conformance level (AAA), the recommended reading level for textual content—lower secondary—is too high. In this sense, then, the whole ID spectrum is not covered by WCAG.

There are a number of practical reasons why the development of guidelines for ID Web accessibility, particularly in the form of explicit testable techniques, is difficult. First and most obvious, the complex diversity of the ID population itself, in which a large proportion of individuals have multiple and pervasive impairments, requires an equally complex set of solutions, not only in terms of design and development, but also with respect to content authoring. As previously noted, although users considered to have mild ID can be included by adherence to WCAG guidance, audiences with more severe manifestations of ID are likely to have limited communication and minimal information technology (IT) capability, thus requiring radical access and information solutions.

Second, lack of standardization with respect to communication systems and assistive technologies used across the ID population creates numerous challenges in relation to accessibility. For example, a range of visual symbol sets is used to aid oral communication, with some aimed at children, some at adults, some international, and others country-specific. Third, WCAG 2.0, like most accessibility guidance, is based on the assumption that accessibility is not achieved unless a user has fully independent access throughout each single process or experience (although it should be noted that WCAG 2.0 supports different levels of conformance for individual pages and discrete processes within a site). However, a critical factor in ID accessibility is human support. For someone with a severe ID who has limited mobility and no conventional communication, human mediation is essential. Thus, accessibility for this ID audience may extend only a single stage within a process—for example, visual review of shopping basket content, where the basket has been filled by a supporter.

Within this context, the absence of academic studies of Web accessibility for ID communities is unfortunate. The "mainstream" accessibility studies tend to focus on accessibility of a particular Web product for particular audiences. A number of tendencies can be observed in these studies. First, they often conclude that the Web site(s) under investigation, or the Web in general, is not accessible. Examples include Kelly (2002), DRC (2004), Coyne and Nielsen (2001), Craven and Brophy (2003), and Lewis (2004), which cover a broad range of public and private-sector Web sites and find diverse and multiple examples of inaccessibility. Although it is true that much of the Web remains off limits to many people with disabilities, we suggest that research into accessibility needs to go further than statements of the Web's inaccessibility, to ask *why* the Web is inaccessible, and whether it is possible to overcome barriers to accessibility. Such research should take into account the range of factors at play in building the Web.

Second, studies of Web accessibility rarely focus on the people who build the Web. Adobe's chief accessibility advisor, Bob Regan (2004), has observed that "in order to understand why there are so few sites that illustrate great design and great accessibility, Web design needs to be understood as a practice of individuals. Sites are built by people, not principles or standards." Likewise, the field of science and technology studies (STS), out of which this research emerges, acknowledges that technologies are "ideas made real," marked by their conditions of production and the people who produce them. Goggin and Newell (2007, 160) point out that accessibility, too, is a relative concept—what is accessible for some people with disabilities may be inaccessible for others. Thus, they argue, "the binary between 'accessible' and 'inaccessible' technology is part of the problem that needs to be addressed." Web technologies, then, and related conditions such as "accessible" are highly contingent. Instead of asserting that a Web site or the Web in general is or is not accessible, we argue that it is more productive to move away from such binaries, and ask "how" and "why."

All of this suggests that use of the Web by people with disabilities could be better understood through an analysis of how it gets made. Yet few studies of Web accessibility have looked into the developmental process. Exceptions include the Lazar et al. (2003) study of 175 Web masters' perceptions of accessibility. Here the authors identify societal value and stakeholder perceptions of accessibility as influences on the processes that shape the accessibility of Web sites. According to their respondents, the biggest challenges to making Web sites accessible are: balancing accessibility and design; convincing clients and managers of the importance of accessibility; lack of funding, time, and training; and technical challenges and the need for better software tools. Thereby their study goes some way toward considering *why* the Web might be inaccessible to some of its users. Another exception is the Law et al. (2005) study of accessibility, which also looks at the people who build Web sites. It focuses primarily on the complexity of Web accessibility guidance as a barrier to accessible Web design, thus ignoring other factors that influence the Web design process. Small et al. (2005).

refer to Web designers rather dismissively when they claim that they build Web sites on the basis of "artistic design parameters developed from personal experience." According to Adams and Kreps (2006), Web designers are empowered to enable or disable Web audiences through their design decisions. This assertion is important in that it draws attention to the social model of disability, but it is also somewhat simplistic for, as we have found in our research, the location of power within Web design is rather more complex than this suggests. To go beyond current preoccupation with whether or not the Web is accessible and to consider whether it can be made accessible to people with ID, we focus on the designers and developers who build the Web, and the environments in which they do this.

None of the research mentioned so far addresses intellectual disability; the Lazar et al. (2009) study considered only visually impaired Web users. Where cognitive disability is considered, it is often in the form of dyslexia, for example, in the UK Disability Rights Commission's (DRC; 2004) report on Web accessibility. The few studies that do specifically address intellectual disability and accessibility are mostly published in specialist journals such as *International Journal of Language and Communication Disorders*, *Journal of Applied Research in Intellectual Disabilities*, or *Journal of Research in Special Educational Needs*, further evidence that ID is its own specialized area, somewhat marginal from "mainstream" disability and accessibility studies. Some studies acknowledge that the Web holds much promise for people with ID (e.g., Bunning et al. 2009), and others point out that even WCAG-compliant sites are inaccessible for this audience (e.g., Small et al. 2005). Other studies identify accessibility issues for people with ID (Harrysson et al. 2004) or accessibility solutions for ID audiences (Brown et al. 2002; Karreman et al. 2007). This research is valuable, as it increases understanding of what does and does not work for intellectually disabled users accessing the Web. But, as we have stated, to understand whether, and to what extent, useful guidance for ID accessibility can be implemented, it is necessary to turn attention to those doing the implementing—Web designers and developers. Thus, our approach to answering the question "can the Web be accessible for people with ID?" is to examine the working conditions of Web designers and developers, the place of accessibility in their work practices, and the social, cultural, political, and economic factors that impact on accessibility practices. In other words, INMD was not a study of the effectiveness of ID accessibility techniques. Rather, it took techniques identified in previous research (and discussed in the next section) and investigated what would (or would not) make it possible for Web professionals to implement them. Can the Web be built to include people with ID? The next section proposes some answers to these questions.

INCLUSIVE NEW MEDIA DESGIN METHODS

Inclusive New Media Design (INMD) grew out of a tradition of involving people with intellectual disabilities in research about their technology use and needs, and so was fully committed to the "nothing about us without us" ethos of disability advocacy movements. Previous action research conducted by two members of the INMD team, alongside teenagers with ID, Web developers, ID support charity workers, and other researchers (Bunning et al. 2009; Kennedy 2008, 2009; Williams and Nicholas 2006), had focused on the development of a virtual learning environment for the teenagers with ID. The research was instrumental in helping to generate the ID accessibility guidelines discussed later in this article, but it had concluded that more understanding was needed of the place of accessibility in the design processes employed by new media workers. Hence INMD was born. Once we had secured funding, the project team held a workshop with eleven ID Web users, to explore opportunities of their involvement in our research. We concluded that we needed to work with people at the mild end of the ID spectrum, in order to be sure that they could (1) use the Web and (2) talk about their Web use. Subsequently, we employed twenty-nine people with ID, recruited from an organization dedicated to finding employment opportunities for this community, to attend four of our nine workshops and to work as experts in their own Web use. Thus people with ID were *colleagues,* not subjects, in our research.

Our primary research subjects were Web professionals, thirty-one of whom worked with us on INMD. Twenty-eight attended our accessibility workshops; the remaining three participated in interviews, but were unable to take time off to attend the workshops. We recruited our participants from a range of sources, including events for Web professionals, targeted e-mails, existing networks, and a project Web site. Thirteen participants were women; eighteen were men. As our workshops took place in London, most participants worked in the South East of England, and a small range of nationalities was represented among participants. Participants' job titles varied hugely (see table 1), and changed during the project, as participants moved among jobs or experienced other changes in their workplaces. They worked in a range of sectors, and had a varying number of years of Web design experience—some less than two, some more than ten. Their ages also varied, although most participants were younger than forty years old. Twenty-five out of thirty-one participants had experience of Web accessibility. However, only eight participants said they were aware of the ID user group, and only two of these eight participants had engaged in Web development work for ID audiences. Six participants had experience of cognitive disability and accessibility in their

TABLE 1
Age range, years of Web work experience, and job titles of Web professionals

Age range	
20 to 29 years	13
30 to 39 years	10
40 to 49 years	6
50 to 59	2
	$n = 31$
Years of Web work experience	
2 or less	6
2 to 5 years	12
6 to 9 years	7
10 or more years	6
2 or less	6
2 or less	6
Participants' job titles	
Accessibility usability specialist	
(Creative) director (3)	
Design consultant	
Digital content producer	
Distributor	
Information architect (2)	
IT coordinator	
IT support	
Knowledge transfer associate	
Learning materials developer (2)	
Learning technology advisor	
Lecturer	
Product development manager	
Technology and information manager	
Trainer	
Web assistant	

Note. IT = information technology.

work, predominantly with accessibility needs of people with dyslexia.

All participants except two knew of the WCAG. But not all had read the guidelines firsthand. Twenty had done so; others had read about them, for example, on the Web sites and blogs of Web design field leaders. In one of the workshops, in response to an ad hoc question about whether participants felt they *understood* the guidelines, only one participant confirmed that he did.

All participants were interviewed before our workshops, to find out about their work and accessibility practices, although previous accessibility knowledge was not a requirement for participation. Workshops ran over a six-month period. Data-gathering methods in the workshops included note-taking, video recording, photography, and feedback forms, filled by the participants at the end of each workshop. Six months after the workshops, we ran a follow-up session to reflect on the extent to which engagement with INMD had affected participants' work and accessibility practice.

One of the central purposes of the INMD workshops was to communicate core principles for ID accessible design to our participants. Since INMD was directed toward the social inclusion of people with ID in the Web, the extent to which participants understood and subsequently acted on these principles was of great concern to us. The principles we used were drawn from previous research, some of which we conducted, and from the experience of one of us who had worked with ID users and observed their Web use for more than fifteen years.

In their small study of IT use by people with ID, Harrysson and others found that these users had difficulty with text input, and concluded that "the processing of text can impede accessibility to the Internet for people with cognitive disabilities" (Harrysson et al. 2004). Brown et al. (2002) examined the usability of an interactive multimedia learning environment for people with intellectual disabilities by consulting an expert panel. They concluded that to be ID accessible a Web site must: provide a speech alternative for all buttons and text; provide a menu that allows the user to jump to anywhere at any time; and use a maximum of three sentences per page. Friedman and Bryen (2007) conducted a review of currently available guidance for ID accessibility. Their most significant recommendations were: use pictures, graphics, icons, and symbols along with text; use clear and simple text; use consistent navigation and design on every page; and use headings, titles, and prompts. However, these guidelines were not validated by users. The Karreman et al. study concluded that the application of detailed guidelines for verbal content and layout of easy-read text, produced by the European Commission (Freyhoff et al. 1998), enhanced comprehension of Web content for the twenty ID Web users who engaged in their study. They also concluded that it is only by testing Web sites with ID users that designers can know whether their sites work for these audiences (Karreman et al. 2007).

From this research and other experience, we identified the following ID accessibility principles around which we developed our workshop activities:

- Include pictures that provide key information and repeat the information provided in text.
- Have simple navigation, with just a few choices, rather than navigation with lots of choices.
- Incorporate movement and interaction to generate interest: video, animation and sound.
- Use voicing to narrate text on the page.
- Use simple, easy-to-read text and short sentences.
- Involve people with intellectual disabilities to advise on design and to user test.

CAN THE WEB BE MADE ACCESSIBLE FOR ID AUDIENCES?: OUR INMD FINDINGS

Through our engagement with Web professionals on INMD, we identified a number of factors that affect the extent to which Web designers can enhance ID accessibility. These include: awareness of and engagement with people with ID and their accessibility needs; barriers to ID accessibility; the lack of ID accessibility guidance; and the need to balance ID accessibility with accessibility for everyone else. Each of these points is discussed in turn in the following subsections.

Awareness of and Engagement with People with Intellectual Disabilities and Their Accessibility Needs

To build Web sites that are accessible specifically for ID audiences, Web designers and developers first need to be aware that ID users exist as potential site visitors. Prior to participating in INMD, most of our participants had no experience or understanding of intellectual disability. "It never crossed my path," said Armando, a Web designer and lecturer. The invisibility of this community leads to a genuine lack of understanding of what intellectual disability is, and a corresponding lack of awareness of the accessibility needs of ID Web users. Meeting people with ID raises awareness of who they are. Further, the diversity and complexity of ID can only really be grasped through contact with people with intellectual disabilities themselves. Because of this, we built user involvement in the form of user testing into the design of INMD. In the user-testing sessions, either participants tested prototype products they had made in collaborative groups, which aimed to incorporate some techniques to enhance ID accessibility, or they carried out a test which the project team designed, of a Web product targeted at ID users.

Our hypothesis that facilitating a dialogue between Web professionals and people with ID would go a significant way toward contributing to the inclusion of people with ID in the WWW proved correct, to some extent. When asked to identify which aspects of the workshops were most beneficial in encouraging them to build ID-accessible Web sites, most participants mentioned the opportunities provided to engage directly with ID users. The user-testing sessions were important in raising awareness and understanding of ID accessibility, particularly the complexities of designing for such a diverse audience. Participants pointed out that despite discussing in detail the accessibility needs of the ID community in workshop sessions prior to user testing, intellectual disability was, as Sofia, a design agency director said, "a very vague thing," and an ID user, "someone I couldn't really judge [before today]."

User testing put a human face on the issues we had previously discussed with participants. "Meeting the user group, seeing their reactions (some as expected, some unexpected), understanding how to prompt for input, getting honest and sincere feedback," were aspects of the user-testing experience that Nadine, a Web designer and lecturer, found valuable. "In order to design for accessibility, you need ID users to test your sites," said Aaron, an information architect from a large media organization. "Things we would not think to pick up get highlighted. There is nothing more effective than getting actual users to test your products."

When asked how to ensure that people with intellectual disabilities are included on the Web, half of those who responded said through user testing and user participation in the process of building the Web. Likewise, when asked how to encourage other Web professionals to create ID accessible designs, and how to spread knowledge about ID accessibility issues, our participants advocated a user-testing approach, suggesting free user-testing days, information about how to gain access to affordable user testing, and user-testing sessions in university and other courses.

User engagement on INMD had a profound impact on the way participants conceptualized accessibility. For most participants this new perspective involved "a general attitude that accessibility covers a broad range of people, all with separate and differing needs that need to be considered" (Poppy, design consultant). "I am more aware of accessibility issues and much more aware of the extent of a diversity of people's uses of online media," said Frances, a lecturer and freelance Web developer. User involvement was clearly much valued by participants, and instrumental to their understanding of the ID audience and their Web use. Engagement with intellectually disabled Web users is therefore an important factor in motivating Web designers and developers toward a commitment to ID accessibility, the first step toward building a Web that is accessible to them.

Barriers to ID Accessibility

Most INMD participants took some action to implement ID accessibility principles and so enhance the digital inclusion of people with ID during the course of the workshops. For example:

> "Used imagery with words. Ensured font is big enough." (Gregory, self-employed Web designer)
>
> "Used more Ajax to make some things more intuitive; tried to offer a tab and hit 'space' navigation for portfolio." (Sofia, design agency director)
>
> "Re-checked existing work to bring up to scratch, but that then led me to learn new techniques to validate certain mark

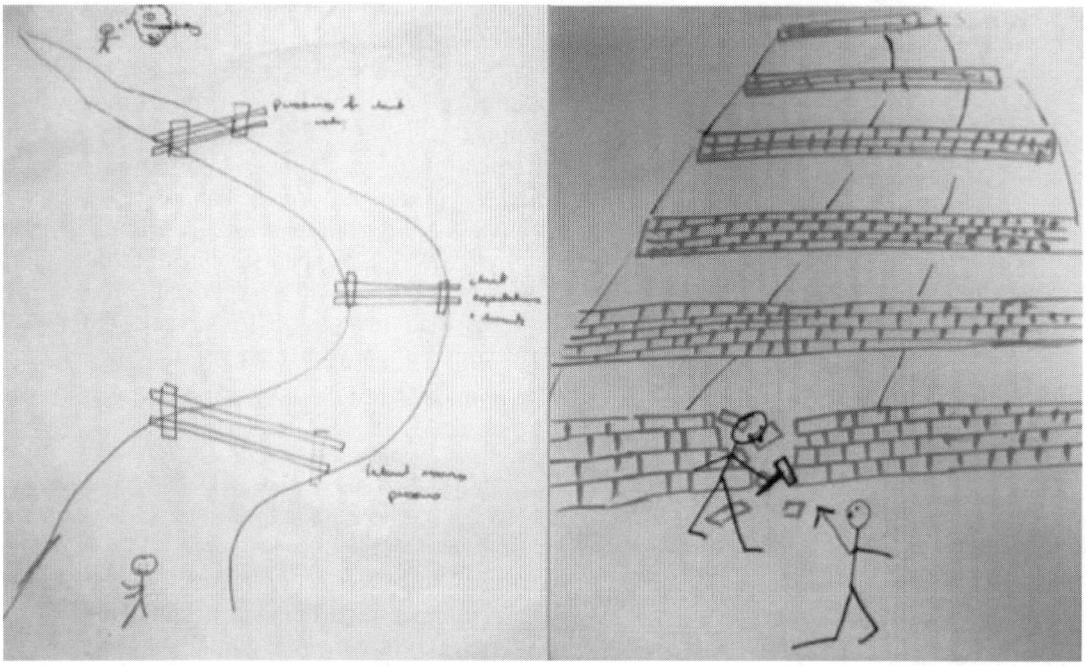

FIG. 1. Two participants' drawings of their actual experiences in the workplace after the workshop. Fences and brick walls represent obstacles to achieving accessibility.

> up (Flash embedding)." (Patrick, learning materials developer)
>
> "We produced an e-learning module on disability awareness and added in both rich media and plain text versions." (Patrick, learning materials developer) "I often re-do previous Web pages and re-visit content to update, used that as an opportunity to rectify [ID] problem areas." (Ayesha, Web developer)
>
> "Circulated slides amongst user experience team." (Aaron, information architect at a large media organization)

This list of action taken suggests that it is technically possible for the Web to be made accessible to people with intellectual disabilities, but of course such processes take place in social contexts, where competing issues influence what can and cannot be done. Not surprisingly, then, INMD participants identified a range of factors that affected their ID-accessible Web design practice, including the attitudes of decision makers and the nature of projects they work on.

The decision makers with whom our participants work affect accessible practice—line managers, clients, content producers, and others may not share our participants' commitment to accessibility. While the workshops were running, we asked participants what obstacles they were encountering in implementing ID accessibility, and a common response was that clients or equivalent decision makers did not care about accessibility, did not want it, or wanted to retain inaccessible elements in their Web sites, such as confusing labels for functional features.

The impact of decision makers on accessible design could be seen in the changes observed among participants between the end of the workshops and our reunion with them six months later. When the workshops finished, most participants had identified some steps that they could take to build a more ID accessible Web, and some had already taken these steps, as noted earlier. At the same time, they also identified barriers to achieving this. When we met again six months later, the realities on the ground appeared to have dampened the can-do spirit generated at the workshop. For many, after six months back in the field, away from the supportive network of the workshops, barriers proved to be overwhelming despite what they learned and applied during the workshops. We asked participants to draw visual representations of their experiences of learning about and trying to implement ID accessibility, and common metaphors were long roads and walls as obstacles, as seen in the two images in figure 1. Some said that they had not taken any steps toward ID inclusion, or that they could not, which contrasted sharply with their earlier statements about the action that they had taken during the course of the workshop program.

Some of our participants, after six months back at work, felt that they did not have the power to affect change on behalf of the ID community. They claimed that we should be targeting not them, Web designers, but "stakeholders"—

line managers, clients, decision makers. Without them on board, there was nothing they, the Web designers, could do.

> "My workplace does not prioritise accessibility at the level of management so there's not much hope." (Frances, lecturer and freelance Web developer)

> "It is really more to do with the people commissioning the websites than the designers." (Serge, corporate Web designer)

Others held the opposite view. As a commissioner, one participant, Lily, said she was committed to accessibility, and needed projects such as ours to show designers what techniques they could deploy. At the same time, some participants identified strategies to work around the obstacle of decision makers' attitudes. Billie, a Web developer in a performing arts organization, said, "I am trying to think about how far our organisation is willing to go. Maybe start to implement 'invisible' elements." As a result of such comments, we argue that when it comes to building an accessible Web, the location of power is complex. It is not simply the case that Web designers, through their choices and actions regarding accessibility, are empowered to enable or disable Web users, as Adams and Kreps (2006) have suggested.

The nature of the projects workshop participants worked on was also a factor affecting accessible design, both general and ID-specific. Some felt that the back-end coding that they work on cannot affect ID accessibility in the same way as front-end design: "I'm still not sure how I can bring this into my everyday work," said Timothy, a self-employed Web developer. "It's something I hope to do some personal projects around, but I'm not sure yet how I can bring it into my client work. Currently I seem to be brought in to help finish off projects that need to get done quickly. If I get to work on any projects from nearer the start then hopefully I can bring these issues to the table." Other participants expressed similar sentiments, such as Frances:

> "Working on projects with larger teams and requirements set by a client means that it is too difficult to build a collective consensus to implement accessibility." (Frances, lecturer and freelance Web developer)

These comments suggest that Web designers and developers have limited power when it comes to enabling or disabling Web users. They suggest that the commitment our participants demonstrated to ID accessibility can often be thwarted by external factors beyond their control. Thus ID accessibility, while technically possible, is often difficult to achieve for reasons that are sociotechnical.

WCAG Guidance and the Absence of ID

When asked what they thought about WCAG guidance, some INMD participants acknowledged their value, some acknowledged their limitations, and some did both. About one-quarter of participants described WCAG 1.0 (current at the time of the research) as good, easy, inclusive or "nice to test against." One said that they were "very thorough documents." But, on the whole, participants were critical of the guidelines, with more than half highlighting the complexity of the language used as a barrier to understanding and, therefore their implementation. In different ways, participants stated that the guidelines were hard to understand or to work with. Tom, an accessibility professional responsible for advising employees of a large telecom company on accessibility practices, said:

> "Because of their nature as standards, the language used and because it is so comprehensive, it can be off-putting. However, if you have a specific query, they can be very helpful, and there are intermediaries which will link to them with explanations. So I think they are useful as a resource, but they can be off-putting because of the language and way they are structured." (Tom, IT support, telecommunications)

A number of participants acknowledged the danger of a tick-box culture that the guidelines can generate, in which Web designers might become more concerned with validating code than with producing a genuinely accessible site. Armando, a trainer at a London-based innovation center, explained the pitfalls of conforming blindly to guidelines:

> "I think they're a lovely, philosophical, well-meaning piece of documentation which causes more harm than good, because too many people, if they think about accessibility, think WAI and that's it. They think as long as they put WAI at the bottom, then their Web site is good, as long as they pass the WAI validation, that's it, they walk away from it. And it's far more sophisticated and important than just passing one specific document." (Armando, Web designer and lecturer)

One of the things at issue here is guidelines per se, not the WCAG guidelines in particular. Guidelines in general are not enough, with their checklist, tick-box orientation, because alone, they do not guarantee genuine inclusion. Consequently, supplemental approaches such as those that we adopted on INMD, where designers and developers seek guidance directly from users, seem necessary.

A further obstacle to designing for ID accessibility was that the WCAG guidelines were perceived by many workshop participants as inadequate in addressing the needs of people with ID. When asked if they could foresee any obstacles to implementation, participants' responses included:

> "Lack of definitions. No standards/recommendations." (Gregory, self-employed Web designer)

> "No real specifications to clearly work towards a better product. Clients don't care. Need formal guidelines to enforce the justification and need for ID accessibility." (Ayesha, Web developer)

The omission of the ID audience from the main international accessibility guidance has an effect on perceptions of what constitutes accessibility. "Accessibility is often viewed as only being about screen readers," pointed out Serge, a Web designer for a commercial Web development company. It also impacts on the strategies that Web professionals develop to address ID accessibility. In the absence of specific guidance, said Ayesha, a Web developer for a government department:

> "It's an area of judgement call, personal perception. It can be quite difficult to achieve effectively for all IDs. A general perception which I took away was to keep language simple as a starting point and possible use of icons, although I'm not sure everyone understands icons in the same way."

In other words, in the absence of clear guidelines, Web designers and developers make their own decisions about what they can and will do to enhance ID accessibility. Thus, although WCAG guidance is a valuable starting point, it is also perceived as too complex, and inadequate in addressing accessibility for the ID user group, and these perceptions can act as obstacles for building ID accessible Web sites.

Accessibility for ID or for Everyone Else? The Pragmatic Approach

Our research was based on the premise that it is possible to take some steps, which had been identified in previous research, toward including people with intellectual disabilities on the Web. But given the diversity and complexity of ID, accessibility steps will work to varying degrees, depending on where on the ID spectrum individual Web site visitors are located. The more intellectually disabled the user, the more extremes the measure to meet his or her accessibility requirements will need to be. Making a Web site accessible for people with mild intellectual disabilities could widen audiences, as everyone can benefit from simple text, nice graphics, simple choices, and a clear message. People with severe intellectual disabilities need Web sites with very little text, lots of sound, a very small number of choices, and very deep structures. Such Web sites will not work for everyone, so additional, easy-read versions of existing sites might need to be created. This can mean more work for Web designers. But that is what is necessary to move toward ID inclusion. The accessibility needs of people with the most profound intellectual disabilities are even more difficult to address, unless the Web site is being built specifically for this group.

Because of the diversity of ID, different ID accessibility measures have different impacts on non-disabled Web users. Some front-end measures might seem more intrusive than other more "behind the scenes" measures typically employed for sensory or physical impairments. The large fonts, simple language, and deep rather than wide structures required for ID accessibility impact the usability of a Web site more than writing code in such a way that it can be read by a screen reader. Conversely, good markup for sensory/physical disability will often result in good search engine optimization, quick downloads, and cross-platform compatibility. In effect, accessibility for people with sensory or physical disabilities has other payoffs beyond accessibility. Because of all of this, most INMD participants concluded that they would adopt "simplifying" measures that would include people with mild ID and also benefit all users. Sofia, a design agency director, said, "Making a site more accessible to ID users will make it easier for everyone." She continued:

> "ID accessibility suggests to make sites more intuitive, a little playful, with images to reinforce meaning, navigation, and not clutter a site too much. Previously, we only concentrated on making navigations text-based for the blind and people with bad eyesight." (Sofia, design agency director)

Most INMD participants said they would adopt this pragmatic approach to ID accessibility, stating that they would cater to mild ID users because this would benefit all site visitors. For example, Jane said:

> "We have the potential to help all users, but unless a client has a specific requirement I doubt we will go further than mild/moderate. I think there are strong advantages to us doing this: by investigating what can be done to help this group of people we will improve our sites for everyone." (Jane, corporate product development manager)

On the one hand, it is a positive sign that, as a result of INMD, most participants appeared to understand how to build Web sites that include audiences with mild ID. On the other hand, participants recognize that designing accessibly for people at the severe to profound end of the ID spectrum would be both costly and obtrusive to other users, and therefore not pragmatic to attempt. This means that the people with profound intellectual disabilities who are already very marginalized members of society, because of the severity of their disabilities, remain at the margins. They remain excluded.

TOWARD ID ACCESSIBILITY

We set out to move beyond claims that the Web is inaccessible, to explore why it might be inaccessible and what can be done about it, particularly for people with ID. In doing so, we have filled a gap in the accessibility literature, which tends to focus primarily on visual impairment and other sensory and physical disabilities, and to ignore the accessibility needs of people who are intellectually disabled. We did this by focusing on those people who build the Web, Web designers and Web developers, which few accessibility scholars before us have done—and the few who have do not engage with ID accessibility.

Our understanding of ID accessibility calls into question the notion of universal design, which is mobilized in a number of discussions of accessibility (e.g., Craven 2006; Ellis and Kent 2008). In these discussions, accessibility and universal design are seen as the same thing, to the extent that Ellis and Kent argue that it is productive to "reframe disability accessibility as a principle of universal access and design" (Ellis and Kent 2008). But so-called universal design solutions are not, in fact, universal, despite the label, as illustrated by our study of ID accessibility.

So, can the Web be made accessible for people with intellectual disabilities? Our findings question the notion articulated by Adams and Kreps (2006) that Web designers and developers are empowered to enable or disable Web users, and point to the more complex social conditions in which the Web gets built. There are things that Web designers can do to enhance ID accessibility—use images to communicate core content; have simple navigation; use simple text and short sentences; use voicing to narrate pages; and incorporate video, animation, and sound. Some of our INMD participants do these things, some of the time. But there are also obstacles—the attitudes of decision makers; the nature of the projects that Web professionals work on; the complexity of existing accessibility guidelines; and the absence of ID in these guidelines. These obstacles limit what Web professionals can do, despite their commitment to ID accessibility. The pragmatic approach to ID accessibility adopted by many INMD participants, where simple ID accessibility steps that improve usability for all site visitors are taken, means that people at the more profound end of the ID spectrum are likely to remain excluded.

Our findings on INMD suggest five possible steps that might result in greater inclusion in the Web of people with ID. First, widely available resources detailing how Web designers and developers can attend to the accessibility needs of ID users are needed. A comprehensive, multimodal resource could provide tips on how to build ID accessible Web sites, examples of both good practice and ID Web use, and information on how to meet and even exceed WCAG standards. Given the desirability of contact with like-minded peers and information sharing by INMD participants, such a resource could also facilitate community building among Web professionals committed to maximizing the accessibility of their Web sites.

In suggesting that WCAG guidelines could be extended and alternative approaches explored, it is not our contention that they are of little value. The reality is that the needs of many within the ID population, and in particular the most intellectually disabled, require very significant adaptations beyond WCAG standards. Given the influence and standing of World Wide Web Consortium's Web Accessibility Initiative (WAI), our second suggestion is that WCAG include explicit additional guidance for the inclusion of people with ID.

Third, to achieve ID accessibility, action researchers like us need to engage with other "stakeholders" who influence the Web design process. Through INMD, we found that the "webs of connections that make up the production of technical systems" (Wakeford 2003, 241) are more complex and dispersed than we originally anticipated. Consequently, it is necessary to engage with a more diverse range of stakeholders—line managers, copywriters, policymakers—to make ID accessibility a reality. To design inclusively, we need to ask questions about who the designers are and where power lies in design decision-making processes.

Fourth, because of a generalized lack of understanding of ID, engagement with people with ID by Web designers, developers, and other stakeholders is essential. The value that our participants attached to engagement with ID Web users suggests that it is important to find ways of facilitating such continued interaction between Web producers and ID users. One participant said: "Theory is pointless without meeting ID users. You can theorise the day away and not understand their issues at all. It is important to meet them to see how they see things and to hear them say what they think and want." One suggestion about how to achieve this was to include information about how to access ID users for user-testing in an online resource. Other participants suggested that a more participatory approach to design than INMD could be explored, where people with ID are expert coproducers in the development process, not just testers. This might result in more genuinely inclusive new media design, but of course it will be costly and time-consuming, and not high on the agenda of those who commission Web sites.

And finally, despite our efforts in INMD, people with severe or profound ID remain an extremely marginalized and excluded community. New media like the Web present a wealth of opportunities for including them, yet the measures that can be taken to do so are often perceived as obtrusive to other nondisabled Web users. As a result, Web designers and developers are more likely to cater for the accessibility needs of people at the mild end of the ID spectrum, and people at the severe to profound end remain excluded. More action research initiatives are needed that specifically address the digital inclusion of people at the profound end of the ID spectrum.

It remains to be seen whether, in the long run, INMD participants will build Web sites that are more inclusive of intellectually disabled Web users as a result of their participation in the project. Their comments suggest that some of them, at least, might take some small steps to include people at the mild end of the spectrum. This can be seen as a modest achievement of INMD. But more needs to be done, to spread information about ID accessibility, to engage an appropriate range of stakeholders, and to include those people at the severe to profound end of the intellectual disability spectrum. Without this further action, the Web will remain inaccessible to people with intellectual disabilites.

REFERENCES

Adam, A., and D. Kreps. 2006. Enabling or disabling technologies? A critical approach to Web accessibility. *Information Technology and People* 19(3):203–18.

Berners-Lee, T. n.d. Web Accessibility Initiative (WAI) Web site. http://www.w3.org/WAI (accessed December 2003).

Brown, D. J., H. M. Powell, S. Battersby, and J. Lewis. 2002. Design guidelines for interactive multimedia learning environments to promote social inclusion. *Disability and Rehabilitation* 24(11–12):587–97.

Bunning, K., B. Heath, and A. Minnion. 2009. Communication and empowerment: A place for rich and multiple media? *Journal of Applied Research in Intellectual Disabilities* 22:370–79.

Coyne, K., and J. Nielsen. 2001. *Beyond ALT text: Making the Web easy to use for users with disabilities*. Fremont, CA: Nielsen Norman Group.

Craven, J. 2006. Web accessibility: A review of research and initiatives. Paper presented at the World Library and Information Congress, 72nd IFLA General Conference and Council, Seoul, Korea, August 20–24. http://e-space.openrepository.com/e-space/handle/2173/5943?mode=simple (accessed June 2009).

Craven, J., and P. Brophy. 2003. Non-visual access to the digital library: The use of digital library interfaces by blind and visually impaired people. Library and Information Commission Report 145. CERLIM. Manchester, England.

Davis, L. J., ed. 2006. *The disability studies reader*, 2nd ed. New York: Routledge.

Disability Rights Commission. 2004. The Web: Access and inclusion for disabled people, a formal investigation conducted by the Disability Rights Commission. Joe Clark.org. http://joeclark.org/dossiers/DRC-GB.html and other URLs (accessed March 2006).

DRC. See Disability Rights Commission.

Ellis, K., and M. Kent. 2008. iTunes is pretty (useless) when you're blind: Digital design is triggering disability when it could be a solution. *M/C Journal* 11(3). http://journal.media-culture.org.au/index.php/mcjournal/article/viewArticle/55.

Emerson E., C. Hatton, D. Felce, and G. Murphy. 2001. *Learning disabilities: The fundamental facts*. London: Foundation for People with Learning Disabilities.

Freyhoff, G., G. Hess, L. Kerr, E. Menzel, B. Tronbacke, and K. van der Veken. 1998. *Make it simple: European guidelines for the production of easy-to-read information for people with learning disabiliy.* Brussels: ILSMH European Association.

Friedman, G., and D. Bryen. 2007. Web accessibility design recommendations for people with cognitive disabilities. *Technology and Disability* 19(4):205–12.

Goggin, G., and C. Newell. 2003. *Digital disability: The social construction of disability in new media*. Boston: Rowman & Littlefield.

Goggin, G., and C. Newell. 2007. The business of digital disability. *The Information Society* 23:159–68.

Harrysson, B., A. Svensk, and G. I. Johansson. 2004. How people with developmental disabilities navigate the Internet. *British Journal of Special Education* 31(3):138–42.

Karreman, J., T. van der Geest, and E. Buursink. 2007. Accessible Web site content guidelines for users with intellectual disabilities. *Journal of Applied Research in Intellectual Disabilities* 20(6):510–18.

Kelly, B. 2002. An accessibility analysis of UK university entry points. *Ariadne* 33. http://www.ariadne.ac.uk/issue33/web-watch (accessed October 2009).

Kennedy, H. 2008. New media's potential for personalisation. *Information, Communication and Society* 11(3):307–25.

———. 2009. Going the extra mile: Emotional and commercial imperatives in new media work. *Convergence* 15(2):177–96.

———. 2010. Net work: The professionalisation of Web design. *Media, Culture and Society* 32(2):187–203.

Law, C., J. Jacko, and P. Edwards. 2005. Programmer-focused Web site accessibility evaluations. In *Proceedings of the 7th international ACM SIGACCESS Conference on Computers and Accessibility,* ed. A. Sears and E. Pontelli, 20–27. Baltimore, MD: ACM SIGACCESS.

Lazar, J., A. Dudley-Sponaugle, and K. D. Greenidge. 2004. Improving Web accessibility: A study of Webmaster perceptions. *Computers in Human Behaviour* 20(2):269–88.

Lewis, A. 2004. A user survey of the experiences of blind and visually impaired people using electronic information services with regard to the practical implementation of these services in public libraries. MS diss., Department of Information Management, Robert Gordon University, Aberdeen, Scotland.

Mitchell, D., and S. Snyder. 1997. Disability studies and the double bind of representation. In *The body and physical difference: Discourses of disability,* ed. D. Mitchell and S. Snyder, 1–35. Ann Arbor: University of Michigan Press.

Regan, B. 2004. Accessibility and design: A failure of the imagination. Paper presented at International Cross-disciplinary Workshop on Web Accessibility (W4A), New York, NY, May 18. http://portal.acm.org/citation.cfm?id=990657.990663andcoll=GUIDEanddl=GUIDEandCFID=51345195andCFTOKEN=92102064.

Small, J., P. Schallau, K. Brown, and R. Appleyard. 2005. Web accessibility for people with cognitive disabilities. In *Conference on Human Factors in Computing Systems: CHI* 2005, ed. G. van der Veer and C. Gale, 1793–96. New York: ACM.

Williams P., and D. Nicholas. 2006. Testing the usability of information technology applications with learners with special educational needs. *Journal of Research in Special Educational Needs* 6(1): 31–41.

"General Aesthesia": Mutations of Value and Cognition in New Media Practices

Helen Grace

Department of Cultural and Religious Studies, Chinese University of Hong Kong, Shatin, Hong Kong

Although penetration rates and other measures of the rapid growth of mobile technologies capture our imaginations, what is not so readily understood is why this "charismatic technology" (Fortunati 2007) has been so adopted—and adapted—in local contexts. In particular, relatively little systematic attention has been given to the *forms* of user-created content. Video- and photo-sharing sites, social networking sites, and blogs have become the space for projection of a range of new user-created content, challenging assumptions about the image's power to universally communicate and presenting a dissolution of the division of aesthetic labor between artists and nonartists (the skilled and unskilled). This results in what the author calls a widespread *general aesthesia* in which an affective state of response, a heightening of awareness, extends users' creative capacities and presents a counter to the widespread assumption of anesthetization in the face of information overload. This research is based on the study of camera-phone practices in Hong Kong in which microlevel adaptations and transformations of technology by users suggest a much more diffused form of innovation than is generally understood within innovation and industry policy frameworks.

> The position that an epoch occupies in the historical process can be determined more strikingly from an analysis of its inconspicuous surface-level expressions than from that epoch's judgments about itself. (Kracauer 1995, 75)

INTRODUCTION: "PHYSICAL REALITY" AND THE TECHNICAL IMAGE

This article explores two key themes or contentions. The first is that a changed relation to memory may be observable in the study of new forms and practices of communication and especially in the use of mobile media, such as camera-phone picture taking. Second, the proliferation of new image production via digital and cameraphone photography and videography and the circulation of images via social networking and image-sharing sites constitutes a new "sphere of innovation" beyond modernist assumptions of innovation at the purely formal level. This establishes what could be called a "general aesthesia," transcending ideas of creativity that we have taken for granted since the Romantic revolution. While it requires a book-length study to fully develop these two contentions, I briefly summarize the main departure points, before focusing on the use of camera-phone pictures in Hong Kong and illustrating some of my arguments via reference to images.

The study of memory has become a deep concern in critical scholarship in the postwar period in the West, surfacing in debates on collective memory (Halbwachs 1992), on the relation between concepts of time, history, and memory (Le Goff 1996), on historical trauma and forgetting (Ricoeur 2004), and on anxieties about amnesia and oblivion (Huyssen 1994). If it seems the case that intellectual history has centralized the problem of memory, where is it situated in popular culture? To answer this question, I consider the emergence of a new class of images that I call "hieroglyphs of affect," and to understand what I mean by this, let us consider a context of their production.

We are in the AsiaWorld Arena in Hong Kong on a chilly night in February 2008, and the city is beginning to thaw in the coldest winter in a quarter of a century. The Icelandic singer Bjork is in full techno flight, in a concert promoting her new album, while around the stadium little blobs of light flash continuously, like dim stars in a firmament. Early in the concert Bjork pauses to ask the audience to put away their camera phones to be "in the moment" (Wright 2008). It is a curious response from this star, one of the most technologized of all performers, but it draws our attention to a particular form of presence that is now a feature of everyday life in many places including Hong Kong and it emphasizes that for each audience member there is a different way of being "in the moment" than there is for the star. For the Hong Kong audience, the use of the camera phone in this context registers its presence more completely "in the moment" than anything else, because the "self-imaging" of the gesture is precisely what produces a sense of presence in the event, securing the very reality of the moment, otherwise unsecured.

The little flashes of light from camera phones have no capacity to illuminate the well-lit star on the distant stage, but they do locate the photographer-subject, enveloping him or her in a halo—a kind of aura—that situates him or her precisely in the moment, registering his or her presence in the event being witnessed. The sheer scale of the huge stadium otherwise reduces audience to an undifferentiated mass in the darkness of the star's shadow. The audience is necessary for the event because of its largely *aural* presence—in the *sound* of response and applause that the performer relies on as an immediate gauge of reaction. So the small pulses of light as camera phones flash in an asynchronous rhythm across the crowd have the effect of making individual audience members visible in a random pattern of light, the flow of which is controlled by audience rather than by technicians sweeping the crowd with choreographed lighting effects. The audience thus disrupts the show, reversing the order of the "distraction" industry's one-way flow of value.[1]

The camera-phone image taken in this context may not circulate at all, or it might be posted to a blog, but in any case, its use is personal and, in its way, disruptive—as the star's request testifies.

So ubiquitous has the use of mobile media become in Hong Kong, and in Asia more generally, that we take for granted the magnitude of image capture made possible by their use. Not much serious attention is given to the worth of the images produced, and if anything there is a tendency to assume their general worthlessness, in the face of social and economic issues of the rate of technology uptake, sales volume of devices, information volume transfers, technological impacts on poverty and development, and so on. Even the highly technologized star in my first example wants to discount the value of the image as an inauthentic attempt at presence. The ephemerality of the images and their low resolution means that even users frequently have a low opinion of them, generally considering them to be substitutes for higher resolution digital camera images in recording events and the everyday. This means that we might regard the camera-phone picture as a "surrogate" image of a particular kind, and I suggest that this apparent "surrogacy" involves a specific development in the nature of communication and sociality, of aesthetics and creativity, and of thought and feeling, which marks a return to more embodied forms of cognition.

Notwithstanding ambivalence toward the images, it is clear that the very ubiquity of their production is a cultural phenomenon of considerable significance, especially within visual culture studies and their overlap with visual sciences and informational aesthetics. Kristóf Nyíri (2006) argues that mobile communication (e.g., the convergence of oral, visual, and written forms in voice, image, and music consumption, MMS and SMS functions of the mobile phone) returns us to more archaic forms of sociality in which a renewed relation to the visual and the oral take precedence over written forms. These apparently unalienated and more direct forms of sociality and more pictorial and hieroglyphic forms of inscription come to the fore as inner mental contents are passed over to external devices in a process that, he argues, liberates rather than alienates the mind. Nyíri refers to film critic Béla Balázs's concept of the "Visible Man" (*Der sichtbare Mensch*; Balázs 1924) whom the development of cinema had brought to the fore, after the age of printing had restricted communication to reading and writing. Nyíri's main argument is that these forms of communication offer the reestablishment of local forms of community connectedness lost within postmodern society and have expanded as a counter to the sense of alienation of excessive mobility and information overload.

Actually the recent revival of interest in film theories such as those of Balázs and also Siegfried Kracauer's concept of "the redemption of physical reality" represents an argument for a sense of cultural reenchantment, balancing developments in communication philosophy—such as Vilém Flusser's (2002) concept of the "technical image" and Friedrich Kittler's (1999) counternarrative of technological subjectivity—approaches that go beyond the more romantic and nostalgic aspects of Baláz's "visible man" in his singularity. This research, focused on the circuits of production and distribution (sharing) and on the images themselves, is concerned that the images—these "inconspicuous surface-level expressions" as Kracauer might have described them or, as I would prefer to see them, these small hieroglyphs of affect—may represent a stage of cultural development the significance of which is inadequately understood. Indeed, these images are so ephemeral one may lose them without knowing what they have recorded of life in these times—or, more important, what "thought processes" they record. In this article, I provide a general background for considering these images, referring to data and observations gathered in a pilot research project recently undertaken to study camera-phone pictures.[2]

In Hong Kong, where this research is based, the mobile phone subscription rate reached 167 percent (Office of the Telecommunications Authority 2009) in August 2009. In June 2007, just a little more than two years ago, the figure was 135.6 percent; by comparison, the broadband uptake rate runs at under half this level, at 78.7 percent. Although higher-end technology interest has focused on the uptake of 3G and other advanced service options, so far only 37.6 percent of total subscriptions are for 2.5G or 3G services[3]—which means the majority of users are not yet engaged in the kind of activities that mobile phone companies foreground in the marketing of their products. Rather, their uses involve a range of lower level uses of technology, which, I argue, are innovative in particular ways and represent a sphere of creativity that has, in my view, transformed how we might understand creativity in general, overthrowing remnants of romanticism that locate creativity predominantly within the activities of self-declared artists.

As previously noted, the ubiquity of image making in this form has been taken for granted, with its subject matter considered unworthy of serious concern because of the limited technical qualities of the pictures—a limitation that users freely acknowledge in their blog comments. Elsewhere I have looked at the proliferation of images in a scene of local activism (the 2006 Star Ferry protests and final vigil; see Grace 2007), and in discussions of new media and user-created content, attention is more likely to be given to activist uses, to ways in which democracy and citizenship are activated by new forms of information circulation and engagement (see Nyiri 2003 in particular, but see also McCaughey and Ayers 2003; Meikle 2002; Rennie 2006; Spyer 2002; Van De Donk 2004; Waltz 2005).

But even this very focus betrays a prejudice, as if the everyday proliferation of images by new technological means is unworthy of attention unless it can be linked to something deemed worthwhile. In studying material of this kind, it is being assumed that everyday practices of image production are part of the processes by which people produce meanings and value for themselves beyond the constraints of conventional political forms and social limitations. Further, it is precisely in these new forms of intentional community formation and network structures that new potentialities are emerging. More especially, it is in these small-scale affective adaptations of technology that one can observe mood and sentiment to understand what mobilizes people—assuming always that one is studying individuals and their thoughts, feelings, and actions and not just a reactive, easily manipulated and undifferentiated mass.

Let me illustrate with a story of improvisation and innovation that you are unlikely to read about in the marketing of all the beautiful new objects we desire and are willing to consume. This is a case of a critical practice, within the constraints of an everyday encounter with commercial culture, which I think is not uncommon in young people's technological use, because they are well aware of the nature of the world in which they live and they are also aware of their own limited resources and futures in the world of consumption, notwithstanding their commoditized surroundings.

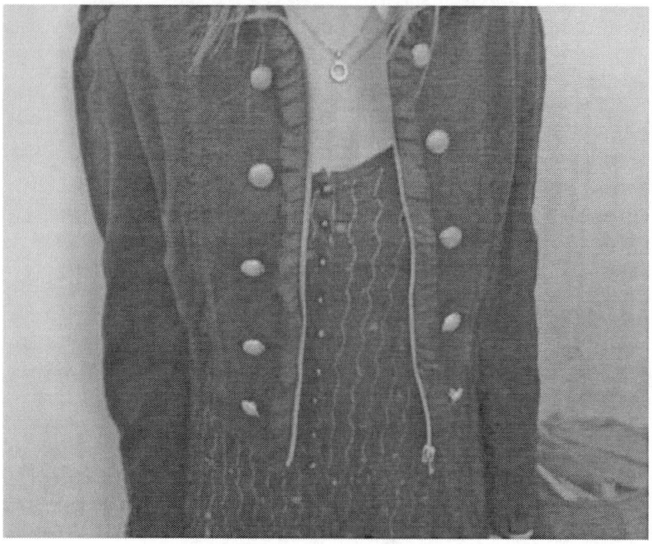

FIG. 1. Teleconferencing.

Three young women (see figure 1) are looking for clothes in one of Hong Kong's big shopping malls; two of them go into a changing room in one store to try on a jacket, which one of them has chosen, while one waits outside (since there's no room for three of them in the cubicle). But they are irritated to find there is no mirror in the changing room—for good reason, in the women's view; the absence of a mirror means that the wearer has to leave the cubicle to use the large mirror outside, and this means the sales assistants can then pressure her to purchase the item she is wearing. The shopper, however, is a creative and innovative person who immediately sees through all marketing and sales tactics, so in this case, one of the women has a mobile phone with which she takes a picture—providing a small mirror for the wearer (women are used to small mirrors in makeup compacts and lipstick cases, so this a new form of an existing everyday practice). However, there is a new capacity in using the mobile phone: The resultant image can be sent by Bluetooth to the waiting friend outside, who is able to reply by sending an SMS message with her own opinion of the clothing item. Let us be clear what has happened here. This is a mini–phone conference vastly different from the kind imagined in corporate advertising of global teleconferences and in describing the exchange; the young woman has no illusions about the nature of power involved:

> The mirror was hanging out of the fitting [room]. The lack of mirror in the fitting room is actually for the advantages of the salesgirls. If the customers need to come out of the fitting room, the salesgirls are able to convince them with the clothes they are on. My friend used the function of the cell phone to resist this institutional violence, structuring a private space upon the institution.[4]

I think it is fair to identify this act as a highly creative one, an instance of innovation of a kind not usually acknowledged in the discourse of corporate entrepreneurship, which focuses only on profit-motivated innovation, and in a sense I want to appropriate the word "innovation" as a synonym for another word we often use in this kind of context: resistance. I am not so naive as to imagine that such acts will bring about "the revolution" or whatever social transformation a radical political discourse dreams of producing, but even if the dreamed-of transformation were to occur on whatever terms, so would resistance and so would the need exist to survive whatever regime is in place. In our search for transformative strategies and tactics, creativity and innovation are required, and it is useful to imagine the everyday form of these adaptive appropriations in terms other than corporate ones on the one hand or romantic and easily recognizable political ones on the other. To this extent, more recent attempts to broaden a notion of the political are useful to us in reconsiderations of what democracy might come to mean (Mouffe 2000, 2005).

EVERYDAY SPHERES OF INNOVATION

In a recent essay on ubiquitous computing based on research in Singapore and Korea, Bell and Dourish (2007) suggest there are particular spatial reasons for rapid adoption in these places (e.g., the embedding of computational technology in daily life in Singapore, the strong relation between public and private sectors in Korea in infrastructure development—as opposed to reliance on the free market in the United States—and the condensed spatiality of Asian cities in general, making the wiring of a building much easier than the slower house-by-house wiring in cultures of urban sprawl present in the United States and Australia, with the very privacy of domestic space in, say, Korea stimulating the development of a "public domain" for gaming activities).

I argue that we need to view everyday uses of technology as a sphere of innovation, to adapt Sawhney and Lee's (2005) description of "arenas of innovation" in their account of higher end networks of innovation in technological development. My principal argument is that innovation is a much more diffuse concept than it is generally understood to be within innovation and industry policy frameworks—and it is these microlevel adaptations and transformations of technology by users that need to be studied and evaluated for fully understanding the processes of social and cultural change that are occurring (a fact acknowledged in the growing number of anthropologists being employed by information and communication technology [ICT] companies and in the expansion of more nuanced ethnographic research methods in industry research).

The emergence of newer forms of visual culture and communication and in particular the rapid adoption of the camera phone is, I argue, one such sphere of innovation, which has received less attention than verbal and textual aspects of communication. Fortunati (2001) notes in particular that the mobile phone was designed for work, but changes identity when it enters the domestic sphere. Although too early to refer to camera-phone use, her qualitative research in this and subsequent studies lays the ground for thinking in a more dynamic way about mobile technology generally and in moving research toward social and cultural questions.

I am interested principally in the social and cultural forms of this material and in the adaptive uses to which the material is put in personal and community contexts—in social networking, identity, memory and narrative formation, relationship maintenance, self-expression and projection, and the symbolic and instrumental meanings arising in the production and distribution of these images for users and how these meanings might be understood interculturally. Such imagery suggests unprecedented creative and cultural expression, as well as the possibilities of citizen journalism and democratic uses (which have been more widely noted).

The images now being produced record particular aspects of everyday experience—in its complete ordinariness—which has never previously been recorded on a large scale, but the ephemerality of the images and the impermanence of the technology itself may mean that this material will disappear within a short time. Although the images might be regarded as banal, there is also the sense in which the very task of producing ordinariness is itself the social activity of "working at being usual" (Sacks, cited in Koskinen 2007)—a key aspect of meaning production on a most basic level.

Preliminary quantitative and descriptive research on camera-phone use has predominantly been initiated by the information and telecommunications industry (Kindberg, Spasojevic, Fleck, and Sellen 2004; Spasojevic 2005). Such work focuses on "future design" to discover emerging value and business opportunities and on the development of applications to encourage use, though it may also acknowledge the affective uses and adaptations which everyday practices themselves initiate (Koskinen 2005).

Some of the most developed research has been presented at the ubicomp (ubiquitous computing) conferences in Tokyo in 2005 and in Orange County, California, in 2006 (Okabe 2005; Ito 2005; Okabe, Ito, Chipchase, and

Shimizu 2006), and methodological design issues are foregrounded in important ways (Van House and Davis 2005; Van House 2006a). As these conferences are principally designed to present research results in the design, implementation, application, and evaluation of ubiquitous computing technologies, they are thus industry conferences, and social and cultural questions are largely peripheral, notwithstanding the efforts of leading researchers in bringing such questions to the attention of the field.

Mobile communication and social change conferences have provided another key venue for the social and cultural consideration of camera-phone use and multimedia messaging (Okabe 2004)—though it should be noted that much of this research is also industry-funded, and Motorola and Nokia have supported important research in Europe (Scifo 2005). Ilpo Koskinen (2005), however, notes that industry research is oriented toward faster results, but that what is really needed is longer term comparative research that can only be carried out in academic contexts.

Some of the most developed work has been undertaken in Japan (Ito, Okabe, and Matsuda 2006) and, more recently, Korea (Lee 2006), where more detailed ethnographic and qualitative research methods are deployed. Lee Dong-Hoo especially emphasizes the gender dimension of camera-phone use, in the particular take-up by young women—suggesting another reason why the area may have been relatively neglected in technological research—and popular images of "geek culture," focusing on tech-savvy young men.

In concentrating on ethnographic and anthropological field work in Korea and Singapore, Bell and Dourish (2007) suggest that laboratory-based work has the tendency to assume a top-down implementation of technology—as something that will, in the future, transform social practice—whereas they argue that the transformation has already occurred in everyday adaptations of technology by users (see also Qiu 2005).

THE CAMERA-PHONE STORY

In the myth-making stories of new technology, the camera phone was ostensibly "born" to record a birth—that of Philippe Kahn's daughter in 1997—and "baby photos" remain a popular subject. The technology, however, was not immediately exploited in the United States but in Japan, with the release in July 1999 of Kyocera's PHS VP-210 "visual phone" and in November 2000 of J-Phone's *Sha-Mail* (写メール—a contraction of the Japanese word for photograph, combined with "mail").

Since then, the rate of the device's adoption has been unprecedented. Market research figures indicate that 500 million mobile phones with cameras were sold globally in 2006 (Strategy Analytics 2007), and by 2010 annual sales are projected to be 903 million (Cellular-News 2006). In the Asian region, latest figures claim 78 million units were sold in the first half of 2007—ten times the sales figure of stand-alone digital cameras (GFK Asia 2007). Projections suggest that by 2010, 228 billion pictures will be captured using the device (InfoTrends 2006). No previous imaging technology has been as rapidly disseminated as this one—and all within one decade. This has seen profound changes in what is considered worthy of being photographed and recorded—changes that have been anecdotally observed but remain relatively uncharted.

Dizzying statistics and market hype, however, cannot explain *why* the device has become so popular, *how* it has transformed the production and consumption of images, and, above all, the significance of these changes. In part, we can attribute the dissemination of these technologies to effective marketing—but the purchase of a tool does not in itself determine the nature of its use. I do not assume that users have no agency and are merely the pawns in a marketing game. Rather, I am interested in the little-studied new forms of everyday creativity that arise in the adaptive uses of technologies and in the cultural specificity of practices.

Although extensive research on the social/cultural impact of mobile phones globally and on new forms of communication and social life arising from the technology's use has been undertaken globally (Katz and Aakhus 2002; Ling 2004; Ito, Okabe, and Matsuda 2005; Höflich and Hartmann 2006; Goggin 2006), and there has been a widespread concern with the impacts on democracy and civil society which are enabled by the mobile phone (Nyiri 2003), this work, as already noted, has focused on the verbal and textual aspects of communication. There has been relatively little research on the camera-phone image itself and on the networks within which it circulates.

Perhaps this is because the initially low-quality images were regarded as largely insignificant and unworthy of serious consideration because of their ephemerality—in the same way that snapshots were largely excluded from the history of photography until it became clear that they provided valuable evidence of social life and history. It may also be that attention to the misuse of the camera phone (CBS News 2003), surreptitious uses of phones and concerns with privacy (BBC News 2004; *Forbes Magazine* 2004) or incidents that give rise to notoriety (e.g., the 2006 "bus uncle" case in Hong Kong) detract from the value of much more typical and everyday uses. It is these everyday practices that are the focus of this cultural research—in other words, the "normal" rather than the "pathological" use (Canguilhem 1991).

IMMERSION, CAPTURING, AND SHARING

In accessing camera-phone images for this research,[5] I noted that there is a greater propensity in Hong Kong for people to upload camera-phone pictures to personal Web sites, blogs, and social networking sites than to photo-sharing sites such as Flickr. Initially, I was interested in the use of camera phones in the documenting of actions around the Star Ferry demolition in 2006, because I am interested in activist uses and in tactical media, but the widespread use of camera phones in this context was not an observed feature—at least in terms of the upload of images to accessible sites, although I analyzed a lot of video material uploaded to YouTube (Grace 2007).

Camera phones seem especially deployed in situations of *immersion* in a public[6] event—for example, June 4 candlelight vigils in Victoria Park, Hong Kong,[7] where several thousand people usually gather. Many photographers cover the event, using a range of devices, from low-end digital cameras to high-end professional single-lens reflex cameras and video cameras. I have observed that the higher-end cameras are generally used on the edges of action, whereas in the middle of the action—in the center of the park and immersed in the crowd, the majority of the photographs taken by participants are captured with camera phones.

These "memory events" are particular to place, and the image produced may be less important than the *act* of production—or the act of "capture"—as a register of *affective* engagement in a moment of *expressiveness* that may have deep local significance, but that subsequently fails to be communicative, beyond the instant of production, for anyone other than those who have been involved. This incommunicability of the image stands in marked contrast to assumptions of the universality of visual language, suggesting a constitution of new private spaces, separate from generalized public space (which now more than anything may merely mean a space in which people are under constant surveillance). It also suggests that new types of imagery are being produced that have a very different function than the analogical photographic image and a very different relation to memory.

THE MUTATION OF MEMORY

Because the Star Ferry actions and the June 4 vigils are particular kinds of "memory events" in Hong Kong, I am interested in how the image itself is constituting memory, both personal and collective, and the extent to which one can say a mutation of human memory is occurring, if one compares the ways in which analog photography functions as memorial and how digital photography operates.

A blurring of the distinction between still and moving images in new technologies means that the still image no longer records a "frozen" moment in time but is rather situated in a generalized dynamic animation of visual space. Ubiquitous user-created imagery may thus involve a different relation to time and memory than exists in the case of analogue photography.

This is because the act of *presence* that it records possesses principally a performative or projective nature, rather than one of memorialization (although this is not excluded); the memorial act assumes the absolute reality of the moment recorded, inaugurating it as a register of the present, which is immediately past—immediately historicized—as soon as the image is taken. The ubiquitous image, on the other hand, has a much more tenuous link to the present, which it does not necessarily accept as real—hence my initial example of the Bjork concert; rather, it is the act of "capture" that brings the present into existence, because ubiquitous image making belongs to a world in which the real is so thoroughly mediated that an event does not exist without at the same time producing an image of itself—and it is this image that secures the lived reality in which the image maker is situated.

In support of this view, I have noted that in interviews carried out so far, interviewees are keen to emphasize that in their use of camera-phone pictures, memory is not the principle reason for taking pictures. Rather, images are produced almost as a form of note-taking or writing—hieroglyphic writing, one might suggest—that relates principally to living in and negotiating the present rather than memorializing (hence it becomes a way of being "in the moment"—so Bjork's exhortation to her audience to put away their camera phones in order to be "in the moment" assumes that photography is primarily about a deferral of presence to remember).

The function of memory is no longer deferred to the negative image as it was in analog photography (because users clearly understand that the "memory card" will be erased), but rather it becomes embodied in the participant, forming what one might call the subject's "body memory" (Damasio 1999) "Body memory" is not only invoked in oral history projects, which seek to recover the memory of experiences not recorded in official histories, but also it implies a more spatial/proprioceptive sense of memory, generated in the use of ubiquitous technologies.

There is an additional factor that is specific to this context. Text messaging is less ubiquitous in Hong Kong because of the complexities of character generation using Chinese—and images are easier to produce.[8] So my research is exploring the kinds of images taken and the circumstances of capture as well as their mode of sharing and storing, and I am looking at these images because of a sense of neglect of the content of such images, in favor of the uses of the images and the manner of their circulation. If these images appear ephemeral, those who make them nonetheless regard them as being worthy of keeping in some form, and in my research, 88 percent of the respondents are quite adamant about archiving the images, usually by downloading them to computers (although at the same time, very few bother to print them, so the computer becomes a kind of virtual shoebox).

New genres are being formed, new narrativizations of the everyday that are specific to place. Many involve fantasies, desire, and wish fulfillment—the desire for love, marriage, and children. So blogs might be written from the point of view of a newborn baby. For example:

> Papa is a photograph enthusiast and he puts a lot of thought when taking photos. Mama found that mobile photos have their own special feel.[9]

There is a whole genre of very immersive images and blogs written from the point of view of a cat or dog, confined in the small space of an apartment, just like the bloggers themselves.

In work so far, I have been struck by the sophistication of images and the understandings that producers have of their values and functions.

Bloggers, for example, frequently refer to distinctions in quality between camera-phone images and digital camera images, identifying specific features of each practice that in the past would only have been made by professional users or very keen amateurs. For example, a blogger writes:

> Comparing to the mobile nowadays, my mobile has a really low resolution. However, I can tell you that I love the texture of the photos it takes. It contains a rugged beauty that I could find nowhere else.

Others identify the value of the diary use of images in blogs and the personal/social value of these uses:

> I've done so many things in July. If I hadn't arranged my mobile photos, I probably wouldn't remember them all. To a lazy person like me, the camera function of a mobile works like a diary, and reminds me what I have done every day. I don't know if anybody who, like me, saves every photo I have taken this month, and filed them like they are documents, putting them into the CD shelf. I do this every month. Sometimes, when I look at the photos, I smile. Happiness can be so easy to attain.

Another notes a way in which the ability to easily take images intervenes in work life, providing a moment of reverie and escape.

> Outside the window the sky is endless, I can't concentrate on my work. I hope to be under the blue sky, feeling the summer air. This is only mobile photo, the quality and the angle isn't great.

There is sometimes a poignant, poetic quality, suggesting an ability to transcend the limitations of the everyday. For example, a blogger posts an image her husband takes of a sunset in front of the mainland factory where he goes to work, giving an indication both of the length of the working day and also of the capacity to see the natural world even in a context in which the worker is not assumed to have the time for looking and appreciating environment.

TOWARD A GENERAL AESTHESIA

A great deal of work has been done on the history of seeing and on the formation of visual codes in media and cultural studies in the last thirty years, so it is a surprise to find so little actual looking at images produced by new information and communication technologies, with their ubiquity seeming to permit a widespread neglect of their content. This is typified in the recently published OECD Working Party on the Information Economy (2007) report, *Participative Web: User Created Content.*

This report emphasizes the use of intelligent web services in empowering users to contribute, rate, collaborate on, and distribute materials, resulting in a "participative Web" embedded in people's lives, and it describes the rapid growth of user-created content, defining it and identifying its key drivers, its scope, and different forms. However, the report foregrounds new value chains and business models rather than social and cultural impacts. The report is focused more on Europe and the United States, and although Japan, Korea, and China are mentioned, there is no detailed discussion of practices in Asia. More particularly, the report merely describes the tools used to generate content and the technological means of its distribution. In other words, it is a report on user-created content that shows no interest in the content itself.

Part of the neglect of the image may arise from a movement away from the practice of "close reading," which has been a key defining feature and analytical tool of classical humanities scholarship, as if a hermeneutics of reading is regarded as a too slow a process for the speed of the world, however much another version of this very practice—pattern recognition—is regarded as central to technocultural concerns in the sciences. Perhaps this has something to do with the fact that "pattern recognition" is increasingly a machinic function rather than a human activity and it seems there is currently much more fascination in discovering the clumsy things that computers are capable of doing than the precise and intricate analytical activity that humans are capable of, unless that activity can be simulated by a computer.

This is not at all to discount the fact that machinic possibilities of pattern recognition do allow us a new means of organizing social data into powerful new visual forms, which extend our capacities to see and know social and cultural patterns and are of increasing value in humanities scholarship in explaining the complexities of cultural adaptations of new technologies. To analyze in any depth the sheer volume of new images being produced (which is in fact one of the features of this new development), one does need to deploy new methods of categorization, which are not merely descriptive but much more affective and visual rather than verbal.

Although much of the critical and analytical work on photography and the status of the image in the last thirty years or so has been principally concerned with the establishment and maintenance (or loss) of *truth value*—in the wake of poststructuralist challenge to the relation between original and copy, real and fake—this emphasis has been replaced by what one might call *face value*: that is, the tendency to take for granted the reality of the image, knowing however that it is an image, which has the capacity to both reflect and produce reality.

When it comes to the actual images being produced by mobile phones, there is a sense that they are individually insignificant because there are so many of them, that they are taken by amateurs and therefore there is no "originality" or formal innovation that is likely to be observable (this is a particular prejudice of modernist criticism's focus on textual forms) and that, in content terms, they are merely snapshots and so of no value to the world beyond the communicative act between individuals at the moment of recording. I do know, however, how historically significant snapshots have become, and although one cannot yet know whether today's ubiquitous images will last, we at least know already how they are affectively used to remap space (Lee 2007) and we know something of their circulation in intimate relations, since many of us have experienced a sharing of images and may even have sent images, within these circuits of "distant closeness" (Van House 2006b).

On the question of the assumed inadequacy of amateur use at the formal level, one can argue that compositional codes have probably become so ubiquitous in themselves—and they are in any case technologically structured in the use of devices ("face recognition," "smile recognition," etc. within devices)—that there is no longer any such thing as a "bad" picture, but what we have instead is the dissolution of the division of aesthetic labor between artists and nonartists (the skilled and unskilled) and the emergence of what I want to call a *general aesthesia* in which everyone's creative capacity has been extended. Aesthesia is the ability to feel and perceive; it is a medical term, but one might appropriate it to describe an affective state of response, a heightening of awareness, which is a counter to the widespread assumption of anesthetization in the face of information overload.

This widened idea of aesthetics may be something like the notion of "social aesthetics" that MacDougall (2006) develops. But something more is involved—what could be called a mutation of aesthetic value, in which everyday and ubiquitous image production acts as a counter to the dominance of professional, artistic, advertising, and celebrity images that otherwise serve to position people as unimportant. The ubiquitous image allows for a self-production—a "self-determination" within blurred public and private spheres.

The "mutation of value" goes further than aesthetics alone, to the general question of value. These images are not merely the manifestations of what Vilem Flusser (1983) calls the "technical image" (a designation that partially removes the image from aesthetic analysis), but are instances of aesthetic/affective ensembles. Something new is involved in their production and circulation that goes beyond conventional value systems and structures, ordering discrete objects and commodities within circuits of acquisition and collection. The very ubiquity of image capture suggests an aesthetics of the immaterial, which I have not yet fully elaborated, involving the production of what one might call "ephemeral value," a strange spectral thing that has no economic function, producing a contradiction at the heart of the commodity form itself, which has the capacity to challenge the apparently overwhelming success of market values globally.

It is the argument of this article that we need to study the nature of the material produced in this new social and cultural phenomenon because it is at the point of production and sharing that affective meaning is produced for users; the technology merely enables expression but it does not *cause* it. It may well be that from the point of view of economic value, the content is irrelevant and only volume matters. However, from the point of view of cultural research, it is precisely the nature of the content that generates energy around particular products, constituting values other than economic ones. My interest is in the extent to which people make meanings for themselves above and beyond their general meaninglessness and insignificance within totalizing and abstract economic structures that otherwise constrain everyday freedom.

NOTES

1. Chris Chesher (2007) describes a more interactive form of use of mobile technologies involving audience and performer in his analysis of a U2 concert—but I am specifically interested here in the audience's agency, rather than the more "engineered" process he discusses.

2. Images and comments were accessed via blogs, interviews, and questionnaires. This research is currently being extended in a two-year Research Grants Council, General Research Fund Grant awarded in 2008. I am grateful to Chan Sum Yee for her research assistance on the pilot project that forms the basis of this article.

3. It must be acknowledged that the rate of subscription for such services is rapidly increasing. In 2007, it was less than 25 percent of all accounts, so there has in fact been a 50 percent increase in the number of 3G subscriptions in the last two years.

4. E-mail to author, November 11, 2006.

5. This research is based so far on analyzing approximately 250 blogs and about 2,000 images; we have also used an online questionnaire and ongoing research involving Web upload of images; a

Facebook group and interviews with bloggers are currently being undertaken.

6. There do appear to be particular local ideas of what is public and private as occasions for taking pictures. For example, from our observations, MTR travel seems to be a "private" space to the extent that, although mobile phones are extremely widely used for conversations and for texting, they are rarely used for taking photographs on the MTR.

7. Commemorating the Tiananmen Square Protests, June 1989, and a specific local focus of mobilization in Hong Kong.

8. One has only to consider the complexities of visual space in popular magazines in Hong Kong to understand how words and images blur together in apparent chaos—compared with a general emphasis on minimalism in "good design" principles, based on a tradition of European modernism.

9. Translation of all comments by Chan Sum Yee. I am grateful for her research assistance on the pilot project, undertaken between May 2007 and March 2008.

REFERENCES

Balázs, B. 2007. Visible Man, or the culture of film (1924). *Screen* 48:91–108.

BBC News. 2004. Camera phones threat to privacy. http://news.bbc.co.uk/1/hi/technology/4017225.stm (accessed September 20, 2007).

Bell, G., and P. Dourish. 2007. Yesterday's tomorrows: Notes on ubiquitous computing's dominant vision. *Personal and Ubiquitous Computing* 11:133–43.

Canguilhem, G. 1991. *The normal and the pathological*. New York: Zone Books.

Castells, M., M. Fernandez-Ardevol, J. L. Qiu, and A. Sey. 2006. *Mobile communication and society: A global perspective*. Cambridge, MA: MIT Press.

CBS News. 2003. Camera phone etiquette abuses: Asia encounters new brands of misbehavior with camera cell phones. http://www.cbsnews.com/stories/2003/07/09/tech/main562434.shtml (accessed September 20, 2007).

Cellular News. 2006. Camera phones account for 87% of mobile phone shipments in 2010. http://www.cellular-news.com/story/15652.php (accessed September 20th, 2007).

Chesher, C. 2007. Becoming the Milky Way: Mobile phones and actor networks at a U2 concert. *Continuum* 21:217–25.

Damasio, A. 1999. *The feeling of what happens: Body, emotion and consciousness*. New York: Harcourt.

Flusser, V. 2002. Line and surface. In *Writings*, ed. A. Ströhl, 21–34. Minneapolis: University of Minnesota Press.

Forbes Magazine. 2004. Phone misuse prompts arrests In Hong Kong. http://www.forbes.com/execpicks/2004/02/23/0223hongkongpinnacor_ii.html (accessed September 20, 2007).

Fortunati, L. 2001. The mobile phone: An identity on the move. *Personal and Ubiquitous Computing* 5:85–98.

Fortunati, L. 2007. *Gender and the mobile phone, Keynote speech*. Mobile Media 2007 Conference. University of Sydney, Sydney, Australia.

GFK Asia. 2007. *Asian mobile sales top $22B as color camera phones continue to dominate*. http://www.wirelessdesignasia.com/article-6628-asianmobilesalestop22bascolorcameraphonescontinuetodominate-Asia.html (accessed August 31, 2007).

Goggin, G. 2006. *Cell phone culture: Mobile technology in everyday life*. London: Routledge.

Grace, H. 2007. Monuments and the face of time: Distortions of scale and asynchrony in postcolonial Hong Kong. *Postcolonial Studies* 10:467–83.

Halbwachs, M. 1992. *On collective memory*. Chicago: University of Chicago Press.

Hjorth, L. 2006. Snapshots of *almost contact*: Gendered camera phone practices and a case study in Seoul, Korea. Paper presented at the Cultural Space and Public Sphere in Asia Conference, Seoul, Korea, March 17–18.

Höflich, J. R., and M. Hartmann, eds. 2006. *Mobile communication in everyday life: Ethnographic views, observations and reflections*. Berlin: Frank & Timme.

Huyssen, A. 1995. *Twilight memories: Marking time in a culture of amnesia*. London: Routledge.

InFoTrends/CAP Ventures. 2005. InFoTrends/CAP Ventures forecasts 2009 camera phone sales at 847 million units. http://www.digitalcamerainfo.com/content/InFoTrends-CAP-Ventures-Forecasts-2009-Camera-Phone-Sales-At-847-Million-Units.htm (accessed September 10, 2007).

Ito, M. 2005. Intimate visual co-presence. Paper presented at the Workshop on Pervasive Image Capture and Sharing: New Social Practices and Implications for Technology Workshop (PICS 2005), Seventh International Conference on Ubiquitous Computing (UbiComp 2005), Tokyo, Japan.

Ito, M., D. Okabe, and M. Matsuda, eds. 2005. *Personal, portable, pedestrian: Mobile phones in Japanese life*. Cambridge, MA: MIT Press.

Katz, J. E., and M. Aakhus, eds. 2002. *Perpetual contact: Mobile communication, private talk, public performance*. Cambridge: Cambridge University Press.

Kindberg, T., M. Spasojevic, R. Fleck, and A. Sellen. 2004. *How and why people use cameraphones* (Technical report HPL-2004-216). Bristol, England: Hewlett-Packard Laboratories.

Kittler, F. A. 1999. *Gramophone film typewriter*. Stanford, CA: Stanford University Press.

Koskinen, I. 2005. *Pervasive image capture and sharing: Methodological remarks*. Paper presented at the Workshop on Pervasive Image Capture and Sharing: New Social Practices and Implications for Technology Workshop (PICS 2005), Seventh International Conference on Ubiquitous Computing (UbiComp 2005), Tokyo, Japan.

Koskinen, I., E. Kurvinen, and L. Turo-Kimmo. 2002. *Mobile image*. Helsinki: IT Press.

Kracauer, S. 1995. *The mass ornament: Weimar essays*. Cambridge, MA: Harvard University Press.

Le Goff, J. 1996. *History and memory*. New York: Columbia University Press.

Lee, D. 2006. Women's creation of camera phone culture. *Fibreculture Journal* 6, http://journal.fibreculture.org/issue6/issue6_donghoo.html (accessed April 3, 2010).

Lee, D. 2007. *Re-imagining urban space: Mobility, connectivity, and a sense of place. Keynote speech*. Mobile Media 2007 Conference, University of Sydney, Sydney, Australia.

Lin, A. 2005. Gendered, bilingual communication practices: Mobile text-messaging among Hong Kong College Students. *Fibreculture Journal* 6, http://journal.fibreculture.org/issue6/issue6_lin.html (accessed April 3, 2010).

Ling, R. 2004. *The mobile connection*. San Francisco: Kaufmann.

MacDougall, D. 2005. *The corporeal image: Film, ethnography, and the senses.* Princeton, NJ: Princeton University Press.

McCaughey, M., and M. Ayers, eds. 2003. *Cyberactivism: Online activism in theory and practice.* New York: Routledge.

Meikle, G. 2002. *Future active: Media activism and the Internet.* London: Routledge.

Mitchell, W. J. T. 2005. *What do pictures want? The lives and loves of images.* Chicago: University of Chicago Press.

Mouffe, C. 2000. *The democratic paradox.* London: Verso.

———. 2005. *On the political.* New York: Routledge.

Nyiri, K. ed. 2003. *Mobile democracy: Essays on society, self, and politics.* Vienna: Passagen Verlag.

———. 2006. The mobile telephone as a return to unalienated communication. *Knowledge, Technology, & Policy* 19:54–61.

OECD Working Party on the Information Economy. 2007. *Participative Web: User created content.* http://www.oecd.org/dataoecd/57/14/38393115.pdf (accessed April 3, 2010).

Office of the Telecommunications Authority, The Government of Hong Kong Special Administrative Region. 2008. *Key telecommunications statistics.* Updated August 2009. http://www.ofta.gov.hk/en/datastat/key_stat.html (accessed October 9, 2009).

Okabe, D. 2004. Emergent social practices, situations and relations through everyday camera phone use. Paper presented at the Mobile Communication and Social Change conference, Seoul, Korea, October 18–19.

———. 2005. Social practice of camera phone in Japan. Paper presented at the Workshop on Pervasive Image Capture and Sharing: New Social Practices and Implications for Technology Workshop (PICS 2005), Seventh International Conference on Ubiquitous Computing (UbiComp 2005), Tokyo, Japan.

Okabe, D., M. Ito, J. Chipchase, and A. Shimizu. 2006. The social uses of purikura: Photographing, modding, archiving, and sharing. Paper presented at Workshop on Pervasive Image Capture and Sharing: New Social Practices and Implications for Technology Workshop (PICS 2006) at the Eighth International Conference on Ubiquitous Computing (UbiComp 2006), Irvine, CA.

Pink, S. 2006. *Doing visual ethnography: Images, media and representation in research.* London: Sage.

Qiu, J. L. 2005. *The accidental accomplishment of little smart: Understanding the emergence of a working-class ICT.* Paper presented at ARNIC High-Level Workshop on Wireless Communication and Development, University of Southern California, October 7–8.

Rennie, E. 2006. *Community media: A global introduction.* Lanham, MD: Rowman & Littlefield.

Ricoeur, P. 2004. *Memory, history and forgetting.* Chicago: University of Chicago Press.

Sawhney, H., and S. Lee. 2005. Arenas of innovation: Understanding new configurational potentialities of communication technologies. *Media, Culture & Society* 27:391–414.

Scifo, B. 2005. The domestication of camera-phone and MMS communication: The early experiences of young Italians. In *A sense of place: The global and the local in mobile communication,* ed. K. Njiri, 363–73. Vienna: Passagen Verlagen.

Spasojevic, M. 2005. Camera phone use and its implications. Paper presented at the Workshop on Pervasive Image Capture and Sharing: New Social Practices and Implications for Technology Workshop (PICS 2005), Seventh International Conference on Ubiquitous Computing (UbiComp 2005), Tokyo, Japan.

Spyer, P. E. 2002. Shadow media and muslim VCDs. In *9/11: A virtual case book,* ed. B. Abrash and F. Ginsburg, http://www.nyu.edu/fas/projects/vcb/case_911_FLASHcontent.html (accessed May 1, 2007). New York: Center for Media, Culture and History, New York University.

Strategy Analytics. 2007. Enabling technologies: CMOS beats CCD in half-billion global camera phone market. http://www.strategyanalytics.net/default.aspx?mod=ReportAbstractViewer&a0=3466 (accessed September 15, 2007).

Van de Donk, W., B. Loader, P. Nixon, and D. Rucht. eds. 2004. *Cyberprotest: New media, citizens and social movements.* New York: Routledge.

Van House, N. 2006a. Interview Viz: Visualization-assisted photo elicitation. In *CHI '06: Extended Abstracts on Human Factors in Computing Systems,* 1463–1468. New York: ACM Press.

———. 2006b. Distant closeness: Cameraphones and public image sharing. Paper presented at Workshop on Pervasive Image Capture and Sharing: New Social Practices and Implications for Technology Workshop (PICS 2006) at the Eighth International Conference on Ubiquitous Computing (UbiComp 2006), Irvine, CA.

Van House, N., and M. Davis. 2005. The social life of cameraphone images. Paper presented at Workshop on Pervasive Image Capture and Sharing: New Social Practices and Implications for Technology Workshop (PICS 2005), Seventh International Conference on Ubiquitous Computing (UbiComp 2005), Tokyo, Japan.

Waltz, M. 2005. *Alternative and activist media.* Edinburgh: Edinburgh University Press.

Digital Cameras, Personal Photography and the Reconfiguration of Spatial Experiences

Dong-Hoo Lee

Department of Mass Communication, University of Incheon, Incheon, Republic of Korea

Digital technology has transformed the nature of photography and its cultural significance. This article addresses how the use of portable digital cameras and the subsequent exploitation of personal photos as major user-generated content on the Internet have transformed the cultural meaning of framing, taking, displaying, compiling, and reviewing photographs. It especially focuses on how digital photographic practices have changed as people are increasingly choosing to carry digital cameras with them at all times and to compile their output on the Web, as well as how these practices have affected people's spatial experiences with and within the physical world. Based on qualitative interview data collected from nineteen Korean digital camera users, this study explores how personal digital photography, as a tool to register personal experiences in physical space as well as a currency for communicating in digital space, has affected people's sense of physical place and thus has contributed to the ongoing hybridization of physical and digital experiences.

One of the main concerns of media studies is the way that changing media environments have redefined the interdependence of the media and its human subjects and consequently how media have shaped the way we perceive and make sense of the world around us. As Marshall McLuhan's (1964) notion of media as "extensions of man" suggests, different forms of media affect the nature of our interactions with the world, and human experiences are conditioned by the specific quality of media technologies. Digital communication technologies, which process all kinds of information in the form of digital bits, have created a new media environment that has transformed the way users access, process, manipulate, store, and distribute information. These technologies have enabled us to select, appropriate, create, and disseminate media contents, as well as to have access to a digital media space of communication that extends beyond the constraints of time and space. Although the asymmetrical relationship between mass-media producers and the audience remains, anyone can become an amateur media producer and participate in diverse communicative activities, thus creating participatory culture (Jenkins 2006). Moreover, the development of mobile personal digital media has provided users with their own portable media space while they move about in physical space (Gumpert and Drucker 2007), thus allowing them to coordinate their temporal, spatial, and sensory experiences in the moment. The portability of personal digital media, coupled with their easy connection to wireless or wired networks, has affected people's experiences both with and within physical places, and has made their media practices in physical space closely interconnected with those in digital space.

The snapshot camera, which was introduced by Kodak in 1883, is an old portable medium that allows users to record personal experiences. The camera makes it possible for anyone to visualize his or her being in the moment, thus pursuing democratized aesthetics. However, these possibilities were not fully explored, as snapshot practices were institutionalized mostly as constituents of family rituals and tourism. The development of digital cameras, and their connection with communication networks, has transformed photo-taking conventions and expanded the range of photography's social usage. Digital cameras are more likely to be carried by people no matter where they go, and their photographs can be compiled and shared beyond an immediate circle of family members and friends. Thus, conventional photographic moments and occasions, the limited post-photo-taking events and photo-sharing practices, and

This work was supported by a University of Incheon Research Grant in 2007.

the cultural meanings of popular photographs begin to transform.

This study attempts to examine how the everyday use of portable digital cameras and the subsequent exploitation of personal photos as major user-generated content on the Web have reconstructed not only people's photographic practices, but also ways of experiencing place. This examination tries to apply qualitative and microscopic research to concrete cases of digital camera users' photo-taking and photo-sharing practices. Based on qualitative interview data collected from 19 Korean digital camera users, this study explores how personal digital photography, as a tool to register personal experiences in physical space as well as a currency for communicating in digital space, has affected people's sense of physical place, and thus has contributed to the ongoing hybridization of physical and digital experiences.

SNAPSHOTS IN A DIGITAL AGE: TOWARD A POSTHOME MODE OF COMMUNICATION

When snapshot cameras became available on the mass market with the advent of Kodak cameras, they were carried to celebrate the rites of family life and to constitute familial self-presentation and memory. Popular practices of photo-taking and keeping a photo album were contextualized by the modern familial ideology that put great value on the "stable and united" family (Hirsch 1997; Holland 1997; Williamson 1993). Snapshot cameras were used to record special occasions such as graduation ceremonies, birthdays, wedding ceremonies, anniversaries, and other family rites, producing indexical references to represent family life and their imaginary harmoniousness. Kodak's early advertising campaigns introduced the adventurous Kodak Girl to promote its easy-to-handle (albeit poor-quality) snapshot cameras, and to emphasize their playfulness and spontaneity in capturing outdoor experiences (West 2000). Still, one of the most popular uses of portable snapshot cameras was to record family life and ceremonial events and to accumulate their idealized images in a personal or family album. Additionally, the production and consumption of snapshots were a constitutive part of modern tourism (Sontag 1977). To carry cameras as "tourist identity badges" and to take photographs were indispensable parts of the tourist experience (Chalfen 1987, 101). As the capitalist commercial projects of leisure industry have formed a significant context for people's photo-taking practices, photo taking has constituted "leisure event-structure" (Slater 1995, 141).

However, traditional methods of compiling and sharing personal photos were usually conditioned by "the home mode of pictorial communication" (Chalfen 1987, 8)—that is, the oral contexts shared by families and intimates. Since photographs are "message without code" that render an awareness of the having-been-there of the thing and, at the same time, its absence in the here and now (Barthes 1977, 1981), they need textual or oral contexts to anchor their interpretations and meanings. Photo compiling and photo sharing are acts of contextualizing the interpretations of pictures and leading their viewership in certain ways. When the compiler organizes photographs into albums, one builds a mnemonic framework for oral presentation and collective conversation that brings one's stories into the presentation of photographs in an album (Lanford 2001). Traditionally, the home mode of communication has constructed meanings and narratives around images of personal photographs, and this communicative practice has helped to foster intimate relationships and communal membership among those photo sharers.

Digital cameras have brought about a transformation of photo taking and photo sharing. As numerous information communication technologies (ICTs) have provided new settings for taking and sharing photographs, they have transformed the nature of photographic performance and its cultural significance. First, the digitalization of photography, which processes images as a form of calculable data, has enabled people to experiment with its presentational form to express their sensory experiences and emotions. Users can easily review, edit, retouch, or collate the photographed images, and enjoy being the active producers and distributors of those images. As digital photography is far less expensive than traditional film and print, it eliminates the expense of wasted shots, and requires no input from external "photo experts" to achieve the final image. This frees the photographer to be more experimental. With digital cameras, people can take as many shots as necessary to get a desirable shot, or they can test various techniques that were previously available only to professionals. Digital cameras enable ordinary users to take "professional-looking" or creative pictures at no further expense (Cobley and Haeffner 2009). The changing materiality of digital photography and its wider availability have extended "the range of potentially photogenic situations and opportunities," and consequently its social practices (Shove et al. 2007, 81). Moreover, as digital cameras have been increasingly adapted as a part of personal media, they seem to revive, in a new way, the early promise of the light-hearted, mobile Kodak Girl who enjoys the pure pleasure and adventure of taking photographs. People can playfully take pictures of moments in their everyday lives, let alone the special moments of family events, holidays, and social occasions. The range of potential photo-taking situations tends to expand beyond the conventions of recording and commemorating the ephemeral but significant past (see Kindberg, Spasojevic, Fleck, and Sellen 2005; Lee 2005; Okabe 2004). Digital cameras as an intimate mobile medium allow people to readily visualize every moment of their experience.

While the altered materiality of photography has transformed the nature of photographic performance, the digital network has recontextualized the oral condition that usually shapes the conventional processes of remembering and interpreting snapshots. Consequently, photographs can be used to enhance people's shared experience in the photo-taking moment, and to help people remember as well as to converse over it later (Kindberg et al. 2005). The oral performance, which used to be a post-photo-taking event to evoke memories, now proceeds in different ways. One can take photos and use them for ongoing conversations with people sitting together or remotely; in turn, this oral performative condition can constitute a playful context for photo taking. Moreover, as photo-sharing practices can now be placed in more diverse communication modes, snapshots and their associated stories are extended well beyond personal or familial communication circles, taking on new social functions and meanings. Photographs taken by individuals have become an integral part of user-created content on the Internet. As they are displayed and circulated via blogs, personal Web sites, or community bulletin boards, personal expressions can be easily accessed not only by intimates, but also by the general public.

Personal photo-taking practices today have new social, public meanings, and are potentially affected by the expansion of communication contexts where they are appreciated and interpreted. Dialogues and social relationships on the Internet can condition photographers' expectations for their output, for their relationships with objects to be photographed, and thus for their experiences with the physical places in which they circulate. Whether people use their photographs to maintain existing relationships, to create social relationships, or to express themselves, their Web activities influence the moment of photographing (Cohen 2005). As Web activities such as blogging become a major way of sharing pictures, these come to constitute another kind of oral performance that makes sense of and signifies photographs. Thus, the Web activities tend to be implicated in the photographic act of framing, taking, displaying, compiling, and reviewing photographs. In addition, they have affected photography's traditional commemorative function by distributing personal pictorial memories over the Web and allowing them to emerge in various unforeseen and public contexts (Van Dijck 2008).

DIGITAL SNAPSHOTS AND SPATIAL IMAGERY

The photographic frame presents a part of infinite and boundless physical space, cut out by a photographer's gaze. This gaze, which demarcates a space inside a frame from the referential physical space, tends to be conditioned by dominant spatial discourses. These discourses construct the cultural codes that define a physical place's social and aesthetic value, and they modify the popular taste of a spatial scene, turning a specific site into an appreciable and visitable one. As a result, they have shaped people's expectations and experiences of a place, as well as their photographic practices (Urry 2002). Photography, as a major medium for representing place and landscape within its frame, has embodied these discourses and has often served as a "pre-text" for consuming places (Osborne 2000). For instance, images of tourist places, projected by mass media and tour marketers, shape people's perception and photo-taking practices at the tourist sites, and those photos of tourist icons, in turn, become another form of image projection that perpetuates the iconic images of the places (Jenkins 2003). The photographic gaze of a place is likely to be subsumed by the discourses where commercialism and stereotypical imagery have articulated the ways of occupying, using, and appreciating a space.

However, the moving public's photographic practices can reconstruct the cultural notion of walking about or strolling. Benjamin's (1973) *flâneur* is fascinated by the urban phantasmagoria of urban streets and arcades that display the spectacles of modern wonders and commodities, and yet scrupulously reads how these modern fetishes and illusions have emerged and how the present has mingled with the past. De Certeau's (1977) association of practices of walking with the speech act also suggests the possible resistance of ordinary people's walking, in opposition to the top-down planning of an urban space and its commodification. Cameras can provide, for these *flâneurs* and pedestrians of "enunciating" spaces, a tool to disclose their reflections on urban contradictions and to enrich their creative tactics of walking against the administrative and commercial organizations of space. Susan Sontag (1977, 55) suggests this possibility by describing the photographer as "an armed version of the solitary walker reconnoitering, stalking, cruising the urban inferno, the voyeuristic stroller who discovers the city as a landscape of voluptuous extremes."

The photographer as *flâneur* extends the voyeuristic vision of the world as spectacle, and yet the photographer can see into, and make visible, "ambiguities and shadows" within spaces. Especially now, with digital technologies that give ordinary people the position of creator and allow them to produce and distribute their own images, individuals' trajectories and spatial stories can be expressed and shared with the public. While, conversely, digital cameras as a personal, portable medium can intensify voyeurism over everyday places, they can serve as a tool with which individuals visualize their place-based experiences and memories during their acts of walking and rewrite the city as their space. The private interpretations of spaces can quietly meddle in the given cultural codes of spaces.

Several studies have explored how user-created content, including photographs, has become a constitutive part of geolocational data on the Web and how it has provided new ways of perceiving and engaging with urban spaces (Hardey 2007; Lee 2007). Blogs and "mashups," which visualize and map everyday urban life, present multilayered spatial imageries that include personal experiences and depictions of particular places at specific moments. These geolocational data and images become a reference from which other people can reimagine and make sense of urban space. People can create new representations of physical locales they visit or move around, share them via wireless and wired networks, and refer to these data for their spatial practices.

Although these studies have examined the role of Web 2.0 resources for geographic imagination and have suggested that individuals, these resources, and spatial practices now share a new "synergistic relationship," we need to further research the characteristics of individuals' agency to transform geographical imagination, as well as the rearticulation of people's senses of place through their use of digital media, including digital cameras.

CASE STUDY

For a closer look at people's everyday photographic practices, their interconnected Web activities, and the subsequent transformation of spatial practices, I have examined Cyworld, which is similar to MySpace and one of the Republic of Korea's leading online social networks. I interviewed nineteen users who actively show their pictures on their Cyworld mini-homepages and other blogs. As of 2008, the Internet usage rate for the Korean population aged six years and above was 77.1 percent, and among these Internet users, 43.1 percent were blog or mini-homepage owners in the previous year. In particular, young people in their twenties show the highest ownership rate (74.4 percent) among all age groups (National Internet Development Agency of Korea 2008). The popular reception of mini-homepages and other blogs, which prominently feature photos, has created or has been accompanied by people's—especially youngsters'—enthusiasm for various types of digital cameras from mega-pixel camera phones and compact digital cameras to high-end digital single lens reflex (DSLRs).

To recruit interview participants, I visited several mini-homepages linked with Cyworld's "Story Map" (http://map.cyworld.com/menu/view.map), where users attach their pictures and "stories" to the map's geographical information. Interviewees comprised those who were contacted via these mini-homepages and who responded to my message requesting that they tell me about their experiences of photo taking, as well as the acquaintances they would introduce to me. I had a face-to-face meeting with each individual for an in-depth interview from January to May in 2008. They were aged from their early twenties to their mid-thirties, and two thirds of them happened to be women (I have received more positive responses to my requests for interviews from female users). I looked at their photographs that were posted on their mini-homepages or blogs before interviewing them, and tried to hear about the interviewee's experiences of taking these pictures in a fairly open framework. Although interviewees' enthusiasm for photo taking varied (they ranged from serious amateur photographers to casual camera-phone users), they all had something in common: They usually carried more than one camera, including a camera phone, to be ready to take pictures, and they posted their pictures on their mini-homepages or blogs. Their accounts give us some insight into what kinds of practices have been newly cultivated with digital camera usage, and how people's experiences with and within places have been reconfigured by digital photographic practices and their associated Web activities. In the next three sections, based on the interviews, I examine the cultural practices of digital photography and their relationship with spatial experiences and spatial imagery.

CULTURAL PRACTICES OF DIGITAL PHOTOGRRAPHY

The changed materiality of digital photography and its connectivity with wired or wireless networks have provided new possibilities for people's photographic practices. The nature of photographic performance has been changed by the lack of need for film, easy operation, instant production and reproduction of photographs, manipulability, and usability within various communicative activities on the Web. With the popular dissemination of various information technologies in Korea since the late 1990s, digital cameras have become a desirable personal item and their ownership has been perceived, especially among young people, as a trend. The proliferation of camera phones has also helped form an environment where people can use photographic functions in their everyday life. People have easy access to digital cameras and are more likely to carry them as a personal belonging. The communicability of photography has been extended, and the wired or wireless networks have become a significant context for photographic practices.

Photography is a distinctive symbolic environment for representing the world. Photographs have functioned as an objective testimony, as well as technical prostheses to memory because of photography's representational form, which can mechanically visualize and reproduce an exact image of a slice of space and time. However, photography can also be used as an expressive tool that conveys an individual's visual experience and feeling at that moment. According to Susanne Langer (1942), its representative form is nondiscursive or presentational photography, which can provide symbolic analogues of our sensory and emotional experiences, in contrast with the discursive forms of language based on syntax, which can offer "propositions" or statements (see also Nystrom 2006). The photograph's nondiscursive signification with "neither fixed connotations nor explicit denotation" can convey factual and sensitive or emotional aspects at the same time (Nystrom 2006, 296). With digital cameras, people have explored this linguistic capability of photography in mundane and private ways. Interview participants have reported that they have taken numerous pictures with digital cameras to record various moments, ranging from special occasions such as a vacation to everyday moments. Digital cameras have allowed them to photograph "recklessly" and "unconditionally" without consideration of the cost of film and printing and to consequently capture moments that traditional photography would not value. Although they have taken photographs to make records of their special trips for a keepsake memory, they captured what would have been considered insignificant details along the way (for instance, a subway exit they passed by on their way to the destination, or the signboard or menu of a restaurant on the site). Digital cameras serve as a tool for memo taking or chronicling what people see and experience. In addition, small things and events in their daily life, as well as microscopic moments, have been captured. Interview participants captured moments such as when "I put on makeup," "I turn up my hair," "I buy a new clothing," "I eat a brand-new snack," "I meet my friend," "I find a crane-like cloud in the sky," and so on. They have documented the detailed experiences of "here I am" in their life-world, sometimes by design and other times improvisatorially, creating evidence of their being in the moment. Digital cameras accompanied by individuals have extended the subject matter of photography. To some degree, they have reproduced traditional photo-taking practices to commemorate specific occasions, and yet they have begun to include mundane and ephemeral images in their photographic repertoire, turning ordinary scenes or banal moments into something noticeable, and thus something recordable.

Digital cameras have also been used to make images of affective moments and to express feelings. One's mindscape can be both a context for photo taking and a subject to be expressed. People have photographed when they were emotionally attached to a sight or their visual sensations were stirred up (for instance, "I felt beauty in the scenery viewed from the rooftop of my apartment complex after pulling an all-nighter," "I was looking at a bus stop near my home, missing my ex-boyfriend," etc.). Personal affections and artistic sensibilities have created situations for photo taking, privatizing a specific time and space. In this process of subjective photographing, any daily scene can be transformed into a personally meaningful and unique one. People's sensory experiences at the moment can also be turned into visual images (for instance, they took pictures because "I wanted to photograph the sound of a wind I liked," or "I had a great appetite for a food"). With digital cameras, people are more likely to represent their ways of sensing, as well as their feelings of a situation at the moment. Digital cameras have facilitated people's visualization and aestheticization of their subjective experiences. Most interview participants believed that photographs would show not only things and events but also themselves: who they are and what their feelings or perspectives are. The more they get into photo taking, the more they look for their unique shots.

The most distinguishable characteristic of digital photographic practices is their close connection with communication activities on wired or wireless networks. The moments captured by our photographic eyes can be shared and interpreted in a present conversation or later in an individual's social space on the Web. Most interview participants' enthusiasm for taking photos is directly related to the need to visually express "who they are," especially in the social network of the Web. Photographs on mini-homepages or blogs are considered to be expressions of an individual's feelings and aesthetic sensitivity, or the images that objectify and testify oneself in a specific time and space. At the same time, they provide material through which one tries to converse with oneself, friends, or the unknown public, and thus function as "the new currency for social interaction" (Van Dijck 2008, 62). Most of the interviewees have routinely spent a certain amount of time selecting, modifying, editing, storing, or uploading numerous photographs they have taken, and they have done so as part of a sort of "self-impression management" on the Web. The classification of photographs into different categories is considered to be a useful tactic to stage communication settings for photo sharing. According to the characteristics and scale of the actual or imaginary audiences for mini-homepages and blogs, an individual tends to divide photographs into classes for one's personal viewing, for interaction with intimates, or for public viewing. When one selects, classifies, and edits photographic images, as well as designating the range of their potential audience, there occurs a self-reflection to ponder on how to negotiate potential viewership on the Web. Sometimes one discloses personal photographs for attention getting, and at other times one keeps them within a private sphere to avoid unwanted responses. The invisible others tend to have a part in an individual's deployment of self-presentation.

Interview participants have considered others' responses as the best reward for photo-compiling efforts. They pay keen attention to the number of clicks, replies, and scrapings. Also, they have a feeling of satisfaction when photo viewers become aware of, and understand, an individual's unspoken emotion or inner mind that lies beneath the photographic images. Three interviewees who had their photographs recommended for placement on the front page of a social network site or a popular photo gallery site have temporarily experienced the fame of the so-called microcelebrity—"the phenomenon of being extremely well known, not to millions, but to a small group—a thousand people, or maybe only a few dozen" (Thompson 2007). Most interviewees tend to be "microcelebrity-wannabes" who want their blogs to get attention from and be well-received by their intimates or the unknown public. Because photographs are a primary vehicle for self-presentation and connection, they become more concerned with the expressive quality of their photographs and the social gaze of viewers on the Web. Moreover, they tend to agree with the idea that an individual's photo album can serve as a public form of a personal statement to promote oneself.

> It's the age of self-promotion, and by exposing oneself, one reveals who one is. These days, the job world is more likely to favor those who own and manage mini-homepages and blogs. These people are followed about by others. . . . I try harder to manage my mini-homepage when I receive messages from people who understand my sensibility and acknowledge my efforts. (Seeun, female, student, age twenty-one years)

Since pictures are significant elements of the individuals' "show-and-tell," this promotes the desire to take better photos, which in turn leads to a desire to buy high-tech cameras. The commercial deployment of mega-pixel camera phones, as well as the popularization of high-end portable digital cameras and DSLR cameras, seems to be closely related to people's intensive use of photographs and their demands for higher quality photographs to enhance their communicative ability on the Web. Most interviewees revealed their desire to buy high-tech digital cameras if their financial conditions allow it. Some interviewees have joined digital camera users' online communities, and others read books or attend photography classes to improve their photo-taking skills. For them, high-end digital cameras represent their enthusiasm to enhance photographic quality, rather than merely self-display to distinguish an individual's sophisticated cultural tastes from the others. They tend to show interest in new camera models and their technological abilities, and to assume that there is a hierarchy among cameras in terms of their photographic qualities, such that high-tech cameras can create better photographs. However, cameras' portability and their ability to express personal feelings rather than mechanically refined images are also valued. While interviewees tend to favor digital cameras or DSLR to capture anything novel and spectacular, they also use camera phones to get self-images and to substitute for other cameras.

The desire for better pictures often leads to an excessive self-consciousness in searching for photographic subjects and frames. Since an individual's photographs signify personal feelings and an aesthetic sensibility that are likely to be reframed as vehicles for interaction and social networking on the Web, one wants to have a better photo-taking ability, and even to go out with a friend who can take "good" pictures. Digital photography technically enhances the malleability of images and increases the user's control over the final image produced. However, as photographs become tools for self-exposure as well as connection, their productions become subject to the forms of circulation, and people begin to use their photographic eye to search for "pro-photographic" events (Burgin 1982, 83). This then intersects with the social gaze of viewers on the Web.

DIGITAL *FLÂNEURS* AND PHOTOGRAPHIC WAYS OF EXPERIENCING PLACE

Physical places have usually been the foreground or background of pictures when people capture a certain scene in a place where a personal act of photography is situated. Cameras have been used to record one's experience of being there, to visualize one's perceptions and engagements with the place, or to explore one's aesthetic, expressive abilities. While traditional snapshots have usually been taken at special places and occasions such as well-known tourist sites and photogenic landmarks for the commemoration of their "having-been-there," digital snapshots tend to be photographed far beyond these traditional sites and circumstances. As they are likely to be personally carried by people at hand, digital cameras tend to extend the range of sites for photography. People have become interested in capturing moments and places that conventional photography has typically disregarded, such as those moments that are banal but personally intriguing, those events that people experience accidentally or instantaneously on a site, or those routine places where people don't usually carry cameras. These places for photography include not only the privatized public places such as restaurants and shops, but also streets and transit stations that people pass by in their travels. From a cup of coffee at a café to goods in a showcase to alleys in the neighborhood and the ever-changing sky on their way to and from work: All have become prophotographic objects. Everyday users do not merely travel to tourist sites but also walk around familiar urban locales as "a strategy for accumulating photographs" (Sontag 1977, 9). Handy digital cameras can easily transform daily life into pseudotouring experiences in which an individual hunts and collects images to be later used for his or her storytelling on the Web. An interview participant reported that the everyday carrying of a camera made him expect something novel or unfamiliar out of routine life, as if he were on a trip. Other participants also identified digital cameras as "a partner" or "a part of oneself," which made them more aware of their surroundings, both visually and in a microscopic way. For them, taking pictures is no longer restricted to special occasions and holidays; cameras in an urban space are no longer "tourist identity badges."

These photographers are a new kind of *flâneur* in a digital age. They observe cityscapes from their point of view or photographic eye and, at the same time, they constitute a part of urban scenery. They are the voyeurs of a city's everyday life, who continuously look around buildings, shops, restaurants, coffee shops, pedestrians, peddlers, and so on, and curiously seek out any eye-grabbing, unique things. They dislocate the specific aspects of an urban space through photographic frames and relocate them in their narratives on the Web. At the same time, their photographic practices often appropriate public or commercial spaces, and induce them to discover that there exist various ways of looking at subject positions.

> There is a telephone pole in my neighborhood. One day, I took a picture of "here" and on another day, I took one of "there." My mom laughs at me, saying, "What is it?" Yet I have a new feeling whenever I see this pole. On one day, there was some liquid at the bottom of the pole, and on the other day, there was a garbage bag there. When I look, I find new things. I always tend to go by the same place, and to have the same subject position toward the scene. When I am about to lose interest in the subject, I move my position a little bit and get a completely different picture. I like this. (Noori, female, student, age twenty-two years)

As one usually takes pictures of a place from a shifting and personally nuanced perspective, the place is signified by a fragment of the reality shaped by the photographer's personal, microscopic gaze. *Synecdoche* (to represent a whole from its part) is a common rhetoric of personal spatial imagery (see figure 1). As they become accustomed to seeing a locale through photographic framing, mobile photographers become more attentive to its details. They often visualize the temporal sequence and path of their trajectories. Strolling about to look for scenic points to be photographed, one is able to become an observer who glances at and collects various signs in a locale. The photographer is privatizing the site for his or her own photography, as well as for sociality in other places—virtual or remote places. Photographs of details often serve as significant material that is to be used later for recollecting spatial experiences, for the blog's creation of personally nuanced micronarratives or for its production of geolocational data. Pieces of photographic images of a locale, which convey an individual's subjective position of photo taking, his or her activities, and feelings on the site, are interwoven to form an imaginary space bounded by the modes of communication on the Web. Then, are these digital camera users mere onlookers who are detached from a locale and carelessly appropriate its images for their private photography?

The act of photographing is not merely the act of pressing a button to mechanically fix a part of the world into an image or to reproduce a standardized gaze of photographic conventions. It can also be a practice of being attentive to a series of temporal and spatial moments in the locale and trying to make sense of and interpret a subject. Through the practice of walking around the site, searching for photographable objects, and framing what one wants to capture, one can face the challenge of how to make sense of what one sees. These practices can induce a curiosity for the memories of the locale and the people who have lived there, or make the viewer see a shadowed reality under the surface of a photogenic site. One can be put into a contradictory position of being both a voyeur with vigor for aesthetic visuals, and a detached onlooker who comes

FIG. 1. Examples of synecdochic spatial imagery.

to be aware of the locale's diverse aspects. Some interview participants expressed cynicism about the tourist-like behavior of other photographers who were moving around in flocks and were only obsessed with their private photo taking of well-known scenic spots. Others tried to create their versions of seeing, framing, and meaning-making at the locale. For instance, an interview participant said the following:

> There is a steel fence at the mid-slope of Cheolsan-dong. From there, you can see one side, where shacks are about to be removed in the near future and where their residents live day by day like a dayfly. On the other side, there are newly built apartments awaiting their new residents. Although everybody works hard from one's given position, there is no case of "a black hen laying white eggs." Will these people have a place to live? Would it be too idyllic for them to have a small nest where their family can live together? I feel the world is too unfair. (Jieun, female, receptionist, age twenty-eight years)

When she went to one of the few remaining hillside slums in Seoul, she found beauty in narrow alleys or worn-out cement walls, but she lamented uneven distribution of wealth caused by urban development and commodification. The camera tends to make photographers voyeurs and at the same time lets them have a reflective distance from their physical surroundings. Photo taking is not only a way to create new iconic images of a place, but it also provides a chance to observe and reflect on a place for those who carry out these photographic practices. The immediate reproduction of photographic images also enables users to examine the difference between reality before one's eye and its image captured on a camera's screen, or the difference between the mechanical eye and human eye. Such differences create another pleasure within photographic practices. Through the processes of photographic representation, a place serves as a physical environment where an individual walks around and plays with cameras and also as an object under the individual's photographic gaze. Bits of image of a place, as framed and defamiliarized by the individual's aesthetic sense, have become materials for self-presentation and a place's referential data that float on the Web.

CIRCUIT OF SPATIAL IMAGERY

Television, films, magazines, books, and newspapers have been important sources for people's reference to places. They constitute spatial discourses, which designate certain locales as "must-sees" to visit or photograph, and they instruct how to see and experience them. These discourses have dominated people's experiences and memories of places, and furthermore have interfered with the formation of people's individualized memories of the site. However, individuals' photographs on the Web have been recently added to this image pool for spatial imagination. As photographic images, taken by individuals, increasingly proliferate and provide unprecedented sources of created content in digital space, they become an integral part of people's spatial imagination. Bloggers distribute place-related images among the various modes of communication and are able to have an influence on the place's reputation. Their images and experiential stories provide another source to which people refer for what they can get from the locale and how they can meet their needs there. Pictorial information on the Web has contextualized people's anticipation of a place, and they are profoundly engaged in how we perceive, orientate ourselves in, and talk about the physical space. These pictures contribute to the formation of a new sense of place and to further making us perceive and interact with space through photographic eyes.

Digital camera users have often posted their pictures on the Web to create self-presentations and to enhance social relationships. As bloggers, they provide particular pictures and information related to a local site, and they share them with their intimates or the public to be acknowledged by them. Even though such practices of photo display and photo sharing don't have an explicit commercial purpose, they ironically tend to create an effect of promoting certain images that marketers, shop owners, or city administrators are upholding. An individual's personal photographic practices can unintentionally coincide with the interests of commercialists and administrators. Moreover, as commercial locales have become more aware of the publicity effects of bloggers' opinions and ratings, they have started to think about how to use microcelebrities on the Web. For instance, an interview participant said the following:

> My blog is usually visited by ordinary people. However, restaurant owners are very sensitive to the data I post. They often send me messages. . . . I think that Samcheong-dong has been changed a lot due to blog culture. During the weekend, it's very crowded with people taking pictures. Newly opened shops welcome these crowds. They know people will upload their pictures, so they serve them very well. (Eunjin, female, a script writer, age thirty years)

Although people search for images that fit into their storytelling on the Web, their pictorial documents with and within places have made details of a cityscape visible. As a result, their spatial imagery enhances the commercial potential of the locale. However, since their efforts are to express themselves and get acknowledgment from others rather than to acquire material reward, they can keep a distance from the commercialists' interests. They are more sensitive to their audiences' responses.

However, personal photographs can inform people of a locale and affect its reputation; they provide one of the references with which people find out about and make sense of the locale. When people search on the Web for information about a locale, they are able to get a sense of place before getting there, and to visit the locale based on this information. Personal photographs provide visual details of numerous places, make them aesthetic and desirable, and consequently extend the pool of destinations that are considered worthy to visit. People's spatial experiences are more likely to be contextualized by these visual images and photographic practices. In the past, mass media imagery was the main source that structured the gaze and experience of a locale, but now personal spatial imagery also provides a source that shapes this gaze and these experiences. Personal photographic images become a part of geolocational data, with which people consult to make plans for visits and to choose a subject position for their photographic gaze. People tend to experience the effects of these images rather than the physical reality itself.

However, when images dislocate certain particulars of locality and turn them into visual icons, people become disillusioned. On the Web, such personal disillusionment coexists with the familiarized iconic images of locales. When they visit the actual places in those images, people are often disappointed with the reality. They come to realize that photos' synecdochical images are only delivering fragmented and dislocated signs. As people take photographs, share them, refer to others' pictures, and compare images with their live experiences, they come to learn the possibilities and limits of photography's visual effects and communicability. They tend to depend more and more on the user-generated information and images as a source for knowing locales, but they do not blindly follow them. The archive of spatial imagery is expanding in the process in which the production of images of locales is continually interacting with responses and reputations on the Web. While individuals' experiential, personal, emotional, and aesthetic interpretations of a place are posted, accumulated, and responded to, the ways of walking, resting, recreating, shopping, and dining are, in turn, affected by this imagery. Through photo-taking and photo-sharing practices, the users are provided an opportunity to participate or intervene in the representation, circulation, and consumption of places, and at the same time their spatial imaginations are more contingent on the floating images and comments on the Web.

CONCLUSION

In discussions of digital media culture, one of the most frequently mentioned concepts is digital media users' activeness, which emphasizes the transformative power of digital media users' participation, interaction, creativity, and subjective choices. This notion tends to focus on the instrumental usability of digital media, and leaves unexamined the ontological question of changes in everyday life, as well as our perception and understanding of the world. For example, what does the phenomenon of people circulating their pictures and self-images via digital networks and pictures culturally mean? How do digital media affect our sense of the world, as we begin to habitually externalize our experiences in visual forms with cameras at hand and then expose ourselves in those forms in various communication settings?

This article has examined how the everyday use of digital cameras and digital networks has reconstructed ways of capturing moments and of experiencing place. People with digital cameras have become urban *flâneurs* who have transformed their spatial experiences and trajectories into visual signs to tell their stories and to call for dialogue in both physical and virtual spaces. Their everyday photographic practices tend to make them urban voyeurs and at the same time give them a chance to be aware of their physical surroundings from their subjective gaze and meaning making. Moreover, people's photographic gazes are affected by, and affect, spatial imagery circulated on the Web. Their digital pictures come to constitute a part of spatial imagery and contribute to shaping and defining people's perceptions of the realities. Individuals' everyday photographic practices provide a new opportunity to reflect on their physical environment and to participate in the creation and circulation of dominant spatial discourses. They can be new *flâneurs*, who continuously look around their surroundings with curiosity and find multifaceted aspects of locales.

Although their photographic practices may be merely kitsch performances that conform to the familiarized, prearranged spatial imagery, their individualized frames and comments of locales may lead to a self-reflection on their practices and disillusionment toward photographic imagery. Through their everyday photographic practices, individuals have a chance to see a gap between the beautified visual fragments and the integrity of a physical place. They can also realize that these practices and experiences are a source for self-empowerment. As personal photographs that express individuals' aesthetic sensitivities and experiences are proliferating on the Web, the ways of constructing spatial discourses and imagery are changing, and so, consequently, is our sense of place.

REFERENCES

Barthes, R. 1977. *Image-music-text*, trans. S. Heath. London: Fontana.

———. 1981. *Camera lucida: Reflections on photography*, trans. R. Howard. New York: Hill & Wang.

Benjamin, W. 1973. *Illuminations*, trans. H. Zohn. London: Fontana.

Burgin, V. 1982. Looking at photographs. In *Thinking photography*, ed. V. Burgin, 142–53. London: Macmillan.

Chalfen, R. 1987. *Snapshot versions of life*. Bowling Green, OH: Bowling Green State University Popular Press.

Cobley, P., and N. Haeffner. 2009. Digital cameras and domestic photography: Communication, agency and structure. *Visual Communication* 8:123–46.

Cohen, K. 2005. What does the photoblog want? *Media, Culture & Society* 27:883–901.

de Certeau, M. 1984. *The practice of everyday life*, trans. S. Rendall. Berkely: University of California Press.

Gumpert, G., and S. Drucker. 2007. Mobile communication in the 21 century or "everybody, everywhere, at any time." In *Displacing place*, ed. S. Kleinman, 7–20. New York: Peter Lang.

Hardey, M. 2007. The city in the age of Web 2.0, a new synergistic relationship between place and people. *Information, Communication & Society* 10:867–84.

Hirsch, M. 1997. *Family frames: Photography, narrative, and postmemory*. Cambridge, MA: Harvard University Press.

Holland, P. 1997. Sweet it is to scan: Personal photographs and popular photography. In *Photography: A critical introduction*, ed. L. Wells, 117–64. New York: Routledge.

Jenkins, H. 2006. *Convergence culture: Where old and new media collide*. New York: New York University Press.

Jenkins, O. 2003. Photography and travel brochures: The circle of representation. *Tourism Geographies* 5:305–28.

Kindberg, T., M. Spasojevic, R. Fleck, and A. Sellen. 2005. The ubiquitous camera: an in-depth study of camera phone use. *IEEE Pervasive Computing* 4:42–50.

Langford, M. 2001. *Suspended conversations: The afterlife of memory in photographic albums*. Montreal: McGill-Queen's University Press.

Langer, S. 1942. *Philosophy in a new key*. Cambridge, MA: Harvard University Press.

Lee, D. 2005. Women's creation of camera phone culture. *Fibreculture 6*. http://journal.fibreculture.org/issue6/issue6_donghoo.html (accessed March 1, 2006).

———. 2007. Re-imagining urban space: Mobility, connectivity, and a sense of place. Paper presented at Mobile Media, Sydney, Australia. July 2–4.

Nystrom, C. 2006. Symbols, thought, and "reality": The contributions of Benjamin Lee Whorf and Susanne K. Langer. In *Perspectives on culture, technology and communication: The media ecology*, ed. C. Lum, 275–302. Cresskill, NJ: Hampton.

McLuhan, M. 1964. *Understanding media*. New York; Methuen.

Okabe, D. 2004. Emergent social practices, situations and relations through everyday camera phone use. Paper presented at International Conference on Mobile Communication and Social Change, Seoul, Republic of Korea, October 18–19.

Osborne, P. 2000. *Traveling light: Photography, travel and visual culture*. Manchester: Manchester University Press.

Slater, D. 1995. Domestic photography and digital culture. In *The photographic image in digital culture*, ed. M. Lister, 129–46. London: Routledge.

Sontag, S. 1977. *On photography*. New York: Farrar, Straus & Giroux.

Shove, E., M. Watson, M. Hand, and J. Ingram. 2007. *The design of everyday life*. Oxford: Berg.

Thompson, C 2007. The age of microcelebrity: Why everyone's a little Brad Pitt. *Wired Magazine* 15. http://www.wired.com/techbiz/people/magazine/15-12/st_ thompson (accessed June 18, 2008).

Urry, J. 2002. *The tourist gaze*. London: Sage.

van Dijck, J. 2008. Digital photography: Communication, identity, memory. *Visual Communication* 7:57–76.

West, N. 2000. *Kodak and the lens of nostalgia*. Charlottesville: University of Virginia Press.

Williamson, J. 1994. Family, education, and photography. In *Culture/power/history: A reader in contemporary social theory*, ed. N. Dirks, G. Eley, and S. Ortner, 236–44. Princeton, NJ: Princeton University Press.

The Reality beyond the Hype: Mobile Internet is Primarily an Extension of PC-Based Internet

Petter Nielsen

Telenor Corporate Development, Fornebu, Norway
Department of Informatics, University of Oslo, Oslo, Norway

Annita Fjuk

Telenor Corporate Development, Fornebu, Norway

The mobile Internet (MI) has been hyped as the next big thing by telecom operators, handset manufacturers, and content providers. However, recent studies indicate that the usage of Internet via mobile phones has remained quite flat. The authors inquire into this discrepancy by focusing on actual usage of the MI and the motivating factors behind its use. Based on focus-group interviews in Norway and Hungary, they argue that MI usage is interrelated with and is an extension of the personal computer (PC)–based Internet. The key motivation behind MI use is to attain information in situations in which the PC is out of reach. In effect, MI has not led to the development of new usages. The expectation that the development of new killer applications will lead to an explosion of new usage is therefore misguided. MI usage is and will perhaps continue to be a mere extension of PC-based Internet usage—and such use activities are the very nature of MI.

The mobile Internet (MI) is hyped as the next big thing for both mobile phone devices and the Internet (Cui & Roto 2008). This hype manifests in widely held beliefs that new mobile handset functionality and new types of content improve user experience to the expectation that increased mobile content will fuel the growth of MI. In spite of its hype and the very real investments made by mobile companies, the current success of MI is questionable. Our studies suggest a contradictory picture with regard to the real use of MI.

Research conducted by Forrester Research shows that only 14% of the Europeans who have a mobile phone use MI regularly, i.e., at least once a month (Nuthall et al. 2008). Furthermore, according to the Norwegian TNS Gallup, the weekly usage of MI (defined as 3G) and WAP in Norway has increased less than 1% from 2005 to 2008.[1] From these studies, we may conclude that MI usage continues to stay flat. Further, as shown by Ling et al. (2010), MI usage statistics are deceptive because of a skewed distribution where a few high-end users account for the vast majority of the data traffic. It is therefore easy to hype MI since statistics based on mean values present a much more optimistic picture than does the more correct median.

Recent research on MI usage has focused on describing and understanding how users are challenged by screen size, input facilities, usability of services, and de facto data traffic costs (e.g., Kim et al. 2005). In this article we seek to advance our understanding further by thoroughly exploring actual usage activities and motivating factors for those who really use MI. Since the average user uses the MI to a very limited extent, we have chosen to focus on and recruit mature and advanced users in terms of volume of data traffic generated from MI usage. Understanding their motivations, experiences, and practices is a powerful way to capture what drives and will drive MI usage in the near future.

We report results from four focus-group interviews with advanced MI users in Norway and Hungary. In many ways, our findings suggest a different story than one of MI hype. In particular, we show that MI usage is limited to reading of e-mails and news and simple inquires to databases like Wikipedia and Google. This is the case both for business and private users. Further, and at the core of our discussion, the MI usage patterns are very much related to that of personal computer (PC) usage. In a nutshell, MI appears as an extension of the PC, which is the primary vehicle for full-fledged Internet use. Used mainly to maintain connectivity between PC-based Internet sessions, MI use tends to be consumption-oriented as the limited input capabilities of mobile handsets make content production difficult. In general, MI usage tends to have a "lean back," as compared to PC-based Internet use.

The rest of this article is structured as follows. First, we present related research on MI usage. We then describe our study and present the results. We conclude with a discussion on key implications of our findings for future development of MI.

RELATED RESEARCH ON MI USAGE

There is only limited academic literature on MI usage (for example, Taylor et al. 2008; Ishii 2004). At the same time, industry-oriented research (e.g., Forrester Research) is growing. This uneven focus may be a result of academia not considering MI usage as a distinct phenomenon (but just a part of Internet usage), while the industry efforts are fueled by the hype emphasizing MI as a new sector of the industry.

A large part of the problem is that there is far from one agreed-upon understanding of what MI really is in academic as well as industry research. The "neutral" definitions of MI are rather vague. For example, according to Wikipedia the definition is "access to the Internet from a mobile device, such as a smartphone or laptop via integrated capabilities or via an independent device" (accessed June 16, 2010). Terms like mobile web, one web, and mobile broadband are also often simultaneously used in this context. The other understandings reflect the position, interests, and motives of their source, such as telecom operators and handset manufacturers. On the one hand, handset manufacturers focus on improving the user experience so as to become the preferred terminal. For example, iPhone is branded as providing the best customer experience—Internet services just one click away—while HTC focuses on easy viewing and effortless navigation of websites just like on PC. Nokia uses the concept of Mobile Web, and has introduced Ovi as a service for easily accessing consumers' existing social networks, communities, and content. On the other hand, telecom operators pursue MI as a major future revenue generator, making up for diminishing revenues from services such as mobile voice calls and SMS. They commonly use mobile broadband to describe any service that operates on a high-speed packet (HSPA) network, including mobile phone and PC connectivity.

In this article, we understand MI as the usage of all kinds of Internet services through mobile phones. Mobile broadband (i.e., PC access to the Internet over the mobile network) is kept out of the discussion. The following literature review is based on a similar interpretation.

Nuthall et al. (2008) argue that MI is on the rise because of faster networks, better mobile devices, and simpler price plans that are both predictable and affordable. However, there are still some challenges left to be overcome. For example, although many users have Internet-capable phones, less than half of the users know they have such phones (Nuthall et al. 2008). Furthermore, only 14% of mobile users use MI regularly, i.e., access MI from the mobile handset least once per month.

Nuthall et al. (2008) show a positive co-relation between MI usage and adoption of more advanced MI services. Also, studies indicate that MI users are more likely to be interested in technology than the average PC-based Internet users (Nuthall et al. 2008) and that men more often actively use MI than women (Cui & Roto 2008).

According to Finnish reports, using nonconventional instruments for measurement such as deep packet inspection, there has been an 11-fold increase in mobile data traffic in 3G networks in Finland from 2005 to 2007 (Kivi 2008). Even if 92% of this traffic is generated by users who are connecting to MI with computers, there has been a significant 160% growth from 2006 to 2007 in data traffic generated by Symbian phones (e.g., Nokia). However, the study clearly shows a huge gap between data traffic that is generated from PCs and data traffic that is generated from mobile handsets, showing that measurements tools that differentiate between the different devices are needed in order to understand the real situation with regard to Internet access from mobile handsets. Such a need is arguably confirmed by a longitudinal survey conducted by Telenor (Ling 2009). The study shows that only 7% of the events in the mobile network are MI. This figure also includes traffic generated from PCs.

Cui and Roto (2008) identified four contextual factors related to MI: spatial, temporal, social, and access. The spatial factor is related to MI use while also engaged in other activities, such as watching TV, or having dinner on the bed. The second factor, the temporal one, relates to moments between planned activities, e.g., waiting for a bus to arrive or for a friend to show up. The third social factor relates to MI's role as a conversation enhancer—i.e., the MI is used to initiate a new topic, expand an ongoing discussion, or settle a dispute. The last factor, access, concerns the different types of networks used in MI usage. Cui and Roto (2008) also very interestingly found different use activities, many of them identical with

PC-based Internet (such as information seeking, transaction, and communication), but one activity that differs from PC-based Internet—personal space extension, wherein people put their content on the Web as part of their public persona.

Usability research has also contributed to a better understanding of the challenges of using MI. Kim et al. (2002), Kim et al. (2005), and Lee and Kim (2005) have investigated MI usability challenges and found that people experience different usability problems in different contexts. While being on the move, the availability of hands varies with circumstantial factors, and the movement of legs has significant impact on usability. For example, scrolling the menu bar or changing pages by pushing small buttons with only one hand is often difficult (Kim et al. 2005). Furthermore, when the user is moving it might be difficult to read what is represented in small displays (Kim et al. 2005). These studies are largely quantitative and provide insight into general usage patterns and corresponding usability challenges. However, they provide limited insights when it comes to motivating factors and drivers for usage.

METHODOLOGICAL APPROACH AND CONSIDERATIONS

The primary data used in this study are drawn from four focus-group interviews. They were conducted in Norway (October 2008) and Hungary (November 2008). The participants were either business or private users of MI. They were recruited on the basis of traffic data from Telenor in Norway and Telenor in Hungary. Based on records from the operators' data warehouses, compiled lists of the most advanced MI users were generated. The rankings of users were based on measurements of their data traffic during the last 3 months. The participants were among the top 1,000 in each segment in each market. To make sure that we captured MI usage according to our definition, users only using their mobile phone as modems were excluded in the screening process (Table 1).

The focus-group interviews were carried out in the native language of the users, Norwegian and Hungarian, respectively. In Hungary the interviews were observed based on simultaneous translation. All focus groups were audiotaped and fully transcribed. Further, the transcripts were analyzed and discussed among the authors to identify key themes and problem areas. All the focus groups followed roughly the same discussion guidelines, particularly focusing on MI motivation and usage patterns.

The choice of markets and segments had several motivations. First, as researchers we had the opportunity to locate the most advanced users of MI in both countries based on access to data warehouses. Second, while Norway has a very strong economy and good Internet access due to high PC and broadband penetration, the Hungarian economy is relatively weaker and PC-based Internet adoption is considerably lower. Therefore, a comparison of these two countries with regard to the impact of the economic situation (buying power and cost sensitivity) and PC-based Internet penetration on MI use was appealing. The focus on both business and private users was primarily motivated by the potential for identifying differences in usage patterns within these different user groups.

The primary aim of our research was to understand MI usage patterns and MI drivers. By using focus-group interviews as our primary data material, we got deep insight into the MI users' points of view and their common reflections on their own practices. Our analysis was carried out in several steps, as suggested by Kvale (1996). We performed an initial analysis of the total corpus of data to get a substantial understanding of the participants' reflections. Then the interviews were systematized according to themes that were most frequent and significant among the participants. The issue of intersubjectivity was attended to with discussions on categorization of the most frequent and significant issues, the interpretation of the extracts, and the analytical findings.

TABLE 1
Focus-group participants

Market	Consumer	Business
Norway	8	7
Hungary	8	6

SNAPSHOTS FROM MI USAGE IN NORWAY AND HUNGARY

All focus-group interviews were directed at gathering insights on actual usage as well as its underlying motivation. This included discussions on why MI is used, which services are used for what purposes, and the motivation for becoming MI users in the first place. We have structured this section around six themes that emerged as interesting and relevant. These were: (1) differences between countries and user groups, (2) MI services usage, (3) the relationship between PC and mobile phone usage, (4) the role of MI as pastime, (5) service discovery, and (6) deployment as well as cost confusion.

Differences Between Countries and User Groups

The focus-group interviews indicated only minor differences between Hungarian and Norwegian users, as well as between business users and consumers. While the motivating factors behind MI usage were largely the same, there were some notable differences.

With regard to the composition of the focus groups (reflecting the nature of the most advanced users of MI in each market), the Hungarian participants were men, primarily techies, and had advanced knowledge about the handsets and their functionality, as illustrated by one of the business users:

> "It's an E51, a thin one, cute and smart, very quick, really. It's a really good handset now. Apart from the GPS it has practically everything. My HP is 3.5G, and has everything, including HSDPA, except for a GPS receiver, which is available in the next handset in the series, the E71, which is a bit wider, and the next handset in the series already has it. . . . The only difference is that it has no separate memory card socket, but the 8 GB Flash is already incorporated in it."

Others have reported the same finding (e.g., Nuthall el al. 2008; Cui and Roto 2008). In Norway we saw a much more nuanced picture. There were women who were among the advanced users, and most of the users were not so much into the technology but rather were interested in the opportunities presented by the technology. The Hungarians, at the same time, seemed to have a much better understanding of the properties of mobile phones. For Norwegians, the cost and the mere looks of the phone were more important than its properties. The common practice of buying cheap, subsidized handsets may have had influence, as suggested by three Norwegian private users:

> "I did love the radio on my previous phone, but this new one doesnot have it."

> "The camera on this phone is of inferior quality compared to the previous I had."

> "I bought this one simply because it was pink."

In a similar way, the focus-group interviews indicated only limited differences between private and business usage. Not surprisingly, business users were somehow less concerned about costs than the private users. What is worth mentioning is that none of the respondents made a clear distinction between private and work-related MI usage. Rather, MI usage was seen as spanning their business and private spheres.

MI Service Usage

The participants in the focus-group interviews were recruited based on the fact that they were among those who generate the most data traffic from MI usage. With this approach to recruiting, we sought to identify the services used by these "advanced" users. With only a few exceptions, the usage was limited to e-mail and news websites and simple inquiries to databases such as Wikipedia and Google. Here is what a Norwegian business user and a private user had to say:

> "Every morning, just when I have gone out the door I check delays and stuff like that. And I check e-mails as a pastime, surf and read online newspapers and watch the news, while I am waiting for the train."

> "I like to Google, to search for addresses, and then you have to turn on the GPS to get the direction, but you can still find the address, and if you have some knowledge about the area, you do not have to. . . . If you are sitting and discussing and do not come to a conclusion . . . just something you do not remember and can check it."

In line with the spatial factor identified by Cui and Roto (2008), the preceding responses indicate that MI usage often occurred along with other activities (eating breakfast, watching TV, etc.). Also, in line with what Cui and Roto (2008) term "temporal factors," MI usage occurred in moments between planned activities, such as while waiting for a train. During the focus-group interviews, we also explicitly probed for usage of services particularly made for the MI, but the responses suggested little activity on that front. We had expected to see more adventurous use of the mobile phones in these user groups. But what we found was that primary use patterns were influenced by the relationship between MI and PC-based Internet.

The Relationship Between PC and Mobile Phone Usage

While the focus-group interviews were focused on use of the MI, the discussions frequently involved the PC-based Internet. In particular, the PC-based Internet entered the discussion from three different angles: MI usage that is *related to* PC-based Internet usage, MI usage that is *different from* PC-based Internet usage, and cost issues influencing the choice between MI and PC-based Internet.

The basic and most important advantage of MI is its accessibility when on the move. This was expressed by two Hungarian business users:

> "Not to have to switch on my laptop on the way, but I had a beep when I received an e-mail, I read it and could answer and make decisions. I could make people do things, manage them. Some people were surprised that I could manage half the company with this handset—yes, that's exactly what I do."

> "I can be more mobile because of it, because I can take it with me. So I'm more marketable. So if I were bound to one place, I couldn't get half the work."

The same advantage is also experienced in the private sphere, as expressed by a Hungarian and a Norwegian private user:

> "For example, it [the MI] gives me more freedom because, [. . .] while sitting in the pub drinking with my friends I don't have to go home to check something on my laptop, but I can check it on my mobile phone. So it gives me something extra."

> "I use Google [on the mobile phone] when we are discussing one thing or another, and then someone says, it happened in that year, and then I am always there to check. It is during the weekends."

Where a PC is stationary, or nomadic with WLAN, or mobile with a mobile phone modem, it is still not considered as mobile as the mobile phone. A Norwegian business user put it this way:

> "I often access the Internet from my mobile phone when sitting in my couch. I do not bother walking over to the PC."

Connectivity and being always on seem to be primary motivational factors for using MI. In addition, the users' perception of immediate access to their mobile phones seems decisive with regard to the choice between using the PC or the mobile phone in certain circumstances.

In certain instances, MI usage is simply a backup solution when no PC is at hand. This was expressed by one of the Hungarian business user as well as a Hungarian and a Norwegian private user:

> "Or you can avoid a conflict like this, e.g., when you get home and see that there is someone else behind the computer. Then I'll grab my telephone."

> "It's [MI] good when the ADSL is not working; it's rather called T-offline."[2]

> "It is not the same to surf the Internet on your mobile phone as it is to enjoy it in your living room with your laptop on the lap [. . .] and download music that you do not need to pay for. It is not exactly the same. And then you pay 150 Kroner[3] for Internet at home that is much faster and you can download much more on it. It is actually only backup solution that you use when you do not have other opportunities."

As described earlier, MI usage is limited to e-mail and news and simple inquiries to databases such as Wikipedia and Google. These services, to a large extent, mirror traditional PC-based Internet services. A plausible explanation for this pattern is that MI is just used as a substitute and backup for the PC-based Internet. But there are also other possible explanations, such as that more advanced services especially developed for the MI are too complicated to access and use. According to a Hungarian private user:

> "You cannot be sure that they [operator customer care] are going to answer [to requests regarding MI]. That's very good too [forums and the PC Internet], it helps a lot. You can find a tremendous lot of things on the Internet."

The respondents also clearly described PC-based Internet and MI as being complementary in that the PC-based Internet is superior with regard to user experience and allows for lengthy input sessions. The convenience of the mobile phones, however, lies in anytime connectivity that allows for constant updates and enables provision of short responses. In a professional context, such usage offers new opportunities to mentally prepare for the working day. In private contexts, it is typically related to, for example, quick fact-finding in heated discussions at the pub. Norwegian business and private users described such usage as follows:

> "I see that there are some new e-mails and then I check on this [mobile phone]. It is only if I see that it is difficult to read or with a lot of attachments then I go to the PC."

> "I check my e-mail on my phone in the morning while eating breakfast . . . but respond when I get to work, think on how I should answer it in meanwhile. Cannot sit and reply to a mail on your mobile."

In this way, the PC acts a means for producing content, while the mobile phone is used for more "lean-back" consumption of information.

Finally, the relationship between MI and PC-based Internet is influenced by cost concerns. In particular, in Hungary, it is considered by many as too costly to use *both* MI and PC-based Internet. This was expressed by three of the Hungarian private users:

> "For me, the price is an obstacle . . . it also depends on if I have ADSL at home."

> "When you are at home it's a problem that you have to have a telephone subscription as well, and the majority of my family needs a landline phone, so even if the MI costs as much as the wired ADSL at home, we won't cancel our subscription, and I'm not going to subscribe to the MI only for myself. That's why."

> "For me the price was an obstacle. If I go to California Coffee, and I buy a muffin for 250 Forints[4] then I can work with my laptop for one and a half hours with WiFi. And then I even had something to eat. . . . When calculating how much I spend monthly on muffins, then I can see how much cheaper it would be if I had a mobile phone that I could use as a modem."

These findings quite clearly indicate a difference between MI and PC-based Internet usage. At the same time, the use activities are related and interdependent. In particular, MI usage is strongly interrelated with PC-based Internet usage in the way it is used as an extension to the PC, offering ubiquitous Internet access, as described by a Norwegian private user and a business user:

> "I bring along the little gadget where I have all kind of information, people can get in touch with you, and I can get out. I do not have to be a particular place because I have this little gadget."

> "When I am sitting on the tram or elsewhere, I pick it up and answer short and briefly on e-mails, and finish off the first five, six that has arrived before I reach my job in the morning. That is ok."

The Role of MI as Pastime

While enabling people to work detached from stationary PCs, the MI is further seen as useful when one wants to kill time while on the move. This can be seen in the comments of three Hungarian consumers and a Norwegian business customer:

> "Some people bite their nails, and others take out their mobile phones."

> "For example, when I go to work by tram rather than by car, I don't want to watch homeless people. Have you ever traveled on tram number 1? . . . So, I build a kind of shell around myself. I have the sequence; e-mail, checking the usual news portals, they are listed."

> "I have a little bit of a claustrophobia, which I usually have in the underground. And I regularly bump into malfunctions. We are stuck for twenty minutes, and I don't need to tell you what it is like . . . It [the MI] certainly diverts your attention."

> "When you are on the station and waiting for the subway or train and read some news . . . checking whether the trains are on schedule."

Downloading ringtones and jokes, watching mobile TV, and browsing are commonly seen as pastime and entertainment activities in situations such as commuting. Our respondents reported MI usage as a more sensible way (e.g., rather than biting nails) of spending time on public transport such as the tram. MI offers the possibility to spend moments that otherwise would be wasted to get up to date (e.g., news) and maintain presence on social networks (e.g. Facebook). In many ways, MI offers relief in boring and stressful situations by what Habuchi (2005) has termed "cocooning."

Service Discovery and Employment

Our research showed that MI usage is still primarily limited to services that users transfer from their use of PC-based Internet. To change their unadventurous user habits, the respondents pointed out the need for help and guidance in discovering and adopting new services. This was expressed by two of the Norwegian private users in the following way:

> "I might miss these applications. If they become easier to download, and more information about how to download, it makes it easier to use the Internet on the phone."

> "I have little interest in this [downloading applications]. It might be genius if the retailer asks me about . . . what things I plan to use, and then he could put everything [on the phone]."

As noted by a Hungarian business user and a Norwegian private user, this low adoption of new services is not because of lack of their availability but rather because of the difficulty of setting up the phone and their poor accessibility:

> "That would be a great thing, you see, if you could buy a mobile phone which is already prepared for using the Internet, so you could avoid going to the Nokia website, call the customer service . . . where they don't know anything."

> "One has to have some interest in the technology, if not, it is about coincidences. There are many opportunities that are available."

In the corporate context, this is not made any easier as the employees' mobile phones are commonly not treated in the same ways as PCs. As commented by a Norwegian business user, the users are by and large left to themselves:

> "We have not received training from our IT department. I had to find out [how to use MI] myself. When I got the phone I did not fully understand how I connect, and it is sometimes still a little unclear to me."

Cost Confusion

At the time the interviews were conducted,[5] *uncertainty about cost* seemed more important that the cost in itself. The technical language used in some marketing communication (data transfer rates, etc.) was often hard to understand. This was pointed out by a Norwegian private user:

> "I have little bearing when it says that it costs so and so many Kroner per kilobyte. When I go into the vg.no,[6] I do not know if it's 1 or 1000 kilobyte as if it costs me 14 or 14 million."

In addition to the difficulties calculating costs, the respondents told stories about the risks of overspending. This was described by two Hungarian and one Norwegian consumer:

> "Yes, but in the summer I made a mistake—I use my telephone with a prepaid card. I was browsing in a hotel in the country, in Hajdúszoboszló. And then a woman came and clicked on a particular download button and she could download a 120 MB file. . . . The next text message was that I am in the red with 2,600 Forints [about $10 US]."

> "There was someone at Telenor who accumulated minus 1,000,000 Forints [about $4,000 US] by downloading the three parts of Star Wars using Edge."

> "I use the phone a lot in my work, both abroad and from abroad, so I have some quite nasty phone bills. The minuscule browsing in Norway—but abroad I do have to be careful because there it is expensive and I do restrict myself, at least if private. But at home, I do not think so much about it."

A perception of high costs, particularly when using international roaming, as well as considerable actual costs are influencing MI usage patterns. The blurry cost picture and rumors about how you can end up with huge mobile phone bills make people refrain from or at least limit their MI usage.

DISCUSSION AND CONCLUDING REMARKS

Quite remarkably, 82% of iPhone users use the MI—five times more than average use of MI. But this is not only a function of the handset design. One reason for this high usage is that Apple sells not only a mobile phone but also a value-added network where new services can easily be bought from an application store. In other words, Apple has managed to create a two-sided market with application providers. In a similar fashion, NTT DoCoMo has managed to develop a popular service platform and marketplace for MI services in Japan (see, for example, Funk 2001; Ishii 2004; Funk 2007). While Apple is a handset producer and NTT DoCoMo an operator, a key factor behind their success has been significant investments in user experience that makes it easy to discover and start using new services.

Putting the MI user experience on the agenda, Apple has also influenced the strategy of other handset manufacturers like the HTC Diamond and Nokia's Ovi. However, even if the mobile industry innovates, improves the MI user experience, and invests heavily in this area, the real users will still be integrated in a rather limited way. Further, as suggested by the analysis presented in this article, it is also highly uncertain whether the MI will develop in a direction where we will see a range of new and innovative usage patterns, or only extension of "traditional" PC Internet usage. Much of MI usage is simple extension of existing PC Internet usage, i.e., activities related to e-mail, news, and simple queries from databases. Here the mobile phone primarily acts as a substitute when a PC is not at hand. The mobile phone and the PC are complementary as the PC offers superior user experience and allows for lengthy input sessions, whereas the mobile phone is always at hand and offers the possibility of getting constant updates and thereby a head start for future activities. On the one hand, users' established mindset and experience with the PC-based Internet act as obstacles for using MI. On the other hand, extension of PC Internet usage is also the primary motivation for using the MI.

The key obstacle for growth of MI lies in the perception that the costs are high, which is understandable because of lack of clear price information. This obviously makes people refrain from using MI, or has them only using it to a limited extent. While "all-you-can-eat" packages for MI are likely to ameliorate this problem, there is at least one area where it will remain—despite new price plans, international roaming is not included and international rates are significantly higher. From the user perspective, this is a paradox. The further a user is away from a PC, the greater value the MI has. While the utility of the MI significantly increases when one is abroad, current price plans are likely to make users to continue to refrain from using the MI.

As we have seen, the primary motivation identified for using MI is to stay connected when a PC is out of reach. This need to be "online" is similar across private and business users for both Norwegians and Hungarians. An implication of this is that the value of MI is limited for those without PC access. Further, the MI is not superior to the PC-based Internet and vice versa; they instead act as complementary technologies. This undermines the leapfrogging argument for MI; i.e., it makes limited sense to start using the Internet for the first time on a mobile phone.

Different implications and approaches may be deduced from the MI practice discussed here. These may motivate us to continue to look for new killer applications or more elegant user interfaces that will create more value and propel MI usage. At the same time, we can argue that such a quest is basically misguided. MI usage is and will perhaps continue to be a mere extension of PC-based Internet usage—and such use activities are the very nature of MI. We may go even further and question whether it makes sense to distinguish between MI usage and PC-based Internet usage, a distinction blurred even more by the introduction of mini-PCs with HSDPA modems. The discussion is then about the same services and applications accessed by slightly different devices—devices that are suited to the situated and context-specific needs of the users. Thus, the challenge arguably is to understand how different services and applications can be made more easily available for the users across a range of different devices. Growth in usage may come from actively helping the users accessing existing services, rather than solely developing new innovative services.

NOTES

1. Use of mobile content Q2, 2008, TNS Gallup, http://www.tns-gallup.no/?did=9080956 (accessed March 13, 2009).
2. Referring to the T-*online* service offered by T-Mobile in Hungary.
3. Norwegian currency Kroner. 7 Kroner is about US$1.
4. Forint is the Hungarian currency. 250 Forints is about US$1.
5. Since we conducted the focus group interviews, both the Hungarians and Norwegians are being offered "all-you-can-eat" packages for the MI.
6. A Norwegian newspaper and the most popular Norwegian Mobile Internet media site.

REFERENCES

Cui, Y., and V. Roto. 2008. *How people use the Web on mobile devices.* Presented at WWW 2008, Alternate Track: Industrial Practice and Experiences, Beijing, April 21–25.

Funk, J. 2001. *The mobile Internet: How Japan dialed up and the West disconnected.* Kent, UK: ISI Publications.

Funk, J. 2007. Solving the startup problem in Western mobile Internet markets. *Telecommunications Policy* 31:14–30.

Habuchi, I. 2005. Accelerating reflexivity. In *Personal, portable, pedestrian: Mobile phones in Japanese life,* ed. M. Ito, D. Okabe, and M. Matsuda, 165–82. Cambridge, MA: MIT.

Ishii, K. 2004. Internet use via mobile phone in Japan. *Telecommunications Policy* 28:43–58.

Kim, H., J. Kim, Y. Lee, M. Chae, and Y. Choi. 2002. An empirical study of the use contexts and usability problems in mobile Internet. *Proceedings of the 35th Annual Hawaii international Conference on System Sciences* (HICSS'02), 1767–1776. Big Island, HI: IEEE Computer Society Press.

Kim, H., J. Kim, and Y. Lee. 2005. An empirical study of use contexts in the mobile Internet, focusing on the usability of information architecture. *Information Systems Frontiers* 7(2):175–86.

Kivi, A. 2008. *Mobile data service usage measurements. Results 2005–2007.* Helsinki University of Technology, PowerPoint presentation. http://www.netlab.tkk.fi/~jakivi/publications/Kivi_Mobile_Data_Service_Usage_2005_2007.pdf (accessed March 13, 2009).

Lee, I., and J. Kim. 2005. Use contexts for the mobile Internet: A longitudinal study monitoring actual use of mobile Internet services. *International Journal of Human Computer Interaction* 18:269–92.

Ling, R. 2009. *The rise of the mobile divides.* Paper presented at the Mobile Communication Forum, Oxford Internet Institute, Oxford, England, March.

Ling, R., and P. Sundsøy. 2010. The iPhone and mobile access to the Internet. In *Mobile media and the change of everyday life,* ed. J. R. Höflich, G. F. Kircher, C. Linke, and I. Schlote, 213–23. Berlin: Peter Lang.

Nuthall, P., M. de Lussanet, and D. Wilkos. 2008. *Mobile Internet users lead in advanced mobile services' adoption in Europe.* Cambridge, MA: Forrester Research.

Van Veen, N. 2006. *Getting consumers to use mobile services.* Cambridge, MA: Forrester Research.

Taylor, C., A. Anicello, S. Somohano, N. Samuels, L. Whitaker, and J. Ramey. 2008. *A framework for understanding mobile internet motivations and behaviors.* Presented at Conference on Human Factors in Computing Systems, Florence, Italy, April.

Cultivating Interaction Ubiquity at Work

Carsten Sørensen

Information Systems and Innovation Group, Department of Management, London School of Economics and Political Science, London, United Kingdom

There is limited debate on what "ubiquity" in *ubiquitous computing* implies, in particular in regard to technological affordances connecting people. The aim of this article is to explore the question: What is the role of technologically embedded assumptions in the cultivation of interaction ubiquity at work? Distinguishing between the embedded support for managing ongoing interaction relationships—as opposed to a series of interaction encounters—and the support for prioritizing interactions—as opposed to priorities per se—yields four analytical categories of affordances: connectors, filters, mediators, and coordinators. These four categories are illustrated through four case studies of mobile working. The author argues that successful cultivation of interaction ubiquity at work relies critically on a portfolio approach wherein the technology is seen as playing a more active role in the management of interaction beyond the simple standardized technical connection.

Mark Weiser's (1991) groundbreaking article formulated the vision of ubiquitous computing wherein the computer merged with ordinary objects and got embedded in physical environments and disappeared as a distinct entity. His work suggests that pervasive access to information will lead to a more harmonious relationship where computing adapts to the human environment, instead of the opposite. However, when a user engages with technology supporting the mobilization of interaction, there is no guarantee that it will lead to the harmonious relationship Weiser anticipated. The technology that supports the user also imposes demands such as that of undertaking everyday maintenance tasks, making backups, ensuring that batteries are charged, ensuring that all necessary cables and connectors are brought along, and occasionally installing firmware upgrades (Sørensen and Gibson 2008). With regard to the relationship between the technology and the user, there are also more substantial conflicts at play. Individual users through their mobile information technology (IT), for example, are both free to roam and at the same time instantly available for interaction requests (Arnold 2003). As Leopoldina Fortunati (2005) notes, the process of adaptation between technological affordances and human activities is a complex arrangement of mediated and body-to-body interaction. Whereas in personal interactions complexities are introduced by demands, purposes, and preferences of individuals involved, in the context of work, additional constraints and opportunities emerge with regard to the negotiation of interdependencies between distributed colleagues, performance measurement, and the degree of individual discretion in decision making.[1]

This article focuses on *individual cultivation of interaction ubiquity at work*, which is the ongoing changes in the relationship between a worker and the technological possibilities offered to him or her to ensure that interaction with remote individuals, groups, or interactive systems best matches the individual user's personal preferences, the requirements of the situation, and other constraints. Michael Arnold (2003) argues, in the context of everyday technology use, that such cultivation must be considered as contrary, in that the same technology in similar contexts may result in different and possibly

This research could not have been completed without a large number of practitioners letting us into their working lives and the doctoral students who did most of the hard lifting. I am also grateful for Leopoldina Fortunati for inviting me to an interesting workshop in Hong Kong. Also a big thanks to the editors and anonymous reviewers of this special issue for helping me improve the article. I of course accept full responsibility for the final result.

contradictory performances. Arnold (2003) rejects the notion of linear performances with an unambiguous and stable relationship between a technical affordance and a specific purpose. He does so by representing the technology as a closed black box of affordances—that is, possibilities for action (Schneiderman and Maes 1997; Dourish 2001). These possibilities for action are evoked in a context of contradictions, tensions, and uncertainty that increase the complexities entailed in the cultivation of interaction ubiquity at work. Furthermore, these complexities increase as the users increase their use of mobile and ubiquitous IT and the diversity of technologies deployed also increases. In a nutshell, I ask the question: What is the role of technologically embedded assumptions in the cultivation of interaction ubiquity at work?[2]

To further this analysis, two distinctions are advanced with regard to how we conceptualize technology supported action: (1) Technology offers embedded support for managing ongoing interaction relationships as opposed to a series of interaction encounters, and (2) technology offers embedded support for prioritizing interactions as opposed to priorities per se. These two "dimensions" yield four possibilities, with each type characterizing a distinct type of embedded technological support: (1) *connectors* offering support for unprioritized encounters; (2) *filters* supporting the prioritization of encounters; (3) *mediators* supporting unfiltered relationships; and (4) *coordinators* supporting filtered ongoing relationships. These four types of affordances are illustrated through case studies of mobile working.

Successful cultivation of interaction ubiquity at work relies critically on a portfolio approach wherein the technology is seen as playing a more active role in the management of interaction beyond the simple standardized technical connection explicitly or implicitly assumed in the majority of research on the social aspects of mobile IT. While the simple connections can be appropriated into complex interactive process, thinking that disregards diversity in affordances will overemphasize the social and neglect the role of explicit technological support in the cultivation of interaction ubiquity. Jarvenpaa and Lang (2005) call for further research on technology support for individuals managing interaction, and this article aims to contribute to such a research endeavor.

I also highlight the role of mobile technologies in the development of interaction ubiquity, a technology that has not received adequate attention in the ubiquitous computing literature. Furthermore, it spotlights a blind spot in the growing body of research that explores the role of mobile information technology (IT) in people's lives (Castells et al. 2007; Akiyoshi and Ono 2008; Barendregt 2008; Donner 2008; Goggin 2008; He 2008; Ling 2008; Ureta 2008). The large majority of contemporary research on mobile IT use is only concerned with a single technology, the mobile phone. Most studies assume that technical possibilities are limited to voice or textual connections through mobile phone calls, short message service (SMS) messages, voicemails, e-mails, and multimedia messages (MMS). In effect, they do not consider mobile technologies as part of the emerging ubiquitous computing environment.

In the following section, I discuss the concept of ubiquity, examining the diversity of affordances supporting individual cultivation of interaction ubiquity in terms of the support for ongoing relationships and prioritization. I use this perspective in the analysis of four cases of mobile interaction at work. Each of the cases illustrates portfolios of technological support for the cultivation of interaction ubiquity. The last two sections discuss the results and provide conclusions.

UBIQUITY

Weiser's vision of ubiquitous computing marked a dramatic departure from previous predictions. In 1943 IBM's chairman, Thomas Watson, stated, "I think there is a world market for maybe five computers" (Berghel 1999, 11). In 1977 the founder of DEC, Ken Olson, predicted "there is no reason for any individual to have a computer in his home" (Berghel 1999, 13). Even Bill Gates's statement that "Microsoft was founded with a vision of a computer on every desk, and in every home"[3] is now a conservative vision considering the range of everyday computing experiences (Yoo forthcoming). Harold S. Osborne's 1954 prediction now seems much more lucid. He foresaw that each individual would possess a device similar to the mobile phone with video connection and a lifelong phone number assigned at birth (Ling 2004).

Today ubiquitous computing is no longer a figment of imagination. Beyond developments in the marketplace, it has also become an area of scholarly research. Now there are research programs such as the Disappearing Computer (http://www.disappearing-computer.net/); research conferences such as Ubicomp; and academic journals such as the *Journal of Personal and Ubiquitous Computing*. Much of this research has been quite technical (e.g., Hansmann et al. 2003; Baresi et al. 2004). However, some effort also has been invested in understanding ubiquitous computer use from a broader social and organisational perspective. Dourish (2001), for example, offers a very comprehensive phenomenological analysis of what he calls embodied interaction.

A significant part of research in ubiquitous computing relates to the design and usability of technology—for example, Adam Greenfield's (2006) excellent presentation of seventy-seven principles for understanding what he calls "everyware"; most of Hiroshi Ishii's work on remote collaboration and on tangible bits (e.g., Ishii and

Ullmar 1997); and Donald Norman's (1999b) work on invisible computers and information appliances. William J. Mitchell (1995, 2003) and Malcom McCullough (2005) consider broader relationships between people, ubiquitous computing, and the built environment in terms of the changing role of the city and the individual inhabiting this world of merging architectural and informational elements. Steve Mann and Hal Niedzviecki (2002) explore the social implications of ubiquitous computing based on Mann's more than twenty years of experience with wearable computing. Kevin Warwick (2002) takes the concept of embodied interaction literally and experiments with radiofrequency ID (RFID) chips implanted in his body, which in conjunction with sensors enable his hand to remote control a mechanical hand via an Internet connection. Within the information systems field, very little effort has been invested in understanding ubiquitous computing. Notable exceptions in the literature that focuses on organizations include Lyytinen and Yoo (2002a; 2002b), Lyytinen et al. (2004), Sørensen et al. (2005), and Kourouthanassis and Giaglis (2008). Katherine Albrecht and Liz McIntyre (2006) offers a techno-political exposition on the relationships between individuals as consumers, commercial organizations, and RFID technology. Furthermore, the substantial body of human—computer interaction (HCI) research in ubiquitous computing has largely devoted little attention to understanding unfolding real-life user experiences with the technology (Abowd and Mynatt 2000; Sørensen and Gibson 2008).

INTERACTION

In this section, I look at the relationships between ubiquity, interactions, and the technological affordances that enable them.

Ubiquity and Interaction

The clear-cut classification of activities into those requiring the use of a computer and those that do not is blurred as computation becomes integral to a broader range of activities, characterized by Yongjin Yoo (2009) as "experiential computing." While Weiser's (1991) vision has been powerful in shaping our understanding of the technical possibilities, it engenders notions of ease of use, harmony, and computation merging into the fabric of life. However, sociomaterial assemblages are "constitutively entangled in everyday life" (Orlikowski 2007, 1437) and are best conceived of as enmeshed in complex, paradoxical, and conflicting relationships (Mick and Fournier 1998; Arnold 2003; Jarvenpaa and Lang 2005).

When ubiquitous computing technology supports remote connections with individuals, groups, or interactive systems, the users' contexts and practices can be shaped by actions of these remote entities. For example, the decision on whether or not to pick up a specific mobile phone call will be informed by a whole range of possible factors. Is it possible to determine the caller's identity? Who is calling? What is the recipient's physical and emotional situation? What image does the recipient wish to display to the caller and what is the relationship between the two people? The rhythms of coupling and uncoupling technology from social action can vary across individuals, situations, and tasks and over time (Dourish 2001; Green 2002; Sørensen and Pica 2005). The user experience of ubiquity is therefore complex and an emerging property of the situation, and is shaped by a variety of factors ranging from practical matters of technology (Sørensen and Gibson 2008) and situation (Ljungberg and Sørensen 2000) to fundamental issues of the person's emotional state (Ciborra 2006).

The global diffusion of mobile telephony has, for example, led to emerging social practices (Licoppe 2004; Ling 2008). The individual user's ongoing relationship with ubiquitous computing technology can contain elements of control, harmony, interruptions, and overload. When users and their immediate ubiquitous technology entirely define the situation, the users may still perceive the relationship as problematic—this is the subject of much HCI research and a valid concern. Here the particular technology and the users are, however, the only factors directly influencing the interaction. When the technology mediates remote interaction, other individuals, groups, and interactive systems can play an active role in the user's perception of ubiquitous interaction.

Ubiquitous technology can provide support for the management of interaction, for example, providing the user information about requests for interaction, supporting the management of information about others, providing an audit trail of past interaction, and by supporting the prioritization and filtering of interaction (Ljungberg 1999) and even the negotiation of availability (Wiberg and Whittaker 2005). This type of support for the individual managing his or her own interaction can be compared with the use of coordination mechanisms in collaborating groups (Carstensen and Sørensen 1996; Schmidt and Simone 1996). The cultivation of interaction ubiquity at work implies coordinating mutual interdependencies in the context of the multiple interests of the individual user, immediate team members, and the rest of the organisation.

Latent and Perceived Affordances

In the remainder of this section, I discuss the diversity of affordances offering possibilities for the user to cultivate interaction ubiquity. My aim is to provide the background for a discussion of how the diversity of technological choices can shape the sociotechnical relationship of the user cultivating their interaction ubiquity.

Arnold (2003) characterizes the use of technology as affordances subjected to simultaneously contrary performances, in contrast to the traditional assumption of the affordances serving as simple means of achieving a purpose. Mobile computing technology will, for example, most often both follow the user and offer access to instant connections with others, and thereby both facilitate the user's mobility and provide an uniquely fixed point of contact (Arnold 2003). Technology performances are results of technological affordances—possibilities for action—meeting inherently contradictory situations. Arnold does not offer a specific definition of technology affordances other than rejecting their place in a linear performance that achieves a specific purpose. Instead he explores the role of affordances in the situated and contradictory use where they are evoked.

James J. Gibson's (1977, 1979) original definition of affordances denotes latent action possibilities independent of perception. Norman (1988) popularized the concept in the discussion of the design of everyday objects and here, as opposed to Gibson, emphasized perceived affordances (Gaver 1991; Norman 1999a). Although Gibson's original definition emphasizes possible usefulness of a technology, Norman's perceived affordances emphasizes the usability of a technology (Gaver 1991). As this article is not concerned with issues of technology usability, the properties of ubiquitous computing artefacts are only characterized in terms of affordances—latent possibilities for future action.

In the next two subsections, I consider a category of technological affordances and the third combines the two categories into a framework characterizing diversity of possibilities for cultivating interaction ubiquity.

Encounter and Relationship Affordances

This article draws on the distinction between technological affordances enabling encounters where memory of the interaction is not supported by the technology, and those mediating ongoing relationships by recording aspects of the interaction (Mathiassen and Sørensen 2008). Encounters imply the technologically embedded assumption of algorithmic codification, whereas the mediation of relationships places importance in the cultivation of data (Wegner 1997). Distinctions between encounters and relationships of various kinds have been discussed widely—for example, Peter Wegner's (1997) distinction between algorithmic codification and ongoing interactivity in computing; problem-solving method assumptions of transformation or interactivity (Mathiassen and Nielsen 2000); organizational information services supporting encounters or relationships (Mathiassen and Sørensen 2008); understanding market relationships as transaction or relationship economics (Zuboff and Maxmin 2002); services as encounters or relationships (Gutek 1995); and marketing as transactions or relationships (Coviello and Brodie 2001). In the context of this article, encounters and relationships specifically relate to technology affordances supporting individual users managing their interaction with remote individuals, groups, and interactive systems.

As an example, consider the core affordance of a standard mobile phone, the possibility of establishing connections with other mobile phones, either synchronously through a voice call or asynchronously by SMS or MMS messages. Each such connection is treated as an instance of an encounter between the two telephones and no specific assumptions are made regarding relationships between individual connections other than their chronological ordering and their type—incoming or outgoing. This core affordance defines the mobile phone as a device for encounters with little or no support for memory management for an ongoing relationship consisting of multiple such encounters (Mathiassen and Sørensen 2008). Messages are organized in separate folders for sent and received messages. Each of these folders lists messages by their time stamp as a record of the stream of encounters. As opposed to this approach, the Apple iPhone implementation of SMS messaging draws on an instant-messaging metaphor. SMS messages are organized as a series of ongoing interaction relationships. The iPhone organizes sent and received SMS messages as conversations between the phone user and contacts in user's address book. Although this organization of messages does not fundamentally alter the core mobile phone affordance to provide possibilities for encounters, it offers the additional affordance of encounters being organized as a series of relationships. By assuming that encounters are part of ongoing interaction relationships, the technology can provide affordances supporting the management of these relationships. This basic example illustrates the essential distinction between affordances offering encounters as opposed to those supporting ongoing relationships. Encounter affordances implement the assumption of atomic, unrelated, interaction instances. Relationship affordances implement memory of aspects of the interaction.

Interaction Symmetry and Asymmetry

The assumption that technology will recede into the background and have a harmonious relationship with the user is questionable if the technology mediates user interaction with remote people and systems. Here the technology will enable the user-technology context to be penetrated by remote requests for interaction, messages, alerts, and the like, as well as extending the user's ability to equally engage in remote interaction with others (Ljungberg and Sørensen 2000; Kakihara and Sørensen 2001). In the simple case of a mobile phone call, anyone possessing the unique telephone number associated with a specific SIM (subscriber identity module) card will be able to instigate a call, which the recipient can decide to accept or reject. If the call is accepted, a simple connection is established allowing the two people to engage in a conversation.

Particularly interesting is the discussion of asymmetry in the situation between instigator and recipient, as the request for interaction may be disruptive or the interaction itself may not suit the recipient (Ljungberg and Sørensen 2000; Nardi and Whittaker 2000; Wiberg and Whittaker 2005). However, even if the interaction is deemed disruptive, it may still be perceived as beneficial (O'Conaill and Frohlich 1995). The technological affordance offering one party remote access to another person raises the issue of interruptions, which has been researched extensively in the context of HCI (see, e.g., the extensive list of references at http://www.interruptions.net/). From the perspective of the recipient, this asymmetry can partly be caused by the combination of a technology affording interaction symmetry and the instigator of the interaction having limited or no insight into the recipient's general context and specific interaction preferences. Providing technological affordances for interaction asymmetry is, therefore, a possible means in redressing the situation. In the preceding example, the recipient may decide to reject the request for interaction based on information about the identity of the caller. The affordance of allowing the recipient to be informed about the identity of the caller, or indeed of the subject to be discussed, can be interpreted as the embedded assumption that this information matters for the decision to accept or reject the call (Ljungberg 1999; Ljungberg and Sørensen 2000; Wiberg and Whittaker 2005).

The affordance of interaction symmetry implies that the technology offers all parties equal status in the interaction. Affording interaction asymmetry conversely means offering action possibilities prioritizing interaction, for example, through rules stipulating how interaction unfolds. SMS messaging affords interaction symmetry, as a text message sent is received, and as the technology does not prioritize messages, people, or contents. Instant-messaging systems typically afford interaction asymmetry by providing rules regulating parts of the interaction, for example, requesting approval for a person to be included with the sphere of possible interaction (buddy list), and indeed the possibility of blocking existing members of that sphere. Technology offering interaction symmetry will leave the cultivation of interaction ubiquity entirely to the user, while technology affording interaction asymmetry supports the user in managing the user's interaction through supporting prioritization.

Diversity of Interaction Ubiquity Support

The previous two subsections categorized technology affordances supporting the cultivation of interaction ubiquity into two categories. The first category distinguished between the technological assumptions of interaction as either unrelated encounters or as ongoing relationships. The second category distinguished between technology affording either interaction symmetry or asymmetry. In this subsection these two categories are combined into four types of technology affordances (see figure 1) providing a diversity of possibilities for the individual to manage their interaction:

Connections offer possibilities of symmetrical encounters.
Filters embedded asymmetrical prioritization of encounters.
Mediators afford symmetrical interaction in ongoing relationships.
Coordinators provide opportunities for interaction asymmetry in ongoing relationships.

The four types represent a diversity of affordances, which will be perceived and instantiated depending on the particular user's preferences, need, and particular situation. The four types can each influence the extent to which the individual can cultivate interaction ubiquity to best suit their perceived needs. Figure 1 illustrates the four categories of affordances through examples. The following section uses this categorization of affordances into four types as the analytical framework for a study of sociotechnical practices in mobile working.

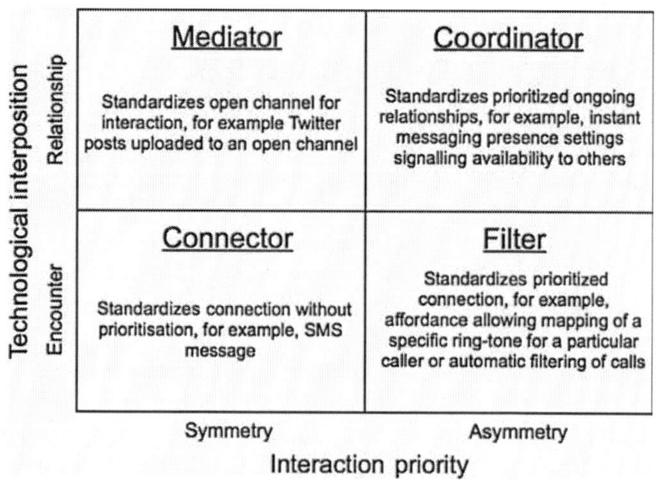

FIG. 1. The diversity of affordances for interaction ubiquity defined in terms of assumptions about technological interposition and interaction priority.

PRAXIS

In this section, I apply the categories established previously in the analysis of the cultivation of interaction ubiquity in mobile working practices. The four empirical studies discussed in this section were all conducted as part of doctoral research work within the mobility@lse unit (http://mobility.lse.ac.uk) at the London School of Economics and Political Science between 2002 and 2005 and form part of a larger body of qualitative empirical studies of enterprise mobility conducted between 2001 and 2008 (Sørensen et al. 2008). Table 1 presents key characteristics for each of the four cases and points toward further sources of information about the studies. In order to advance the understanding of interaction ubiquity in mobile working, the four cases have been reanalyzed. The following four subsections each present one case, and each case represents a diversity of technology affordances. Technology affordances are classified from the perspective of the mobile worker described. The outcome of this analysis is an understanding of how the cultivation of interaction ubiquity is constituted by appropriation of a diversity of technological affordances. Figure 2 summarizes the findings.

Study 1: Interaction Ubiquity at High Speed

In the study of operational policing, the technology subjected to most intense cultivation of ubiquity and most highly rated by the police officers was the personal radio mounted on the officer's shoulder (Pica 2006). The radio was usually the only remaining technology in use during critical incidents demanding the officer's full attention and thereby in this situation offering the optimal sense of interaction ubiquity. Officers would remain in constant contact with the control room during incidents to report progress, to rapidly gather information, to coordinate efforts with other officers, and to request further assistance in case it was needed. In terms of technical affordances, the two-way radio system offered unprioritized constant two-way connection between the police officer and the control room. For this to work, the police apply strict discipline as to how the shared radio waves

TABLE 1
Summary of key aspects of the four case studies reanalyzed in this article

Case	Workers	Years	Place	Method	Topic	References
1	Police officers	2002–2004	UK	250+ hours participant observation with 40+ officers and managers. 20+ interviews; two focus groups	The rhythms of interaction with mobile information technology by operational police officers	Sørensen and Pica (2005); Pica (2006)
2	Off-premises foreign exchange traders	2003–2004	Middle East	102 interviews and participant observation of traders	Discretion and control in mobile working for off-premises foreign exchange traders	Al-Taitoon (2005); Sørensen and Al-Taitoon (2008)
3	Security guards and industrial waste workers	2004–2005	UK	Action research with 350 hours of meetings, interviews, and observation	Real-life experimentation with RFID (radiofrequency ID) enabled mobile phone technology supporting new ways of working	Kietzmann (2007); Kietzmann (2008)
4	London cab drivers	2004–2005	UK	39 interviews and 14 hours of videotaped observations	The choice of location as core business strategy and the role of mobile technologies in pooling resources and informing individuals	Elaluf-Calderwood (2008); Elaluf-Calderwood and Sørensen (2008)

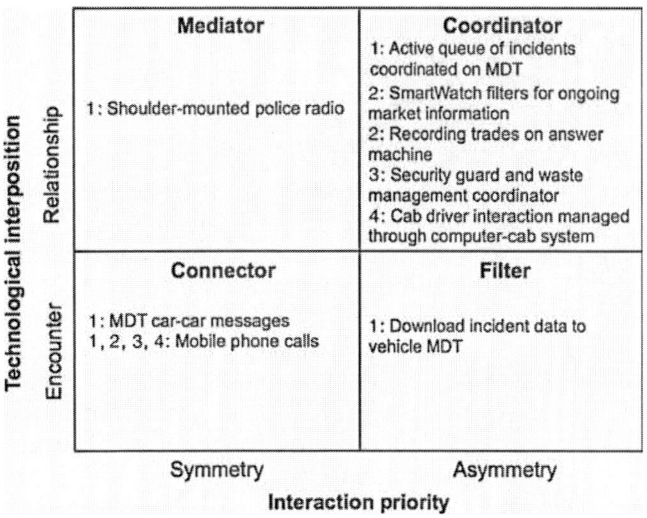

FIG. 2. The diversity of affordances in the four case studies: (1) police; (2) mobile traders; (3) security guards and industrial waste management; and (4) London cab drivers.

are used. Officers themselves also apply highly selective audio filtering to the stream of radio messages broadcast and through this maintain peripheral awareness of ongoing and upcoming incidents similar to that documented from studies of traders and underground train control room operators (Schmidt 1993; Heath and Luff 2000).

The radio has now been supplemented with vehicle-based mobile data terminals (MDT). These terminals provided officers with a more effective means of gaining detailed case information about an incident before they arrive at the scene. The technology could also provide information about related incidents involving the same address or the same citizens. This allowed much more comprehensive briefing as the information would be filtered and only sent to the particular vehicle deployed for dealing with the incident and not on shared frequencies, with implicit demands of keeping interaction brief and to the point. Streaming data to the car also suited the officers as the officer in the passenger seat could read out the information and continue to negotiate over the radio at the same time. This system was so effective that over time there was a gradual shift away from using the two-way radio system for preincident briefing and toward reliance on the more effective dedicated streaming to the relevant car. One side effect of this shift from an ongoing relationship with interaction symmetry, in which information was freely pulled by all officers listening to the main frequency, toward dedicated and filtered push of information, was that only those obtaining the information had an overview of the situation while everyone else was more or less in the dark.

The data terminal also embedded a updated list of current incidents registered, which, much like the queue of customer requests in a taxi system, presented for the dispatch office a semiautomated way of coordinating the allocation of incidents to police vehicles simply by allowing officers to pick incidents themselves on the touch screen in the vehicle. From the point of view of the individual officer in a vehicle, the active queue of incidents represented mediation of ongoing available and completed jobs. The officers evoked connectors when sending messages similar to SMS messages between the mobile data terminals installed in their patrol cars as well as using mobile phones to contact witnesses and colleagues to gather critical information or for instant microcoordination (Ling 2004).

Study 2: Trading Foreign Exchange Out and About

At a large Middle Eastern bank, mobile foreign exchange traders would spend their days in the trading pit and then continue to trade foreign currencies after normal working hours (Al-Taitoon 2005). This arrangement enabled the bank to continuously engage with the market twenty-four hours each day of the week. In the past, the bank had experimented with three-shift pit-based trading, distributing trading across time zones in branches, and selected traders trading out of hours from a stationary personal computer at home. All these attempts to extend trading hours beyond normal working hours proved unsuccessful primarily because they did not yield satisfying results when traders engaged in an individual process of cultivating interaction ubiquity (Sørensen and Al-Taitoon 2008). The traders needed to get on with their private lives while continuing to engage in trading.

Eventually, success was achieved with a system that supported traders' out-of-hours work through a combination of Reuters SmartWatch, a small trading information device showing rate changes, a mobile phone for coordinating trading limits with colleagues, and an answering machine at the office to leave auditable details of the trades made out of hours. A highly select and trusted subset of traders engaged voluntarily in this around-the-clock work. This work required very high levels of technological support to enable the individual to cultivate an acceptable level of interaction ubiquity.

As the traders were subjected to various coordination mechanisms and control systems throughout their working day, they were allowed significant discretion when engaging in mobile trading. Accordingly, they did things such as set up limits on triggering alarms on their Reuters SmartWatch and used filters to view messages. Traders kept interaction with colleagues through mobile phone and other technologies to an absolute minimum and generally were left to trade on their own. In rare cases a trader would call a colleague to coordinate trading limits. An organizational coordination mechanism imposed some minimal interaction asymmetry from the trader to the organization as each trader was required to record details for each trade on an automatic answering machine for subsequent processing the following day. Their individual cultivation of filters for tracking rate changes and for providing a constant stream of information on the Reuters SmartWatch was entirely unregulated and allowed the individual trader to accommodate his own rhythm of work.

Study 3: Loosely or Tightly Coupled Relationships

An organizational system with RFID-enabled mobile phones that recorded RFID tags and automatically sent SMS messages with the readings to a central server enabled coordination of the work force in two different organizations (Kietzmann 2007).

In a security firm the guards would swipe the phone over passive RFID tags embedded in the walls along their route. After each swipe the phone would automatically send an SMS message to a central server updating it with the security guard's position and the situation status selected by the guard on a menu in the phone. For the individual guard, this was a case of explicitly imposed coordination. The security guards generally found it easy to cultivate their interaction ubiquity with the new system as the main difference from the existing system, where a torch-like tag reader was used, was the immediate update of position instead of infrequent batch updates. Because the work was already highly regulated with little scope for individual discretion, the guards did not find it difficult to cultivate interaction ubiquity with the new system. The security guard would occasionally also use the mobile phone for calls.

A similar system was also implemented in another organization to help track industrial waste barrels with RFID tags. In this domain, however, the workers found this particular type of mediated coordination problematic as they were used to having considerable discretion in the organization of work. Now they had to check with central management, which felt it had a good overview remotely through the information fed by the RFID-based system (Kietzmann and Sørensen forthcoming). The embedded coordinator mechanism automated aspects of the work previously conducted by the user and also provided the possibility of real-time interactivity, as opposed to data being recorded in the centralized system with some delay.

Study 4: Finding Fares in London

There are around 21,000 of the famous London Black Cabs and most of them are owned by the licensed cabbie driving each one. Each Black Cab driver has, since 1865, been required to pass a difficult set of exams, "The Knowledge," covering more than 300 routes[4] and all streets in a six-mile radius from the center of London. The drivers rely extensively on mobile phones to exchange information on available customers, roadwork, and for engaging in general social conversation with fellow taxicab drivers, friends, and family when on a job or when waiting for one to emerge (Elaluf-Calderwood 2008). Most London taxicab drivers traditionally work entirely on their own with no overall support for coordination of their efforts. They have appropriated the mobile phones as a means of obtaining work, and for staying in constant touch through mobile phone connections. However, competitive pressures from minicabs, who can hire less qualified drivers, has meant that London taxicab drivers increasingly seek membership in computer-cab organizations, which dispatch jobs to taxicabs through a computer system based on drivers continuously updating their position to the central dispatch office. The embedded rules for allocating jobs are a subject for much discussion among drivers as they greatly influence the overall performance and perceived fairness of the dispatch system (Elaluf-Calderwood 2008). Further innovation led to a system wherein the driver's location as signaled by mobile phone is updated automatically in a central system. The matching of customers and drivers is then almost automatically resolved when customers call the company from their mobile phones and thereby reveal their locations to the system, which in turn automatically seeks out the nearest available Black Cab. The drivers of these cabs will be called on their mobile phones and can then accept or reject the fare. This coordination is an example where the customer and the cab driver are matched automatically through coordination, as opposed to the traditional system where the customer would either call one cab directly or a human operator who would locate a cab.

CHOICES

Several researchers have explored the complex and contradictory relationship between individuals and technology (e.g., Mick and Fournier 1998; Arnold 2003). Such studies tend to place strong emphasis on the social context in which the technology is used, with little or no attention directed toward the role of different technological affordances. Technology is generally seen as a black box. Sirkka L. Jarvenpaa and Karl R. Lang (2005) explore the paradoxes of mobile phone use and suggest a range of design features for supporting the users as they coped with these paradoxes. In particular, they suggest increased support for presence management, collaboration, context awareness, location awareness, and role management. All these capabilities are directly related to affordances offered by the technology.

In the four case studies it was shown how ubiquitous interaction was enabled by a diverse range of affordances. This diversity of affordances marks a departure from studies emphasizing a single technology, most often the mobile phone (e.g., Mazmanian et al. 2005).

It is of course important to understand both the diversity of affordances and the contradicting performances when the technology is situated in social and organizational contexts. Human interaction is always conducted within a complex context of assumptions about others and about the interaction. This has been described best by Erwin Goffman (1963) in his study of the ongoing social processes of seeking to shape others' opinions of oneself, while they seek to gain the truth behind the masquerade. Goffman argues that in this ongoing process, we will always be a bit better at uncovering the true intentions of others than they are at developing further strategies for obscuring them. Rich Ling (2008) offers an extensive analysis of how the ideas of colocated interaction as studied by Emil Durkheim, Goffman, and Randall Collins can be understood in the context of new forms of technology-mediated interaction.

An interesting duality can be identified in the tension between the overwhelming success of connections assuming encounter symmetry, and the assumptions governing social interaction of relationship asymmetry. E-mails, SMS, and mobile phone conversations are popular means of engaging flexible encounters in social situations of ongoing interaction relationships characterized by asymmetry. While relying on *connection* and *mediation* embed assumptions of symmetry in the interaction, *filtering* and *coordination* directly stipulate assumptions of interaction asymmetry and through this support the user in prioritizing the interaction. These dimensions offer a span of possibilities for designing interaction support.

However, problems of interaction overload and addiction alert us to the downside of interaction ubiquity (Mazmanian, Orlikowski, and Yates 2005; Jarvenpaa and Lang 2005). As interaction and requests for interaction intensify, this becomes increasingly problematic, and there will be a need to establish principles, rules, and mechanisms for managing the use of technology. On the surface, the problem with interaction symmetry seems worse in the case of obtrusive interaction, such as phone calls, as opposed to asynchronous text messages or e-mails, which seem more inconspicuous because they need not disturb right away. However, any initiation of interaction can be viewed as a request for someone else's time, and although missed calls only leave behind information that they are missed, e-mails and SMS messages leave themselves behind entirely as long-lasting requests for attention. One of the useful features of buddy lists in instant messaging clients, or the invite system in social networking sites, is the ability to include and exclude—applying *filters* and *coordinators* stipulating asymmetry in instant encounters or ongoing relationships.

The underlying assumption of interaction asymmetry also relates directly to the ongoing and relational nature of interaction at work mediating, negotiating, and resolving mutual interdependencies (Schmidt and Simone 1996; Karsten 2003). Much of the literature on meetings assumes these to be relatively long-lasting atomic encounters, few in numbers, several in participants, and based on a predetermined agenda. Empirical studies of interaction at the workplace have, however, found that the most frequent meetings are unplanned and involve two people discussing ongoing issues for around 90 seconds (Whittaker et al. 1994; Wiberg 2001; Wiberg and Whittaker 2005). Assuming this to be the case, it is not a surprise that technologies such as mobile voice calls, SMS messages, and mobile e-mail have turned out successful as they directly support such microcoordination activities (Ling 2004). However, this leads to users spending considerable time managing multiple contacts as well as many ongoing conversations (Whittaker, Jones, and Terveen 2002). Steve Whittaker, Quentin Jones, and Loren Terveen (2002) illustrate how a desktop-based coordinator can support both remembering the content of conversation and tracking status of conversations and outstanding actions, as well as maintaining contact information. Mikael Wiberg (2001) identifies how ongoing interaction consisting of multiple concurrent conversations can be supported and here identifies the ability of the technology to mediate the relationship through *mediators* and *coordinators*.

The successful cultivation of ubiquity relies critically on the specific context. Although some work contexts, as in the case of security guards, require the explicit mediation of ongoing relationships through *mediator* or *coordinator* mechanisms ensuring sufficient technological support, other contexts, such as the Black Cab drivers, mainly require relatively simple *connector* mechanisms to ensure the appropriate levels of individual discretion for the user. Extensive changes in the ways the ubiquitous services relate to the individual, for example, in terms of shifting from symmetry to asymmetry, can make it problematic for users to cultivate interaction ubiquity and the mechanism may be seen as foreign and inappropriate. For the security guards, the added interactivity and transparency of their movements did not impose a critical barrier for ubiquity as they already were used to being closely managed, whereas the industrial waste management workers found the added visibility problematic as it led to more intervention from management and less discretion for the workers. For the mobile traders, there was an absolute premium on individual discretion even if they worked in the highly regulated banking business. They would, however, on their own cultivate ubiquity through asymmetry embedded in profiles and alarms on their Reuters SmartWatch. This cultivation was, however, entirely determined and controlled by the individual trader (Al-Taitoon 2005; Sørensen and Al-Taitoon 2008).

Working life represents a myriad of emerging relationships continuously connecting and disconnecting social activities through technological capabilities and face-to-face engagements. Some of these connections are relatively easily established and broken, for example, in close-knit networks of mobile phone connections. Others take hard work and significant organizational commitment to establish and to get accepted, such as establishing more significant direct support for collaboration through *mediators* and *coordinators* where the technology directly supports work processes. In general, symmetry, such as that offered by e-mail systems and telephones, has easily found a place in organizations as flexible means for instant negotiation and microcoordination. These connections offer flexible complements to interaction conducted by a variety of technology affordances embedding assumptions of interactional asymmetry, such as coordination mechanisms, schedules, and organizational procedures and forms (Yates 1989; Carstensen and Sørensen 1996; Schmidt and Simone 1996).

CONCLUSION

This article argues that the study of ubiquitous computing must take into consideration the primary ubiquitous technology of the past 20 years, the mobile phone. However, the abundance of studies emphasizing the social context for mobile phone interaction must be balanced with the awareness that a diverse range of affordances support interaction ubiquity. Correspondingly, our thinking should not be limited to affordances that offer interaction symmetry between the parties. We need to consider the entire array of situations and affordances.

Based on the analysis presented in this article, we can see that the diverse technology affordances that support interaction ubiquity are of four types: (1) *connectors* providing support for symmetric encounters with no assumptions about the process or the relative importance of elements; (2) *filters* embedding assumptions of interaction asymmetry supported through encounters with no memory of the process; (3) *mediators* providing support for ongoing symmetric interaction; and (4) *coordinators* embedding assumptions of asymmetry in the unfolding of events as well as mediating support for the process.

With rapid innovation in the diverse range of technologies and services available for the support of interpersonal and organizational interaction, there is a great need for reflection on what the consequences of these technological choices may be once the technology engages in a process of social appropriation. The emerging debate of information growth, overload, and other unforeseen consequences of the broader digitization project can greatly inform such discussions. However, this article argues that there is a need for an additional vocabulary for discussing the intimate relationships forged between individuals and technologies. This vocabulary must support us in understanding the consequences of sociotechnical choices, as well as guiding our decisions on how to design further support. The analysis presented in this article marks one small step in this direction.

NOTES

1. Similar concerns are reflected in the paradoxical relationship between consumers and technology in general (Mick and Fournier 1998), and Jarvenpaa and Lang (2005) extend this analysis to the study of mobile information technology. The mobile phone can, for example, simultaneously fulfill the need for instant contact with someone else and create further need for contact. This complex and paradoxical relationship between user and technology results in the users cultivating their own individual coping mechanisms to resolve everyday conflicts (Mick and Fournier 1998; Jarvenpaa and Lang 2005). The users may decide to look at their mobile phone display before accepting a call to decide whether they wish to engage in the conversation. When confronted with the conflicting demand of not disturbing a meeting and yet remaining available for interaction, the mobile phone may be set to silently vibrate, and the user may here choose to interact through text messages instead of calls.

2. Interaction ubiquity relates to the Arnold et al. (2008, 49) argument that "things do not speak." For example, the telephone disappears from our attention when we recall having spoken with a friend on the telephone and recall this as having spoken to the friend and not as having spoken to the friend through the telephone. However, this scenario assumes that the telephone is not perceived as a disturbance and does not invite interaction to occur in situations deemed inappropriate.

3. See http://en.wikipedia.org/wiki/Microsoft (accessed April 13, 2010).

4. See http://en.wikipedia.org/wiki/Taxicabs_of_the_United_Kingdom (accessed April 13, 2010).

REFERENCES

Abowd, G. D., and E. D. Mynatt. 2000. Charting past, present, and future research in ubiquitous computing. *ACM Transactions on Computer-Human Interaction* 7:29–58.

Akiyoshi, M., and H. Ono 2008. The diffusion of mobile Internet in Japan. *The Information Society* 24:292–303.

Al-Taitoon, A. 2005. Making sense of mobile ICT-enabled trading in fast moving financial markets as volatility-control ambivalence: Case study on the organisation of off-premises foreign exchange at a Middle-East bank. PhD diss. London School of Economics and Political Science.

Albrecht, K., and L. McIntyre. 2006. *Spychips: How major corporations and government plan to track your every move with RFID.* Nashville, TN: Nelson Current.

Arnold, M. 2003. On the phenomenology of technology: The "Janus-faces" of mobile phones. *Information and Organization* 13:231–56.

Arnold, M., C. Shepherd, and M. Gibbs. 2008. Remembering things. *The Information Society* 24:47–53.

Barendregt, B. 2008. Sex, cannibals, and the language of cool: Indonesian tales of the phone and modernity. *The Information Society* 24:160–70.

Baresi, L., S. Dustdar, H. Gall, and M. Matera, eds. 2004. *Ubiquitous mobile information and collaboration systems: Second CAiSE Workshop (UMICS 2004), Riga, Latvia*. Berlin: Springer-Verlag.

Berghel, H. 1999. The cost of having analog executives in a digital world. *Communications of the ACM* 42:11–15.

Carstensen, P., and C. Sørensen. 1996. From the social to the systematic: Mechanisms supporting coordination in design. *Journal of Computer Supported Cooperative Work* 5:387–413.

Castells, M., J. L. Qiu, M. Fernandez-Ardevol, and A. Sey. 2007. *Mobile communication and society: A global perspective*. Cambridge, MA: MIT Press.

Ciborra, C. 2006. The mind or the heart? It depends on the (definition of) situation. *Journal of Information Technology* 21:129–39.

Coviello, N. E., and R. J. Brodie. 2001. Contemporary marketing practices of consumer and business-to-business firms: How different are they? *Journal of Business and Industrial Marketing* 16:382–400.

Donner, J. 2008. Research approaches to mobile use in the developing world: A review of the literature. *The Information Society* 24:140–59.

Dourish, P. 2001. *Where the action is: The foundations of embodied interaction*. Cambridge, MA: MIT Press.

Elaluf-Calderwood, S. 2008. *Organizing self-referential taxi-work with mICT: The case of the London Black Cab drivers*. PhD diss., London School of Economics and Politcal Science.

Elaluf-Calderwood, S., and C. Sørensen. 2008. 420 Years of mobility: ICT enabled mobile interdependencies in London hackney cab work. In *Mobility and technology in the workplace*, ed. D. Hislop, 135–50. London: Routledge.

Fortunati, L. 2005. Is body-to-body communication still the prototype? *The Information Society* 21:53–61.

Gaver, W. W. 1991. Technology affordances. In *CHI'91: Proceedings of the SIGCHI Conference on Human Factors in Computing Systems: Reaching through technology, New Orleans,* eds. G. M. Olson and J. S. Olson, 79–84. New York: ACM.

Gibson, J. J. 1977. The theory of affordances. In *Perceiving, acting, and knowing*, ed. R. Shaw and J. Bransford, 67–82. New York: Wiley.

———. 1979. *The ecological approach to visual perception*. New York: Houghton Mifflin Harcourt.

Goffman, E. 1963. *Behavior in public places: Notes on the social organization of gatherings*. New York: Free Press.

Goggin, G. 2008. Reorienting the mobile: Australasian imaginaries. *The Information Society* 24(3):171–81.

Green, N. 2002. On the move: Technology, mobility, and the mediation of social time and space. *The Information Society* 18:281–92.

Greenfield, A. 2006. *Everyware: The dawning age of ubiquitous computing*. Berkeley, CA: New Riders.

Gutek, B. 1995. *The dynamics of service*. New York: Jossey-Bass Wiley.

Hansmann, U., L. Merk, M. S. Nicklous, and T. Stober. 2003. *Pervasive computing,* 2nd ed.Berlin: Springer.

He, Z. 2008. SMS in China: A major carrier of the nonofficial discourse universe. *The Information Society* 24(3):182–90.

Heath, C., and P. Luff. 2000. *Technology in action*. Cambridge: Cambridge University Press.

Ishii, H., and B. Ullmer. 1997. Tangible bits: Towards seamless interfaces between people, bits and atoms. In *Proc. ACM Conference of Human Factors in Computing Systems CHI' 97*, ed. S. Pemberton, 234–41. Atlanta, GA. New York: ACM.

Jarvenpaa, S. L., and K. R. Lang. 2005. Managing the Paradoxes of mobile technology. *Information Systems Management* 22:7–23.

Kakihara, M., and C. Sørensen. 2001. Expanding the 'mobility' concept. *ACM SIGGROUP Bulletin* 22:33–37.

Karsten, H. 2003. Constructing interdependencies with Collaborative information technology. *Computer Supported Cooperative Work* 12:437–64.

Kietzmann, J. 2007. In touch out in the field: Coalescence and interactive innovation of technology for mobile work. PhD diss., London School of Economics and Political Science.

———. 2008. Internative innovation of technology for mobile work. *European Journal of Information Systems* 17:305–20.

Kietzmann, J., and C. Sørensen. 2010. Ubiquity and RFID: Combining mobile landscapes with pervasive ecosystems. Unpublished manuscript. http://mobility.lse.ac.uk/workingpapers.html

Kourouthanassis, P. E., and G. M. Giaglis, eds. 2008. *Pervasive information systems*. Armonk, NY: M. E. Sharpe.

Licoppe, C. 2004. Connected presence: The emergence of a new repertoire for managing social relationships in a changing communication technoscape. *Environment and Planning D: Society and Space* 22:135–56.

Ling, R. 2004. *The mobile connection: The cell phone's impact on society*. Amsterdam: Kaufmann.

———. 2008. *New tech, new ties: How mobile communication is reshaping social cohesion*. Cambridge, MA: MIT Press.

Ljungberg, F. 1999. Exploring CSCW mechanisms to realize constant accessibility without inappropriate interaction. *Scandinavian Journal of Information Systems* 11:25–50.

Ljungberg, F., and C. Sørensen. 2000. Overload: From transaction to interaction. In *Planet Internet*, ed. K. Braa, C. Sørensen, and B. Dahlbom, 113–36. Lund, Sweden: Studentlitteratur.

Lyytinen, K., and Y. Yoo. 2002a. Issues and challenges in ubiquitous computing. *Communications of the ACM* 45:62–65.

———. 2002b. The next wave of nomadic computing: A research agenda for information systems research. *Information Systems Research* 13:377–88.

Lyytinen, K. J., Y. Yoo, U. Varshney, M. Ackerman, G. Davis, M. Avital, D. Robey, S. Sawyer, and C. Sørensen. 2004. Surfing the next wave: Design and implementation challenges of ubiquitous computing. *Communications of the AIS* 13:697–716.

Mann, S., and H. Niedzviecki. 2002. *Cyborg: Digital destiny and human possibility in the age of the wearable computer*. Scarborough, ON: Doubleday Canada.

Mathiassen, L., and P. A. Nielsen. 2000. Interaction and transformation in SSM. *Systems Research and Behavioral Science* 17(3):243–53.

Mazmanian, M. A., W. J. Orlikowski, and J. Yates. 2005. Crackberries: The social implications of ubiquitous wireless e-mail devices. In *Designing ubiquitous information environments: Socio-technical issues and challenges*, ed. C. Sørensen, Y. Yoo, K. Lyytinen, and J. I. DeGross, 337–43. New York: Springer.

Mathiassen, L., and C. Sørensen. 2008. Towards a theory of organizational information services. *Journal of Information Technology* 23:313–29.

McCullough, M. 2005. *Digital ground: Architecture, pervasive computing, and environmental knowing*. Cambridge, MA: MIT Press.

Mick, D. G., and S. Fournier. 1998. Paradoxes of technology: Consumer cognizance, emotions, and coping strategies. *Journal of Consumer Research* 25:123–43.

Mitchell, W. J. 1995. *City of bits: Space, place and the Infobahn*. Cambridge, MA: MIT Press.

Mitchell, W. J. 2003. *Me++ : The cyborg self and the networked city*. Cambridge, MA: MIT Press.

Nardi, B., and S. Whittaker 2000: Interaction and outeraction. In *Proceedings of Computer Supported Cooperative Work, Philadelphia, USA*, ed. W. Kellogg and S. Whittaker, 79–88. New York: ACM.

Norman, D. 1988. *The psychology of everyday things*. New York: Basic Books.

———. 1999a. Affordance, conventions, and design. *Interactions* 6(3):38–42.

———. 1999b. *The invisible computer: Why good products can fail, the personal computer is so complex, and information appliances are the solution*. Cambridge, MA: MIT Press.

O'Conaill, B., and D. Frohlich. 1995. Timespace in the workplace: Dealing with interruptions. In *Proceedings of CHI'95: Human factors in computing systems, Denver, Colorado*, ed. I. Katz, R. Mack, and L. Marks, 262–63. New York: ACM Press.

Orlikowski, W. 2007. Sociomaterial practices: Exploring technology at work. *Organization Science* 28:1435–48.

Pica, D. 2006. The rhythms of interaction with mobile technologies: Tales from the police. PhD diss., London School of Economics and Political Science.

Schmidt, K. 1993. Modes and mechanisms of interaction in cooperative work. In *Computational mechanisms of interaction for CSCW*, ed. C. Simone and K. Schmidt, 21–104. Lancaster, England: University of Lancaster.

Schmidt, K., and C. Simone. 1996. Coordination mechanisms: An approach to CSCW systems design. *Computer Supported Cooperative Work* 5(2–3):155–200.

Schneiderman, B., and P. Maes. 1997. Direct manipulation vs software agents: Excerpts from debates at IUI 97 and CHI 97. *Interactions* 4(6):42–61.

Sørensen, C. Forthcoming. Mobile IT. In The *Oxford handbook of management information systems: Critical perspectives and new directions*, ed. B. Galliers and W. Currie, chap. 16. Oxford: Oxford University Press.

Sørensen, C., and A. Al-Taitoon. 2008. Organisational usability of mobile computing: Volatility and control in mobile foreign exchange trading. *International Journal of Human-Computer Studies* 66(12):916–29.

Sørensen, C., A. Al-Taitoon, J. Kietzmann, D. Pica, G. Wiredu, S. Elaluf-Calderwood, K. Boateng, M. Kakihara, and D. Gibson. 2008. Enterprise mobility: Lessons from the field. *Information Knowledge Systems Management Journal* 7(1 & 2): 243–71.

Sørensen, C., and D. Gibson. 2008. The professional's everyday struggle to ubiquitize computers. In *Computerization movements and technology diffusion: From mainframes to ubiquitous computing*, ed. M. Elliott and K. L. Kraemer, 455–79. Medford, NJ: Information Today.

Sørensen, C., and D. Pica. 2005. Tales from the police: Mobile technologies and contexts of work. *Information and Organization* 15:125–49.

Sørensen, C., Y. Yoo, K. Lyytinen, and J. I. DeGross, eds. 2005. *Designing ubiquitous information environments: Socio-technical issues and challenges*. New York: Springer.

Ureta, S. 2008. Mobilising poverty?: Mobile phone use and everyday spatial mobility among low-income families in Santiago, Chile. *The Information Society* 24:83–92.

Warwick, K. 2002. *I, cyborg*. London: Century.

Wegner, P. 1997. Why interaction is more powerful than algorithms. *Communications of the ACM* 40:80–91.

Weiser, M. 1991. The computer for the twenty-first century. *Scientific American* 265:94–104.

Whittaker, S., D. Frohlich, and O. Daly-Jones. 1994. Informal workplace communication: What is it like and how might we support it? In *ACM 1994 Conference on Human Factors in Computing Systems, Boston, MA*, eds B. Adelsom, S. Dumais, and H. Olson, 131–37. New York: ACM Press.

Whittaker, S., Q. Jones, and L. Terveen. 2002. Managing long term communications: conversation and contact management. In *35 Hawaii International Conference on System Sciences (HICSS-35), Maui, HI,* ed. R. Sprague, Jr., 115–24. New York: IEEE Computer Society.

Wiberg, M. 2001. In between mobile meetings: Exploring seamless ongoing interaction support for mobile CSCW. PhD diss., Department for Informatics, Umeå University, Sweden.

Wiberg, M., and S. Whittaker. 2005. Managing availability: Supporting lightweight negotiations to handle interruptions. *ACM Transactions of Computer-Human Interaction* 12(4):1–32.

Yates, J. 1989. *Control through communication: The rise of system in American management.* Baltimore, MD: Johns Hopkins University Press.

Yoo, Y. Forthcoming. Computing in everyday life: A call for research on experiential computing. *MIS Quarterly*. Earlier version available at: http://www.lse.ac.uk/collections/informationSystems/newsAndEvents/2009events/SSIT9/yooPaper.pdf (accessed April 13, 2010).

Zuboff, S., and J. Maxmin. 2002. *The support economy: Why corporations are failing individuals and the next episode of capitalism*. London: Penguin.

The "Crisis of the Summons": A Transformation in the Pragmatics of "Notifications," from Phone Rings to Instant Messaging

Christian Licoppe

Department of Economics and Social Sciences, Telecom ParisTech, Paris, France

This article analyzes a class of interactional devices that share the property of being "designed-to-occur" (e.g., alerts, alarms, warnings, calls, summons) and that can be more generally categorized as "notifications." This class of devices is directly related to interruptions and to attention-management issues, and is crucial to the unfolding of communication events. In reviewing the last thirty years of human-computer interaction research on this topic, this article highlights the transformation of the meaning of interruptions and notification devices. Initially perceived as disruptions in the accomplishment of tasks, interruptions have gradually acquired a positive value as "notification" devices and are meant to be subtler and to embed some degree of "intelligence" of the recipient's context. The article provides two empirical case studies on the uses of mobile musical ringtone and of instant messaging in organizations, showing the kind of work that users actually do to pattern their environments with an orientation toward shaping in advance the way in which they might be interrupted and notified. Concerned with how they might be notified, the users are becoming more skilled and turning into "pragmatic amateurs," less inclined to accept the imposition of a summons (which also testifies to a kind of "crisis of the summons"), and with a keener sense for appreciating the working and pragmatic consequences of a given type of notification.

What we consider here is a set of particular devices: alarms, alerts, stock tickers, phone rings, pop-up windows, computer notifications, automated announcements, flashing electronic displays, and so on. One common feature of the items in this list is their orientation toward supporting the occurrence of various perceptual events, which they are precisely designed to enable. This property separates them from the kinds of artifacts that have been discussed by various authors interested in technologies, such as keys, key holders, "sleeping policemen" (Latour 1993), or door handles (Norman 1988). A chair can, for instance, be said to "happen" in the sense that I make it relevant to what I am doing through my unfolding activity, but such an event has a different quality from my kettle starting to whistle. The latter has been designed to produce a meaningful noise when the water is boiling. More generally all such devices are designed to produce accountable, mundane, perceptual microevents. They "occur" in a way that a simple chair cannot. Whenever a boat horn blows, a warning light flickers, a phone rings, or a pop-up window appears on my screen, such occurrences reshape the context of the unfolding activities in the situation in which they occur: They stand for various chains of other events (e.g., a boat passing by, someone trying to reach me on the phone, some trouble revealing itself on my computer), and they project a normatively organized set of alternative possible responses. Because all these devices compose a class in themselves, they deserve a closer examination.

The way communication events begin and end is a crucial topic for the "ethnography of communication" research program (Hymes 1964). A majority of communication events, and particularly "mediated communication events," have to start with some form of notification. That is because a central problem in networked (tele)communications is to get a remote *alter* to somehow "appear" in *ego*'s environment and experience in a proper way, and his or her "appearance" to be acknowledged by the latter. Such inaugural sequences therefore rely on the use of many devices in the class we study, with the phone ring being a commonplace example. It informs and warns that an *alter* is trying to reach *ego*, and marks the

This research was undertaken partially under the project "Ecologie et Politiques de l'Ecriture," and funded by a grant from the *Agence Nationale pour la Recherche*.

kind of sharp boundary that characterizes telephone calls (Hutchby 2001). It also appears as the first move in a well-ordered interactive game in which participants orient toward the relevance of a canonical form of opening of phone conversations (Schegloff 1986), and which is marked by an asymmetry between the participants, that is, the "hegemony of the caller" (Hopper 1992).

The development of computer-mediated communication (CMC) has led to the generalization, multiplication, and trivialization of such notification devices, as well as to the refinement of their pragmatic functions. Because the development of the first graphic user interfaces, our computer screens have become a locus for the frequent appearance of many so-called "pop-up" windows that may signal events as different as a system failure, a wait, the success of a connection, or the arrival of a message, or else, in more specialized environments, the fact that a stock has reach a critical level, etc. The recent success of social networking sites (Web 2.0) strengthens this trend, for such sites make social networks visible and lively through the multiplication of announcements regarding what a member of the network is currently doing, feeling, thinking, or whatever.

More and more invitations to (inter)act materialize through the occurrence of cues in their recipients' environments: alarms, alerts, warnings, announcements, summonses, and the like. On a cognitive level, these cues are usually described as signaling or announcing something, and on a pragmatic level, as presenting such information as relevant and inviting the recipient to treat it accordingly. There is no single word to design this class of "designed-to-occur" devices. To avoid relying too often on such a neologism, I use the term "notification" device, because it is the word used in computer interface research (which is studied in the next section) and because it presupposes less the eventfulness of the information it is meant to convey than words such as alerts, alarms, announcements, or warnings. However, a word of caution is necessary here, because the concept of notification in computer research embeds a cognitive bias for it is usually understood as an event implying the presentation of some "information that X." This may not be too problematic in the case of an error message window in a computer operating system, which actually frames such an "information that X," but understanding a phone ring as the notification of the information that someone is trying to reach may constitute a more troublesome formulation. To paraphrase Ludwig Wittgenstein, replacing "I hear a phone ring" here by "my ears are providing me with the information that a phone is ringing" or that someone is trying to reach me is putting an informational-cognitive gloss on the use of the ring, which does not bring us any closer to understanding how we actually hear a phone ring (Wittgenstein 1958, para. 356). So we have to remain cautious regarding some of the cognitive implications that the use of "notification" to categorize the class of designed-to-occur-devices may have.

Notifications occur, appear, and surge up in our environments, and their occurrence is understood as a possible source of interruption. Notification devices shape the type of interruptions they occasion. They materialize the tension between focus and dispersion, between the "internal" guiding of the activity (on the mode of an internalized plan) and an "external" guiding by sociotechnical "*assemblages*." Turning notification devices into an object for research allows documenting and empirically analyzing attention-related practices and the way involvements are shaped, within a pragmatic frame. If we look at how notifications are designed, accomplished, and treated, attention and involvement do not have to remain in individuals' minds; they may be located in the publicly observable and accountable relationship of such an individual with an environment saturated with devices competing for attention and projecting relevant sets of alternative responses.

Bernard Stiegler typecasts notification devices into the larger set of what he calls *psycho-technologies*: "the aim is to replace the social formation of attention by its automated management, reduced to a minimum on the side of the human 'subject', who is no longer between deep attention and hyper attention; he or she merely delegates his or her attention to automata that become sensors, counters, alarms, warnings, etc." (Stiegler 2008, 183–84). This author goes on to remark that by "grammatizing" and standardizing attention-based processes, these "psycho-technologies" sever the relationship between attention and individuation. Only the experience of events within a continuing involvement frame supposedly allows the kind of transformation of past experiences and future expectations that is required for the constitution of the individual as a moral and desiring subject. In contrast, the media and communication industries support a new "industrial populism," with the construction not even of a public or an audience but of aimless crowds with transient attention spans and few deliberative capacities (Stiegler 2006). In this framework, notifications lie at the heart of emergent forms of capitalism, and their design and uses support a critique of the way it shapes attention-based processes. Such a dystopian critique may, however, be pushing things too far. Although it is true that, in the design orientation underlying distributed cognition and the development of computer interfaces since the 1980s, a well-conceived device is one whose perceptual grasp immediately lends itself to proper use, automatically, such quasiautomatic perception-action chains only operate in parts of our activity settings. They cannot account for the organization of all of our actions and activities. Rather than denouncing notification systems as the sole nexus of a whole new form of attention-based exploitation, it may be interesting to study how such unreflexive cognition-action chains are geared to more complex forms of individual and collective involvements (Licoppe 2007).

The aim of this article is to analyze the ways interruptions and notifications are produced and treated, and to make such a study into an entry point for an anthropology of involvement and activity. How do we accomplish switches from one type of involvement to another in practical terms? What makes those switches, transitions, and interruptions noticeable and recognizable as such? What actual devices and practical procedures constitute resources (and constraints) for the accomplishment of such transitions in an orderly way? Have there been significant changes in the last thirty years in the way we think about interruptions and about the design and uses of notification devices? First, I show that this last is indeed the case, by analyzing a corpus of human-computer interaction research dealing with the topic of interruptions and notifications. Second, I look at how users choose and design musical ringtones as a resource to shape phone ring notifications in a way that testifies to a possible "crisis of the summons." Third, I use naturally occurring data from an ethnography of the uses of instant messaging at work to show how users themselves continuously shape their "notification-scape" and modulate the force of the notifications that might occur in a way that is reflexively tied to the accomplishment of their activity and that displays different regimes of involvement.

RESEARCH ON INTERRUPTIONS AND NOTIFICATIONS IN HUMAN-COMPUTER INTERACTION (HCI) RESEARCH

Interruptions and Notifications: Historical Perspectives

A Short History of Alerts, Alarms, Warnings, and the Like

What might a tentative history of these devices look like? The transition between the modern period and early industrial capitalism has been related to the experience of time (Thompson 1967). To this historian, the scansion of time in the modern period could be symbolized by the sounding church bells in the countryside, which could be described as collective notifications and warnings addressed to whole communities, at a time when individualized clock time was not the norm.

He goes on by arguing that one aspect of the Industrial Revolution was precisely the growing pervasiveness of clock time, associated to the disciplining of individual time, for instance, in factory work. The need for individual alarm clocks and time devices was certainly also amplified by the development of steam-based mobility systems: Widespread railway networks went along with train schedules and timetables, calling both for standardized time zones and individual alarm clocks (Cresswell 2006). Unsurprisingly, the late nineteenth century saw a great number of patents issued for various alarm and warning devices. At the same time, the development of telecommunication systems introduced other "designed-to-occur" devices, such as the telephones' electromechanical rings, or stock tickers to inform traders of telegraph-transmitted variations of stocks (Prada 2006). Although collective alarm and warning devices had not disappeared, the industrial capitalism of the nineteenthth century seems to have enjoyed a strong mutual affinity with individual, standardized notification devices.

It was unavoidable that notification devices would stir some interest in the late twentieth century, marked as it was by a strong emphasis on flexible organizations, reactive individuals, and the widespread diffusion of digital networks (Castells 2000). I subsequently argue that part of the issue during this period was to replace individual standardized notification devices with personalized, adaptive, context-aware notifications, adjusted to the circumstances in which they might be activated, and somehow made sensitive to the way they might be received and to the kind of interruptions that might ensue. A good part of the research on these devices in the last thirty years was conducted in the HCI field by computer scientists and psychologists (as well as a few anthropologists and sociologists). In the next paragraphs I analyze the transformation of this research domain. My analysis is based on the analysis of papers relating to interruptions and notifications, published in the proceedings of conferences on computer-human interfaces (CHI), computer-supported cooperative work (CSCW), and ubiquitous computing (UbiComp) since the end of the 1980s.

The 1980s: The development of desktop human-computer interfaces. One of the origins of this research field probably lies in the studies undertaken in the 1980s, aimed at developing user interfaces based on the desktop metaphor, with which most personal computers are now equipped. This type of interface enables the user to have several "windows" of different applications open simultaneously and thus to perform several tasks at the same time. An analysis of their usability has to take into account problems of multiactivity and transitions between activities. In a seminal article, Yoshiro Miyata and Don Norman (1986)—the latter was one of the founding fathers of the distributed cognition model—examined the way in which computer systems could "notify" the user that engagement in a task was relevant at a given point in time. As any notification of this type could lead to the interruption of other tasks underway, the authors suggested that it could be important to take into account the timing of such notifications. For instance, their occurrence would be more appropriate in moments of transition between different tasks (when the subject is partially disengaged from the preceding task but has not yet engaged completely in the following one), than in the middle of a task.

Research during that period and later had four main characteristics related to the pervasiveness of a cognitive psychology paradigm: (a) The typical situation of use was considered to be that of the isolated user, absorbed by his or her screen and the management of multiple documentary tasks in parallel, sometimes online with someone else[1]; (b) interruptions were seen as an unavoidable consequence of operating systems that proposed desktop-type interfaces and that routinely had to "notify" the user that something relevant had happened concerning an ongoing task; (c) interruptions were seen as disruptions in the accomplishment of ongoing tasks and were therefore perceived negatively; and (d) the experience of interruption could be adjusted to the form of its external cause (notification), so that it was possible to intervene on the design of notification in a way that would make relevant interruptions more acceptable.

The 1990s: From the "discovery" of the ambivalence of interruptions to the emergence of autonomous research on systems of notification. The perspective changed considerably during the 1990s. Although researchers who focused primarily on design carried on seeing interruptions as a disruption of ongoing tasks (MacFarlane and Latorella 2002), several ethnographic studies on managerial staff in professions with intensive networked computer use showed the fragmented nature of their work. These managers' days were punctuated by multiple interruptions and very short, often unplanned face-to-face interaction (Whittaker et al. 1994), and the tasks underway were not always resumed after an interruption (O'Connail and Frohlich 1995). In particular, the idea emerged that interruptions could play a positive part. For the sake of reactivity, certain managers deliberately allowed their activity to be "steered" by interruptions rather than accomplished according to a plan (Hudson et al. 2002). The very notion of interruption became ambivalent.

This ambivalence was reinforced by the awareness that many interruptions were linked to communication events initiated by other parties. During this period the development of instant messaging contributed substantially to this growing awareness of the role of communication, since the use of this type of device occasions many invitations to interact. These are in the form of notifications on the screen and make the context of the interrupted person partially visible through the indicator of presence. Instant messaging appeared as a new and ideal field for studying interruptions and notifications (Cutrell, Czerwinski, and Horwitz 2001). Lists of typical examples of notification devices grew: "Commonly known notification systems include stock tickers, *instant messaging tools*, system load monitors or alerts and the like" (McCrickard et al. 2003, 510, emphasis added). Interruptions linked to communication tools became more and more the focal point of research on interruptions and notifications: "With the increasing volume of wireless communication, users are now frequently interrupted by auditory or visual alerts from cell phone calls, email and instant messaging notifications. This is because each of the user's computing appliances is designed to independently vie for the attention of the user with each message delivered, regardless of the current engagement with other devices or people" (Danninger 2005, 211).

The intensification of interruptions was attended by a growing concern to reshape their causes, that is, the notifications. These were defined as the presentation of relevant information for users, in a particular perceptual, graphic and linguistic format. A notification took the form of a perceptive occurrence conducive to it being noticed and to the processing of the information presented. For instance, the sound of my telephone ringing could be described as a presentation of the information that someone was calling me.

The concern to adjust the timing and format of the notification was expressed in many of the terms used to qualify ideal notification: for example, "subtle cues" (Hansson and Ljungstrand 2000), allowing for "graceful switching" between tasks (Gievska and Sibert 2004), possibly with "aesthetically pleasing" visuals (Zhang, Tu, and Vronay 2005). Researchers explored the modalities of presentation and graphic animation in relation to the nature of what was being notified (McCrickard, Czerwinski, and Bartram 2003). They studied the possibility of using the movement of icons and frames on a screen by developing so-called "moticons" to impact on users' peripheral vigilance (Bartram, Ware, and Calvert 2003), and compared the effects of different sensorial, visual, auditory, tactile (heat), and other modalities (Arroyo and Selker 2003). Questions of notification were no longer dealt with on an ad hoc basis for each system; they became the subject of a research stream in its own right, "notification system research," which aimed to develop general design frameworks (Shen and Sun 2002). Research on notifications had to become autonomous as it had the potential "to become one of the farthest reaching areas of HCI in terms of impact and contribution to people's daily lives" (McCrickard et al. 2003, 513).

The 2000s: From ubiquitous computing to Web 2.0. The development of ubiquitous computing, in which people are seen as constantly having their computer terminals with them (Weiser 1991), poses the problem of managing a continuous flux of mediated interaction. Interruptions concern all the situations experienced by users, and all the terminals they use, including in the domestic sphere (Nagel, Hudson, and Abowd 2004; Takemae,

Ohno, Yoda, and Ozawa 2007) and in mobile situations (Abowd and Mynatt 2000). This research field also encompasses mobile phones and personal digital assistants, which, in addition to computers, seek to capture the user's attention and can thus induce "irritability to interruption" (Ho and Intille 2000). Mobile telephone rings and announcements of mobile text messages, along with computer screen notifications, compose a new landscape of interruptions and notifications: "With the larger volume of mobile communications, users are now frequently interrupted by auditory or visual alerts due to mobile phone calls and to notifications of email and instant messages" (Danninger, Vertegaal, Siewiorek, and Mamuji 2005). As competition for attention has become a constant issue, it is necessary to "design for attention" (Roda and Thomas 2006). Designers have to make notifications more intelligent, that is, to introduce enhanced knowledge of the user's context into the notification, in order to reduce her/his cognitive load (Fallman and Yttergren 2005) and to build notification systems capable of "reasoning" on users' attention (Ho and Intille 2005) and of winning their "trust" (Tullio et al. 2007).

The most recent development has been Web 2.0 (with which instant messaging is sometimes associated), on which sites propose services oriented toward social networking. They either facilitate encounters (e.g., romantic relationships, finding old friends) or make social networks visible to support bonding (e.g., Facebook, Friendster). Even though they are rarely considered from this point of view, these services rely on a stream of notifications about the fact that someone went onto your site, winked at you, sent you a message, etc. in the case of dating sites, or about what members do, feel, think, etc. in the case of social networking sites. This endless "notification buzz" is the basic resource of the kind of social networking provided by Web 2.0 sites.

Toward a "Pragmatics of Notifications"

These three trends reinforce the relevance of understanding the pragmatic properties of interruptions and notifications, because they are currently becoming pervasive "psycho-technologies" of attention. We nevertheless need to bear in mind that, situated at the intersection of research on computing and psychology, all the studies carried out on the subject contain certain biases:

- Users are mostly treated as *individual* subjects engaged in specific tasks.
- They deal mostly with screen-based activities.
- They have an informational-cognitive bias, which expresses itself in the use of the "notification" category, which imposes a gloss that such occurrences offer the recipient some "information that," made relevant here and now in the notification event.
- Their focus is on attention as a perceptive and cognitive resource (which constitutes a research theme for psychology) rather than on notions such as involvement and/or commitment, that is, forms of participation in activity that take into account their meaning and purpose, and include interpretive and normative dimensions into the analysis. This makes it possible to confine the treatment of interruptions and notifications to the problem of an optimal allocation of information, given the limits of "simultaneous" treatment due to limited attention.

The aim of a pragmatics of notification is to remedy these biases and to examine and explain what notifications actually do and how they are treated by their recipients. It shifts the perspective of notification itself toward the understanding of observable notification/answer sequences. Notwithstanding the often trivial nature of these objects, this is a key question for a sociology or ethnography of communication.

Studies by designers of software and communication technologies, who have treated notification increasingly as a generic problem, have instituted a separation between notification devices and what they are likely to announce. Notifications are understood more and more as a way of displaying the relevance of a piece of information or communication, without in many cases referring to its content (which is often provided later, after the initial, inaugural event has been treated). The notification (and the interruption it causes) is thus often a separate move, distinct from the provision of the information it announces.

Becoming more widespread and autonomous, notifications do not presume that what they project as a relevant follow-up move will be of any kind of importance. They may preface (and most often do) routine communication events. This may be understood in the context of the contemporary salience of the imperatives of availability, flexibility, and reactivity, the configuration of notifications that favors a proliferation of interruptions and informal interactions, which in many cases will be brief and trivial (Kraut et al. 1990; Whittaker et al. 1994; Hudson et al. 2002). Notifications are designed to signal both the most ordinary "communication events" (often) and the most alarming ones (seldom). Unlike a "pragmatics of warnings," sensitive to the way in which problems are brought to collective attention and turned into general, public issues (Chateauraynaud and Torny 1999), a pragmatics of notification must also account for the joint effort of designers and users to trivialize and routinize such occurrences.

Because of the proliferation of notification events, mediated by "designed-to-occur" devices, it is the interruptive experience and the discomfort that interruptions might produce that become an issue. Their pragmatic side concerns the modulation of the "force" with which they project some response or other from the recipient. Notifications become paradoxical in the sense of necessarily remaining performative semiotic occurrences that call for some response, while aiming at being subtle and fleeting enough to allow their treatment to be easily delayed or sometimes even ignored, at both practical and normative levels. The traditional summons, symbolized so well by the phone ring, makes way for subtler forms of attracting attention, at the limit of which the summons might lose any form of performativity and blend into a "culture of immanence" (Augé 2008, 503). This expression refers to an alleged contemporary orientation toward a "theory of the event" that negates its very eventfulness.

To go one step further in our pragmatic approach to notifications we must study the way in which they are configured, produced, and treated, and therefore look closely at the way users manage their notification landscapes and actually treat incoming notifications. Two empirical cases show the very concrete work accomplished by people to configure the notifications to which they could be subjected and to orient their consequences. The first deals with the *strategies* users follow in their use of mobile ringtones, which, as we have just seen, have become one of the examples of notifications often quoted by researchers in this field, so as to render their phone rings more subtle and equivocal in order to fit their particular communicative needs. The second example deals with instant messaging, which is another paradigmatic example of communication-related interruptions and notifications, and more specifically with the *situated* management of notification landscapes, which is continuously adjusted to changing circumstances.

The Design and Uses of Mobile Musical Ringtones: Managing the Notification Landscape as a Way to Cope with a "Crisis of the Summons"

Users, and not only designers, are concerned with the performative force of notification and active in shaping it. In this section I discuss the transformations in the design and use of a commonplace form of notification, the phone ring, which, as we have just seen, has been introduced in the domain of notification research with the development of wireless communication and ubiquitous computing. Until the 1980s, telephone calls were initiated primarily by standardized and repetitive electromechanical rings. This produced conventional opening sequences of the type:

1. (ring) . (ring) . (ring) . (ring)
2. A: lifts up the receiver and says "hello."

When understood as an auditory perceptual event that informs that someone is calling, the telephone ring is an example of notification that acts as a cue for a conventional response ("answering the phone").[2] Because of its repetitive organization, incorporated into the electromechanical device itself, the ringing can be interpreted as a summons. In the interactional perspective of conversation analysis, its occurrence constitutes the first part of a summons-answer duo (Schegloff 1972).

The appearance of mobile phones with their capacity to store an address book and musical extracts has profoundly transformed telephone ringtones. It is now possible for users to choose or to design almost any form of sound extract for their ringtone. This is, moreover, one of the rare cases where users agree to pay for downloading music. I did an interview survey of how and why phone users chose or designed their mobile ringtone(s), which shed some insight on how they appreciate what the ring does and highlighted some of their mundane tactics for shaping what they expect it to do (Licoppe 2008).

The first one consists in personalizing the sound extract in order to be able to answer "automatically," "without thinking," as the users themselves put it. This shows call receivers' concern with increasing their possibility to delegate the evaluation of the relevance of responding or not to the notification. The second one consists in symbolically manipulating the summons function, which is usually done in three very different ways: (a) accentuating the summons by lengthening it and/or intensifying the repeated sound occurrence, for example, "beep—BEEEEP—**BEEEEEEEEP**—"; (b) weakening the summons by choosing a melodious musical extract that no longer "rings" like a telephone, so that its occurrence is also an invitation to listen and enjoy the fleeting musical experience that it proposes and to take the call; or (c) maximizing the ambiguity of the summons by making a highly rhythmical short musical extract played in a repetitive loop, so that the repetition exists but seems to be part of the music, thus producing ambiguous artifacts that can be perceived alternately as music or as summonses. The common point of all these practices is that they directly manipulate the traditional sequential organization of the ring, and reshape the way in which it summonses. The latter two (b and c) support the user's notion that experiencing the ringtone as music might compensate for experiencing the ring as a summons. Such users argue that the music "softens" the summons; it enriches it with an opportunity for a fleeting moment of pleasure, in passing, that the coerciveness of the ring *qua* summons seems to make increasingly welcome.

The unforeseen success of mobile phone ringtones therefore suggests the emergence of a "crisis of the summons." Users see benefits in softening the imperativeness that characterizes the summons and is embodied in the repetitive sound organization of traditional phone rings. They look to musical ringtones as ways to "soften" it. But softening the imperativeness of the phone ring in this way also partially cushions the obligation to answer that a "pure" summons entails, which makes users more directly accountable for the fact of answering or not. Why might phone users be more sensitive today to the coerciveness of the summons that traditional fixed phone rings seemed to express and materialize? This tendency could be related to the development of "connected presence" in communication practices. In a "connected" mode, where the social link is maintained, it is the multiplication of contacts via all available media that guarantees the strength of a particular link. This form of maintenance of social relations allows for and contributes toward the proliferation of impulsive calls. "Connected presence" is therefore particularly trying with respect to the recipient's availability (Licoppe 2004; Licoppe and Smoreda 2005) and the management of accessibility and availability (Licoppe and Heurtin 2001). Recipients are expected to participate in such a management of social relationships by taking (and making) many calls, but their availability is constrained by their other activities and is often tested with the frequency of calls, many of them being trivial or even "phatic" calls, for which a summons enjoining an immediate answer might appear retrospectively as an excessively imperative form of notification. "Connected presence" seems to call for ways to make the call recipient less obligated by the ringing of his or her phone.

The success of musical ringtones then appears as an outcome of such a "connected presence"-related "crisis of the summons." The two strategies we identified for mobile ringtone users exemplify the way such devices may be used to modulate the summoning force of the phone ring, and the way it projects some forms of user response as an expected course of action: (a) weakening the summative force of the ring, by replacing it by a musical melody that is an invitation to listen, however fleetingly, and aims to provide a short-lived compensatory pleasure; and (b) facilitating the decision to answer by personalizing the sound extract with respect to the callers (and thus having several different ringtones), which amounts to introducing a form of knowledge about the caller into the summons, and delegating to the ring device some agency in the shaping and the production of a proper response.

The success of mobile ringtones may also appear as a cause, and not only an outcome, of the "crisis of the summons." The tools that mobile ringtones make available for modulating the pragmatic force of the ring also make the ring more visible and enable users to become more sensitive to it, to evolve more subtle appreciative skills for experiencing and realizing what the phone ring does. This is evidenced by the kinds of appreciations and judgments that underlie their strategies in reshaping the ring. The evolution of the notification device toward more subtlety and flexibility goes hand in hand with a refinement in interpretive skills regarding the pragmatic effects of notifications. It could be described as a kind of acquired taste, for like taste (Hennion 2004), it is an enactive process, constructed through a succession of trials whose outcomes rely on collectively evolved and shared inference practices, embodied experience, and what the notification artifacts do. This coevolution of interpretive skills and notification devices involves a reflexive performativity loop in which the properties of notification devices are co-produced with the sensemaking resources to appreciate their effects.

I move on now to a slightly different but related issue, that of the users' situated management of their notification landscapes in a way that is adjusted to the changing circumstances of their activities, based on video recordings.

Management of "Notification Landscapes" and Interactional Engagements: The Case of Instant Messaging

Like many recent computer-based communication services, instant messaging proposes several different notification formats. On most systems, when someone belonging to a user's contact list signs in, a pop-up window appears with a message like "X has just signed in," sometimes with the contact's photo. The arrival of a message may be signaled in two ways: directly in the dialogue window if it is open on the screen or, if the dialogue has not been interrupted and the window is not active on the screen, by means of a task tab at the bottom of the screen, which changes color (to bright orange or dark blue) and starts flickering when a message arrives. This format therefore incorporates a lasting perceptive change (the change of color) and a summons (the flickering). Some notifications are nested. When the dialogue window is open, a notification like "X is busy writing" may appear at the bottom of the reception window (see figure 1).

Such a screen environment can be described as a "perspicuous setting" (Garfinkel 2002) that makes the temporal organization of the activity visible in the spatial arrangements produced during the course of that activity (Lynch et al. 1983). In this respect, the notification resources and the way in which they are used make accessible and intelligible the continuous work of the actors to (a) format their orientations and expectations regarding certain types of occurrence likely to arise contingently during their work; (b) prefigure their status as events and their response to them; and (c) configure in a visible and accountable way the forms of their engagement in the activity. Thus understood, the management of the notification landscape consists of practices that are contingent on the circumstances of the activity. It is based on operations that are most often accomplished automatically (and

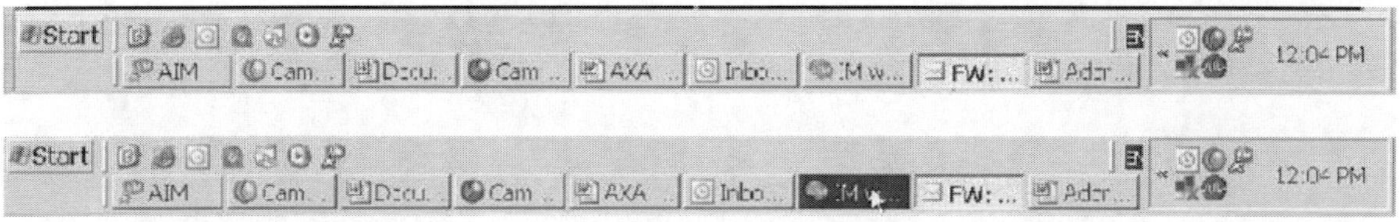

FIG. 1. Change of color of the instant-messaging tab when a new message is received.

that may not have a name), and that become visible only in the systematic analysis of sequences of action. The case analyzed here is drawn from a study based on ten interviews and video observations of managers at work in two high-tech firms that have generalized the use of instant messaging to the whole of their organizations.[3]

Negotiating the Legitimacy of an Isolated Request via Instant Messaging, and the Interruption That It Is Likely to Cause

During one of these one-hour recordings, we observed the following instant messaging sequence.

Transcription 1.

1. NicoleOMTL (12:10:57 PM): Hey Albert!
2. NicoleOMTL (12:11:03 PM): Do you plan to watch the LiveMeeting on mixed initiative?
3. albertrobson2356 (12:11:26 PM): What's that?
4. NicoleOMTL (12:11:31 PM): ☺
5. NicoleOMTL (12:11:50 :PM): Never mind then. It's that email that was sent out. I'm sure you received it.
6. albertrobson2356 (12:12:13): i'll take a look .. i'm at home today, not sure i can log in from there.
7. NicoleOMTL (12:12:39 PM): ha! sorry to bug you at home, i thought you were here . . .
8. NicoleOMTL (12:12:44 PM): never mind.
9. NicoleOMTL (12:12:49 PM): go back to sleep! ☺
10. albertrobson (12:13:05 PM): you couldn't bug me
11. albertrobson (12:13:06 PM) :)
12. albertrobson (12:13:19 PM): i'm wfh
13. NicoleOMTL (12:13:19 PM): ?? hu ??

Before the initiation of this sequence, Nicole was busy with an e-mail invitation to a videophone meeting. After reading it, she sent the same message to two of the addressees of the initial e-mail, asking them whether they were going to attend the meeting. This corresponds to the use of instant messaging for requests for clarification or verification that concern an activity underway and are configured so that answers can fit into a single message without needing further elaboration. It is one of the most typical uses of instant messaging at work (Nardi et al. 2000; Quan-Haase et al. 2005).

The interaction starts with a greeting ("Hey Albert," message 1). Nicole does not wait for her correspondent's answer; she immediately follows on with a question (message 2). This shows the routine nature of this type of request. albertrobson does not return the greeting but initiates a repair sequence by a request for clarification ("what's that?," message 3). Nicole answers with a smiley (message 4), followed by an expression indicating that an answer is no longer relevant because she is not informed on the matter ("never mind," message 5). Finally, she concludes by referring to the invitation e-mail and the fact that he was on the list of recipients. This legitimizes her initial question—a legitimization made necessary by the fact that there was no immediate answer.

After about twenty seconds albertrobson indicates that he will check, that he is working at home and that, due to the difficulty of logging on, he may not be able to do so that day (message 6). She answers with a message of excuse for bothering him (the word "bug" refers to the irritation that one sometimes feels when one is disturbed or interrupted for little things), justifying her request by the fact that she thought he was at the office (message 7). She thus orients herself in relation to the potential inconvenience of making such minute work-related requests when the addressee is at home and may be busy with personal matters (which excludes any interruption of a professional nature, except in case of emergency), or else may be working but stayed at home precisely to get on with a very absorbing task, shielded from interruptions. She then repeats that her request is unimportant (message 8), and follows with a joke about the difference of contexts between work at the office and teleworking from home (the injunction "go back to sleep," message 9). The idea of sleep topicalizes once more the notion that at home one may not be interrupted for short requests of a professional nature. He answers by reaffirming that she is not disturbing him and could not disturb him (message 10), followed by a smile and the acronym "wfh" for "work from home" (messages 11–12). He thus reaffirms the legitimacy of Nicole's initial request by emphasizing a conception of telework that demands one's availability for colleagues—an availability that must be asserted and shown even more visibly and conspicuously (hence, his justification) to avoid criticism (for instance, the accusation of skiving). The dialogue then moves onto a playful conversation about acronyms based on the lack of understanding that she indicates when he uses "wfh" (message 13).

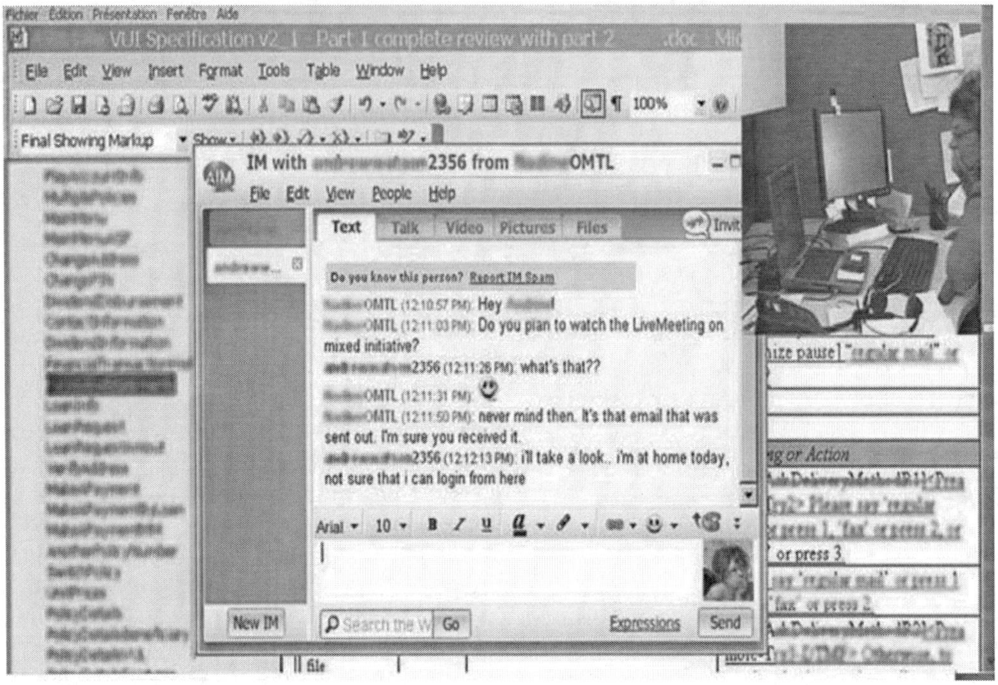

FIG. 2. Nicole's screen when she reads message 6, with the video camera image in the top right-hand corner. Some areas have been blurred for confidentiality reasons but one sees clearly how the instant-messaging window is opened and centrally positioned on the screen.

We thus observe how (1) the participants orient themselves toward the sending of requests via instant messaging as a potential source of interruption; (2) such interruptions are warranted between participants who have frequent contact, when the addressee is supposed to be at the office and the presence icon indicates that he or she is online; and (3) once it appears that the addressee is online but at home, the interaction and its interruptive nature are negotiated by orienting in relation to two opposite maxims: If one is at home, one is not available for interruptions of a professional nature, for minor reasons, but if one is teleworking, one can be interrupted, and perhaps even more than at the office (to display that one is indeed teleworking, and to justify the right to telework, considering the ceaseless demands of distributed teamwork and the fact that telework is still a fragile institution).

Two Modes of Engagement in the Conversation via Instant Messaging

In the rest of this section I adopt a perspective that is no longer that of the instant messaging (IM) interaction itself, but is centered on Nicole's activity and based on both screen capture and videorecording. I consider two different moments in the interaction in more detail.

Dialogue window open full-screen, with "focused engagement." I first consider what happens after the opening and reading of Message 6, in a simplified transcription.[4]

Transcription 2.

1. albertrobson2356 (12:12:13): i'll take a look .. i'm at home today, not sure i can log in from here. [figure 2]
2. NicoleOMTL: (3.0)
3. NicoleOMTL (12:12:39 PM): ha! sorry to bug you at home, i thought you were here . . .
4. NicoleOMTL (12:12:44 PM): never mind.
5. NicoleOMTL (12:12:49 PM): go back to sleep! ☺
6. NicoleOMTL : (readjusts her position on her chair and rearranges her hair, smiling) [figure 3]
7. NicoleOMTL : (leans forward toward the screen, with the remains of a smile) [Fiure 4]
8. NicoleOMTL : (13.0)
9. albertrobson (12:13:05 PM): you couldn't bug me

During this sequence (and in fact for the rest of the instant messaging interaction), one can describe Nicole as fully involved in the IM interaction in several respects. The dialogue window remains open all the time at the center of her screen, covering all the other documents. The open window "on top" corresponds to the most relevant active task at that moment. In the desktop metaphor, perceptive salience corresponds to a hierarchy of relevance.

FIG. 3. Readjusting her posture after sending "go back to sleep."

In this mode, the messages are fully displayed as they arrive. Their arrival can be anticipated only through the notification that the correspondent is busy writing, which leaves imprecise the exact moment of their "occurrence." Following the exchange in this configuration therefore supposes maintaining a relatively continuous orientation and vigilance with respect to the screen.

Which is what Nicole clearly does. For sixteen seconds after sending the message "go back to sleep," she stares at the screen, and most of this time is spent in a position of expectation, her chest and chin tilted forward. This corporeal and attentional orientation displays the fact that she is "waiting for" the answer, and is completely absorbed in that waiting. At other similar moments, a little later on, she will alternate this waiting position with quick glances to the side, small rearrangements of her position, or a sip of coffee—all recognizably subordinate activities that require only minimal and occasional rearrangements of her posture and orientation. Even in these moments that may seem to be distractions, it is clear that watching the screen remains her base orientation,[5] and that she carries on waiting for the next message without allowing herself engagement in activities that could significantly challenge the prevalence of this principal involvement.

Nicole's body language also marks her appreciation of the ongoing interaction. After sending the message "go back to sleep" she smiles, partly in anticipation of the reception of her joke. Later in the sequence she marks the reception of messages in the same way. She thus indicates her orientation toward what the messages say and "do" (since the interaction has shifted to a playful mode, close to a kind of professional banter between colleagues). This justifies the use of the term involvement, rather than attention, insofar as it is not simply an attentional orientation toward what is happening on the screen, but also a visible appreciation of the performative effects of these screen-based communicative events. Moreover, these embodied marks of appreciation lend meaning to the way in which Nicole "waits for" messages for long seconds, rather than engaging in another activity, as she would on other occasions, for example, in the waiting periods during the running of a computer application.

For long minutes Nicole visibly accomplishes only one main activity: this "instant messaging conversation." She manifests what I would qualify, by analogy with Erving Goffman (1963), as a focused engagement in the conversation via instant messaging. This is, however, simply an analogy. The participants are not caught in an "eye-to-eye ecology," so that her correspondent knows nothing about how she is engaged in the mediated conversation, and is waiting for messages (he has no way of knowing whether she is doing something else at the same time). Moreover, her appreciation of the messages, especially their reception, concerns "whole" messages in so far as she does not have access to the way in which they are written moment by moment, as she would have in the case of a turn-at-talk in a face-to-face or telephone conversation. It is nevertheless still meaningful to describe her involvement as "focused," in view of the way in which she produces a visible impression of absorption in the exchange via instant messaging, and the contrast with other types of engagement such as the one I analyze next, which occurred earlier in the sequence.

Reducing" the instant messaging (to a tab) and "doing" unfocused involvement in the communicative event. Consider what happened during the thirty seconds preceding the arrival of the message that inaugurated the sequence analyzed in the preceding section.

1. NicoleOMTL (12:11:50 PM): Never mind then. It's that email that was sent out. I'm sure you received it.
2. *NicoleOMTL : (goes to the window of another correspondent whom she had asked whether he was going to the same meeting, looks at the incoming message, treats it as a closing message by completely closing the conversation, which brings her to the screen with the window of dialogue with albertrobson)*[6]
3. *NicoleOMTL : (5.0)*
4. *Nicole OMTL : ("reduces" the window of dialogue with albertrobson)*
5. *NicoleOMTL : (following this "tabbing" of the instant messaging window, the initial mail mentioning the LiveMeeting returns to the foreground of her screen, as does the list of instant messaging contacts that she used to initiate the dialogue with albertrobson)*
6. *NicoleOMTL : (closes the window of the list of contacts)*

FIG. 4. Nicole, oriented toward the screen, in what I describe as a "posture of expectation."

7. *NicoleOMTL : (6.0)*
8. *NicoleOMTL : (closes the email so that her list of incoming messages is displayed on the screen)*
9. *NicoleOMTL : (3.0)*
10. *NicoleOMTL : (puts her cursor on the AXA tab at the bottom of her screen, corresponding to a file of specifications on which she was working; this brings this file back onto the screen)*
11. *NicoleOMTL : (the instant messaging tab corresponding to the dialogue with albertrobson turns dark blue)* [figure 5]
12. *NicoleOMTL : (as soon as the flashing starts she shifts the cursor onto the tab and clicks, which reopens the instant messaging window and produces a screen similar to the one in figure 2)*
13. albertrobson2356 (12:12:13 PM): i'll take a look.. i'm at home today, not sure i can log in from there.

Nicole first closes the first instant messaging dialogue window concerning the videoconference meeting. She then reduces the window corresponding to the dialogue with albertrobson to an active tab. She closes the list of contacts that she used to initiate the conversation with him. She then closes the message about the future LiveMeeting, the opening and reading of which had triggered the two instant messages. She closes her e-mail application. Finally, she opens a reference file (still open) on which she was working just before dealing with that e-mail (the treatment of which appears with hindsight as a sequence "inserted" into another activity thread). The series of actions from 2 to 10 can be interpreted as a near-complete closing of everything concerning the search for information on the LiveMeeting, and the reorientation toward another activity pertaining to a technical draft.

The only thing she does not close is the dialogue window with albertrobson. It is only reduced to an active tab. This operation consists in clicking on the small minus-shaped icon that appears in the top-right corner of most windows in Windows environments. It causes the open IM window to disappear from the screen and to be reduced to an active tab, often situated at the bottom or the side of the screen. "Reducing" an application to an active tab means it will not be visible any more, but it can still be made so with a single click on the tab. Such a reduction leaves the screen free for other windows while maintaining the corresponding activity thread open.

Why did Nicole not completely close the instant messaging application? albertrobson had shown that he was not aware of the meeting and Nicole had made it unnecessary for him to look further, so that nothing interesting concerning the initial question could be expected from the dialogue. But there had been no recognizable closing sequence. It was therefore possible for the conversation to die there (if he did not produce a new turn) or to be revived (if he produced a new turn). In the latter case, as it was Nicole who initiated the conversation with a request, she was in a relative obligation to answer this possible turn, even if it was largely unrelated to her initial question. This makes relevant and warrants the "reduction" of the dialogue box at that precise moment in the IM conversation.[7]

This "tabbing" of the instant messaging dialogue window constitutes a form of management of the notification landscape in which Nicole's screen activity takes place. Reduction to an active tab is a recognizable way of shaping in advance the occurrence and the eventfulness of a future message. In this mode, incoming messages will be notified by the change of color and flickering of the tab. This orients the user toward a different form of vigilance from the preceding situation where messages were open full-screen—that is, a peripheral awareness where the waiting and the concern about receiving the correspondent's next message are delegated to the microevent constituted by the change of state of a notification device, such as the flicker and change of color of the tab. Just after Nicole opens the specification draft, the tab changes color and Nicole reacts by quickly clicking on it (in the space of a flicker). This opens the message and inaugurates the sequence of focused involvement that I analyzed in the preceding section.

This reconfiguration of the notification landscape and of the type of awareness that it induces constitutes another particular mode of involvement in the instant messaging exchange. By "reducing" the dialogue window rather than closing it, Nicole orients toward the possible arrival of another message. By not keeping the instant messaging fully open, she displays that she possibly expects the occurrence of a next message, but that she is not waiting for it. Because of the sequential placement of this reduction operation, she shows an anticipatory appreciation of the fact that this message might be only marginally

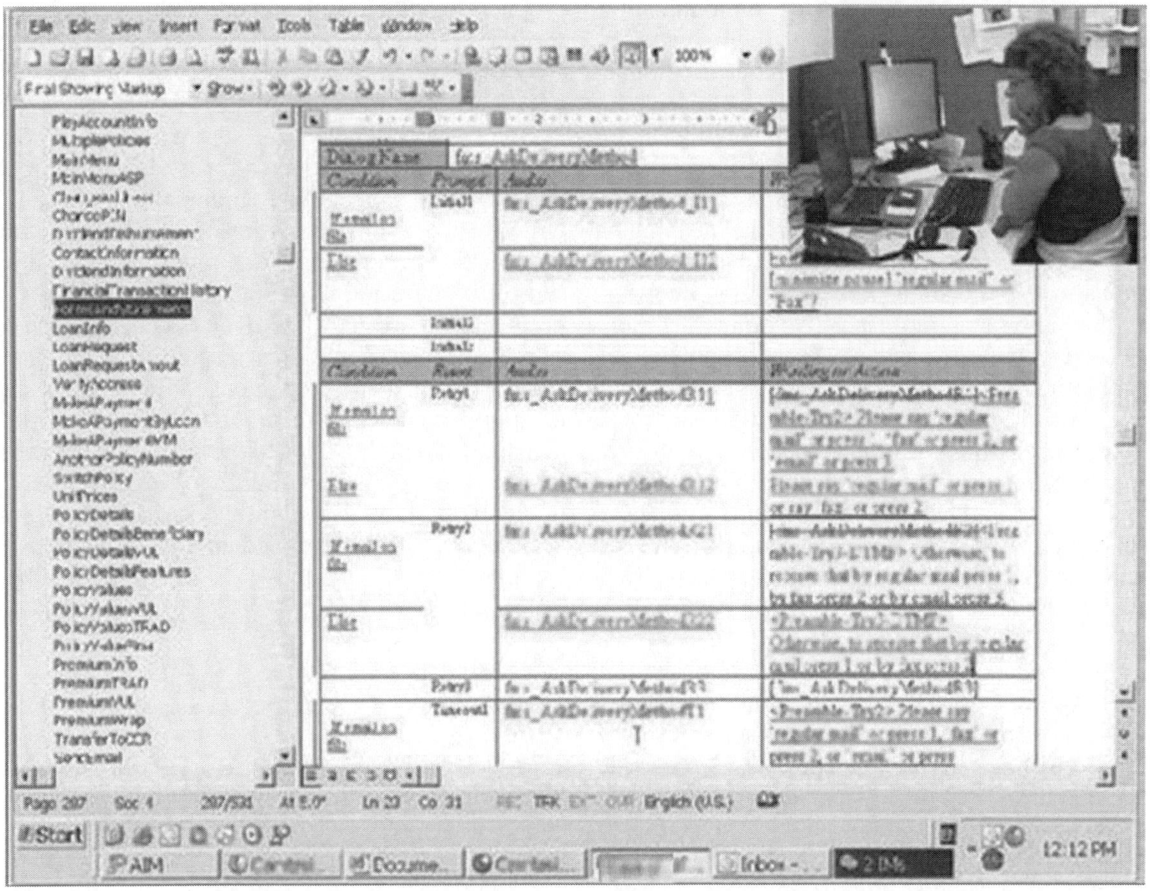

FIG. 5. State of Nicole's screen when the instant messaging (IM) screen changes color. Some areas are blurred for confidentiality. One can see the colored active IM tab on the bottom left on the screen (actually flickering on the video.

relevant compared to the initial object of her request. It will consequently not be much of an "event" from the point of view of the communication under way. The intelligibility of the reduction operation, the minimization of the eventfulness of the message that might follow, and an orientation to treat this message if it arrives without waiting for it, are constituted mutually and reflexively. Our example shows how an operation directly pertaining to the management of the notification landscape, the reduction of the instant messaging window to an active tab, probably accomplished without thinking, constitutes an artful accomplishment, finely tuned to the changing details and contingencies of the activity.

The whole sequence shows how the fine-grained management of the notification landscape and the type of involvement of the subject in the activity are mutually elaborative, and constitute a joint accomplishment. The different ways of organizing the notification of incoming instant messages and of shaping in advance the kind of event that the occurrence of a message is likely to be and how it might be treated are based on standardized and conventional operations allowed by the software operating system. They are publicly intelligible for any member of the community competent in using this type of software at work. In this respect, the notification landscape, constituted moment by moment during the activity, presents a form of "scenic intelligibility" (Jayyusi 1988) within a computer-literate community. It makes visible to the competent observer the relevance of different modes of involvement with respect to the ongoing communicative event.

CONCLUSION

I have studied in this article a class of interactional devices that share the property of being "designed-to-occur" (e.g., alerts, alarms, warnings, calls, summons, etc.) and that I have categorized as "notifications" to stay in line with current HCI research. This class of devices is directly related to interruptions and to attention management issues. The increasing emphasis on the reactivity and availability of individuals and the sharp development of communication networks have led to the proliferation of such devices in our information ecologies, since most mediated communication exchanges start with a microevent occasioned by the activation of such devices, or at least involving such a device.

In a review of the last thirty years of HCI research on this topic, I have shown a significant change in the meaning of interruptions and notification devices. Initially perceived as disruptions in the accomplishment of tasks, interruptions have gradually acquired a positive value. Workers (and particularly managers and workers in knowledge-intensive activities) say that they let themselves be driven by them in the course of their work, for they have realized that noticing and dealing with interruptions may ensure some degree of adaptation and optimization of their activity with respect to rapidly changing environments. There has been a simultaneous and correlated change in the design rationale of "notification" devices. They have been made more autonomous with respect to the occurrences they signal. They are more independent from the "eventfulness" of such occurrences, in the sense that they are now designed to notify users of events of all kinds: routine and trivial (mostly), as well as momentous ones with far-reaching consequences (rarely). They have been made more subtle and have been given some degree of "intelligence," in the sense of being endowed with capacities to anticipate some of the circumstances in which they might be used. Their design is therefore more and more marked by a tension between the need for them to be perceptually salient (to be noticed), while proving less intrusive, causing less of an imposition on their recipient, and allowing her/him more leeway in their acknowledgment and treatment.

In the two empirical case studies discussed here, the first one on users' strategies for choosing or designing a mobile musical ringtone and the second on video recordings of the use of instant messaging in organizations, users are shown to pattern their environments with an orientation toward shaping in advance the way in which they might be interrupted and notified. In the case of mobile ringtones their strategies display an orientation toward softening the potential coerciveness of the ringtone, a "crisis of the summons" that is probably a more general phenomenon. The cleverness and delicacy of their strategies for choosing or crafting mobile musical ringtones (e.g., "compensating" the coerciveness of the ring *qua* summons with the pleasure of the ring *qua* music) go hand-in-hand with increased pragmatic competencies, such as skills in assessing and appreciating what a given ringtone does. In the instant-messaging video study, I was able to show how the management of notification landscapes constituted a situated, artful accomplishment, sensitive to the particulars of the unfolding situation and reflexively tied to the production of intelligible forms of involvement in relevant activities. Here also, interpretive skills and competencies) coevolve with the resources available to users for managing their notification landscapes.

The systematic study of the pragmatics of notification devices that this article calls for is also a way to research how we may be becoming "pragmatic amateurs," less inclined to accept the imposition of a summons (which testifies to a kind of "crisis of the summons"), and with a keener sense for appreciating the fine details of the way a given notification is crafted, of how its occurrence produces us as subjects, makes relevant a response, and orients the possible forms that such a response may take, as well as its meaning. If such pragmatic amateurs are the most likely denizens of a highly connected world that praises flexibility, reactivity, and accessibility, in the sense of adapting to it and evolving with it, then the varied forms of notification devices that I have studied are a constitutive part of its "*umwelt*."

NOTES

1. In the early 1990s the CSCW community sought to orient the design of technical devices and especially computer technology, with a view to facilitating the collaborative activities of several individuals. One of the typical situations envisaged at the time was the problem of the collective writing of a document, where every author had to be informed of the actions of the other authors, and a "mutual awareness landscape" had to be created.
2. Except in the case of certain practices, common in developing countries, in which the sound is used as a way of "beeping" the receiver, not for him or her to answer but so that he or she can call back (Donner 2007).
3. I thank Renato Curicio and Serge Proulx, with whom I carried out this study.
4. To maintain a certain degree of legibility in the argument, I have not accounted here for certain details of the activity, like the hesitations and repairs in the typing of messages.
5. The bottom half of her body remains constantly oriented toward the screen (Schegloff 1996).
6. I am summing up the complex actions related to the fact that she holds two conversations simultaneously on the same subject, a point that I do not have the space to consider here.
7. As regards the position of the "tabbing" in the order of closures, independently of the dialogue itself, the applications are closed almost in the same order as that in which they were opened.

REFERENCES

Abowd, G. D., and E. D. Mynatt. 2000. Charting past, present, and future research in ubiquitous computing. *ACM Transactions on Computer-Human Interaction* 7:29–58.

Arroyo, E., and T. Selker. 2003. Self-adaptive multimodal-interruption interfaces. In *Proceedings of the 2003 International Conference on Intelligent User Interfaces*, 6–11. New York: ACM.

Augé, M. 2008. *Où est passé l'avenir ?* Paris: Editions du Panama.

Bartram, L., C. Ware, and T. Calvert. 2003. Moticons: Detection, distraction and task. *International Journal of Human-Computer Studies* 58(5):515–45.

Castells, M. 2000. *The rise of the network society. Vol. 1. The information age: Economy, society and culture*. Oxford: Wiley-Blackwell.

Chateauraynaud, F., and D. Torny. 1999. *Les sombres précurseurs. Une sociologie pragmatique de l'alerte et du risque*. Paris: Editions de l'E.H.E.S.S.

Cresswell, T. 2006. *On the move: Mobility in the modern Western world*. London: Routledge.

Cutrell, E., M. Czerwinski, and E. Horvitz. 2001. Notification, disruption, and memory: Effects of messaging interruptions on memory and performance. In *Proceedings of IFIP INTERACT'01: Human–computer interaction,* ed. M. Hirose, 263–9. Tokyo: IOS.

Danninger, M., R. Vertegaal, D. P. Siewiorek, and A. Mamuji. 2005. Using social geometry to manage interruptions and co-worker attention in office environments. In *Proceedings of the 2005 Conference on Graphics Interface,* ed. K. Inkpen and M. Van de Panne, 211–18. Victoria, Canada: Canadian Human-Computer Communications Society.

Fallman, D., and B. Yttergren. 2005. Meeting in quiet: Choosing suitable notification modalities for mobile phones. In *DUX '05: Proceedings of the 2005 Conference on Designing for User eXperience*, 55. New York: ACM.

Garfinkel, H. 2002. *Ethnomethodology's program. Working out Durkheim's çphorism*. Lanham, MD: Rowman & Littlefield.

Gievska, S., and J. Sibert. 2004. A framework for context-sensitive coordination of human interruptions in human–computer interaction. In *Proceedings of the 8th ERCIM Workshop on User Interfaces for All,* ed. C. Stary and C. Stephanidis, 418–24. Vienna: Springer.

Goffman, E. 1963. *Behavior in public places*. New York: Free Press.

Hansson, R., and P. Ljungstrand. 2000. The reminder bracelet: Subtle notification cues for mobile devices. In *CHI '00: CHI '00 extended abstracts on human factors in computing systems*, ed. G. Abowd, B. Brumitt, and S. Shafer, 323–24. New York: ACM.

Hennion, A. 2004. Pramatics of taste. In *The Blackwell companion to the sociology of culture*, ed. M. Jacobs and N. Hanrahan, 131–44. Oxford, England: Blackwell.

Ho, J., and S. S. Intille. 2005. Using context-aware computing to reduce the perceived burden of interruptions from mobile devices. In *Proceedings of ACM CHI 2005 Conference on Human Factors in Computing Systems,* ed. C. Gerritt and C. Gale, 909–18. New York: ACM.

Hopper, R. 1992. *Telephone conversation*. Bloomington: Indiana University Press.

Hudson, J., J. Christensen, W. Kellogg, and T. Erickson. 2002. "I'd be overwhelmed, but it's just one more thing to do": Availability and interruption in research management. In *Proceedings of ACM CHI 2002 Conference on Human Factors in Computing Systems,* ed. L. Terveen, 97–104. New York: ACM.

Hutchby, I. 2001. *Conversation and technology*. Cambridge, England: Polity.

Hymes, D. 1964. Towards ethnographies of communication. *American Anthropologist* 66:1–34.

Jayyusi, L. 1988. Toward a socio-logic of the film-text. *Semiotica* 68:271–96.

Kraut., R., R. Fish, R. Root, and B. Chalfonte. 1990. Informal communication in organizations: form, function and technology. In *Human reactions to technology: Claremont Symposium in applied social psychology,* ed. S. Oskamp and S. Spacapan, 287–314. Beverly Hills, CA: Sage.

Latour, B. 1993. *La clef de Berlin et autres leçons d'un amateur de sciences*. Paris: Eds. La Découverte.

Licoppe C. 2004. "Connected presence": The emergence of a new repertoire for managing social relationships in a changing communication technoscape. *Environment and Planning D: Society and Space* 22:135–56.

———. 2007. De la communication interpersonnelle aux communautés épistémiques: Le développement des TIC et l'enracinement du paradigme de la distribution. *Hermès* 47:59–68.

———. 2008. The mobile phone's ring. In *The handbook of mobile communication,* ed. J. Katz, 139–52. Cambridge, MA: MIT Press.

Licoppe C., and J. P. Heurtin. 2001. Managing one's availability to telephone communication through mobile phones: A French case study of the development dynamics of the use of mobile phones. *Personal and Ubiquitous Computing* 5:99–108

Licoppe, C., and Z. Smoreda. 2005. Are social networks technologically embedded? How networks are changing today with changes in communication technology. *Social Networks* 27:317–35.

Lynch, M., E. Livingston, and H. Garfinkel. 1983. Temporal order in laboratory work. In *Science observed: Perspectives on the social study of science,* ed. K. Knorr Cetina and M. Mulkay, 205–38. London: Sage.

McCrickard, D. S., M. Czerwinski, and L. Bartram. 2003. Introduction: design and evaluation of notification user interfaces. *International Journal of Human-Computer Studies* 58:509–14.

McFarlane, D. C., and K. A. Latorella. 2002. The scope and importance of human interruption in HCI design. *Human-Computer Interaction* 17:1–61.

Miyata, Y., and D. Norman. 1986. Psychological issues in support of multiple activities. In *User centered systems design: New perspectives on human-computer interaction,* ed. D. A. Norman and S. W. Draper, 265–84. Hillsdale, NJ: Erlbaum.

Nagel, K. S., J. M. Hudson, and G. D. Abowd. 2004. Predictors of availability in home life context-mediated communication. In *Proceedings of CSCW'04 Conference on Computer-Supported Cooperative Work,* ed. J. Herbsleb and G. Olson, 497–506. New York: ACM.

Nardi, B., S. Whittaker, and E. Bradner. 2000. Interaction and outeraction: Instant messaging in action. In *Proceedings of CSCW'04 Conference on Computer-Supported Cooperative Work,* ed. J. Herbsleb and G. Olson, 78–88. New York: ACM.

Norman, D. 1988. *The psychology of everyday things*. New York: Basic Books.

O'Conaill, B., and D. Frohlich. 1995. Timespace in the workplace: Dealing with interruptions. In *Proceedings of CHI'95 Conference on Human Factors in Computing Systems*, ed. I. Katz, R. Mack, L. Marks, M. B. Rosson, and J. Nielsen, 262–63. New York: ACM.

Orlikowski, W., and J. Yates. 1994. Genre repertoire: The structuring of communicative practices in organizations. *Administrative Science Quarterly* 39:541–74.

Prada, A. 2006. Socio-technical agency in financial markets: The case of the stock ticker. *Social Studies of Science* 36:753–82.

Quan-Haase, A., J. Cothrel, and B. Wellman, B. 2005. Instant messaging for collaboration: A case study of a high tech firm. *Journal of Computer-Mediated-Communication* 10, http://jcmc.indiana.edu/vol10/issue4/quan-haase.html

Schegloff, E. 1972. Sequencing in conversational openings. In *Directions in sociolinguistics. The ethnography of communication*, ed. D.

Hymes and J. Gumperz, 346–80. Cambridge: Cambridge University Press.

Roda, C., and J. Thomas. 2006. Attention aware systems. Theories, applications and research agenda. *Computers in Human Behavior* 22:557–87.

Schegloff, E. 1986. The routine as achievement. *Human Studies* 9:111–51.

———. 1998. Body torque. *Conversation* 65(3):535–96.

Shen, H., and C. Sun. 2002. Flexible notification for collaborative systems. In *Proceedings of the 2002 Conference on Computer Supported Cooperative Work CSCW '02,* ed. E. Churchill and J. MacCarthy, 77–86. New York: ACM.

Stiegler, B., and Ars Industrialis. 2006. *Réenchanter le monde. La valeur esprit contre le populisme industriel.* Paris : Flammarion.

———. 2008. *Prendre soin de la jeunesse et des générations*. Paris: Flammarion.

Takemae, Y., S. Chaki, T. Ohno, I. Yoda, and S. Ozawa. 2007. Analysis of human interruptibility in the home environment. In *CHI '07: CHI '07 extended abstracts on human factors in computing systems*, ed. M. B Rosson and D. Gilmore, 2681–2686. New York: ACM.

Thompson, E. P. 1967. Time, work-discipline and industrial capitalism. *Past and Present* 38:56–97.

Tullio, J., A. K. Dey, J. Chalecki, and J. Fogarty. 2007. How it works: A field study of non-technical users interacting with an intelligent system. In *CHI '07: Proceedings of the SIGCHI conference on human factors in computing systems,* ed. M. B. Rosson and D. Gilmore, 31–40. New York: ACM.

Weiser, M. 1991. The computer for the twenty-first century. *Scientific American*. September. 94–104.

Whittaker S., D. Frohlich, and O. Daly-Jones. 1994. Informal workplace communication: What is it like and how might we support it? In *Proceeding of the CHI'94 conference on human factors in computing systems,* ed. B. Adelson, S. Dumais, and J. Olson, 131–7. New York: ACM.

Wittgenstein, L. 1958. *Philosophical investigations*. Oxford: Basil, Blackwell & Mott.

Zhang, L., N. Tu, and D. Vronay. 2005. Info-lotus: A peripheral visualization for email notification. In *Proceedings of ACM CHI 2005 conference on human factors in computing systems,* ed. C. Gerritt and C. Gale, 901–4. New York: ACM.

Living in the Mediatope: A Multimethod Study on the Evolution of Media Technologies in the Domestic Environment

Thorsten Quandt and Thilo von Pape

Institut für Sozialwissenschaften, Universität Hohenheim, Stuttgart, Germany

Domestication is a productive concept for analyzing the sense-making processes behind the integration of media technologies into everyday life. However, researchers have yet to take advantage of the full heuristic potential of this metaphor. So far, most studies have focused on single devices and employed qualitative methods, mainly case studies, to generate insights into the process of domestication. The authors suggest broadening of perspective to the overall domestic ecology within which media cohabitate and compete. Toward this goal, they conducted a large-scale multimethod study involving observations and interviews in 100 households, thereby analyzing not only the "birth" of individual media devices into households, but also examined how these devices reside in certain "mediatopes" (media environments), how they compete as different media "species," and how they change their social and spatial positions during their lifecycle. More generally, the study demonstrates how to apply domestication research to the topography of a domestic media environment that is complementary to the ethnographical descriptions that have dominated the literature thus far.

THE RAPID EVOLUTION OF MEDIA TECHNOLOGIES

With the advent of new digital media and mobile communication devices, the lives of media users in postindustrial countries have changed considerably. Cutting-edge computer companies such as Apple are forcing the transformation of computers into entertainment devices; their strategy is to make the computer the central node of a networked home—a "digital hub." With similar ambitions, Microsoft has released the gaming device Xbox 360. Designed as a stylish multimedia machine, it also plays CDs and DVDs, connects to the online service Xbox live, and is even (partially) compatible with Apple's iPod. Clearly, these companies have opted for a seamless integration of functionalities in computer-based devices that no longer resemble traditional computers. Other companies have focused on the integration of telecommunications, broadband applications, and entertainment media (like television)—the so-called "triple play." All these strategies are directed to the vision of the future, in which people live in connected multimedia environments pervaded by computer technology.

One would expect this emergence of new media environments to be a central topic for communication and media studies, but for a long time, "mainstream" communication studies have been predominantly interested in the messages of the media, their production, their effects or use, and various aspects of the media system (see the special issues of the *Journal of Communication* published in 2005, 55(1–3)). The carriers of the content, i.e., the media devices themselves, in their physical existence as technological artifacts, were only of peripheral interest. Studying this domain—or "doing technology," as Sørensen (2006) puts it—was neglected. We thereby see a technology-driven perspective of producers, on the one hand, and communication studies, which considers the user perspective but neglects technology, on the other hand. However, the question of whether a technology will find its place in a user's everyday life does not depend on either one of these two sides, but on the interplay between technology and the user-sided context: How do the social sphere of the user and the technological sphere of the communication technologies affect each other mutually over the lifespan of a communication technology? The aim of this article is not to formulate new hypotheses, but rather to present a new way of addressing this general question.

The underlying processes involved in adopting new devices into households, "taming" them, and giving them meaning in the social context have been successfully described by various empirical studies, most notably qualitative studies employing the concept of "domestication" (Silverstone & Haddon 1996; see also Berker et al. 2006; Haddon 2006; Livingstone 2007). These successes notwithstanding, there remains some scope for additional research in this robustly developing field. We believe that the approach's basic idea can be extended beyond the existing conceptual and empirical advances. Employing a biological metaphor, one could say that individual media species and their "taming" in specific mediatopes (media environments) have been observed and described in detail (Hirsch 1992; Bakardjeva & Smith 2001; Ward 2006; Frissen 2000; see also Haddon 2006). However, the larger context of "media ecosystems" has been little studied. Such a holistic perspective was attempted in the early days of domestication research (Silverstone & Hirsch 1992) when the household was considered as a "moral economy" (Silverstone, Hirsch, & Morley 1992) of shared identity and values. More recently, new media have been considered as "media repertoires" (Haddon & Vincent 2004; cf. Haddon 1992) or as "technospace," an approach close to the domestication perspective (Licoppe 2004). Methodologically, most of these approaches draw on qualitative data, as is the tradition within the domestication research. However, as we argue in this article, a quantitative perspective on mediatopes can give additional insights, namely, on the relation between the individual media devices, their users, and the domestic environment.

To this end, we propose a theoretical model that specifies quantifiable equivalents for some of the concepts of domestication research. To further extend the original metaphor behind domestication, we treat media technologies as living organisms cohabiting and competing in the domestic space and focus on questions of their interaction and integration into the domestic environment.

On the basis of these analytical foundations, we develop the instruments of the multimethod study, including observations, "modular" interviews, and a collection of pictures for 100 households selected on the basis of a quota sample. The findings are presented in accordance with a process logic, as described earlier, starting with the "birth" of devices into households, their positioning and development, and finally their "aging" process. Thereafter, a case study is used to exemplify the general findings in a more detailed way. Finally, we critically assess ways in which our approach provides insights into the development of domestication, and whether there is potential for further development.

TOWARD A THEORETICAL MODEL OF DOMESTICATION IN MEDIATOPES

Research Overview: Theories and Observations of Media Wildlife

The long period of relative neglect of media as technological devices by mainstream communication studies has led to the discussion being dominated by technologically determinist approaches that are commonly derived from technologically oriented disciplines. Thus, the early "convergence" debate (see Baldwin et al. 1996; Nora & Minc 1978), the idea of a "smart home" (for a critical overview see Aldrich 2003), and the vision of "ubiquitous computing" (Tolmie et al. 2003; Weiser 1993) focus strongly on the technologies as the driving force behind the developments and their "impact" on society.

In response to this rather one-sided discussion, social sciences, and cultural studies in particular, have developed concepts that stress the users' contribution to media development. Different aspects of social change in the context of technological evolution have been analyzed using a variety of approaches, including social constructivism applied to technology (Pinch & Bijker 1987; MacKenzie & Wajcman 1985; Latour & Woolgar 1979; Williams & Edge 1996) and the domestication approach (Silverstone & Haddon 1996; Berker et al. 2006). The latter has a strong sociological basis, and arguably offers the most complex explanations for the social reconstruction of technologies by consumers in their domestic environments. Most studies in this tradition focus on how new technologies—metaphorically speaking, "wild species"—are being integrated into cultivated home environments, thus being "tamed" and "domesticated."

The basic idea of considering individual cultural objects as biological beings and analyzing their "life" has been developed by the anthropologist Kopytoff (1986), who describes how objects cease to be commodities when they are culturally redefined in the specific household's context. Drawing partially on this idea, Silverstone and Haddon (1996; cf. Haddon & Silverstone 1994; Haddon 2003) have further differentiated the integration and (re)definition of technological artifacts into everyday life as an ongoing process of objectification, incorporation, and conversion. "Objectification" describes integration into the domestic space, such as the physical placement of a TV set in a living room. "Incorporation" denotes the integration into time routines and rituals of everyday life (e.g., watching TV at a certain time of the day, such as watching the news after dinner), and "conversion" represents the symbolic promotion of one's public image by presenting the new devices to the outside (e.g., showing off a new plasma television set to neighbors and friends). The "two articulations" of communication technologies (Silverstone & Haddon 1996) permit a differentiated view of these processes in the household—media in their physical presence as objects on the one hand and in their function as symbolic transmitters of messages on the other hand (see also Livingstone 2007; Hartmann 2006).

In domestication research, a holistic perspective has so far proven especially fruitful when media change is concerned. Haddon (1992) analyzed the introduction of home computers into households, which did not simply add one activity to the existing repertory—and one object to the living room—but had an impact on the overall communication (reading specialized press, talking about video games, etc.) and social relations. In a similar way, Haddon and Vincent analyzed the impact of the mobile telephone (Haddon & Vincent 2004) on the domestic management of communication repertories. In close connection with domestication research, Licoppe (2004) has developed the concept of "technospace," to study how people use communication technology today to gain presence over distance, beyond the compensation or substitution of presence that has been realized by media in the past (see also Gergen 2002; Fortunati 2002). Research based on these approaches especially considers the changes brought about by mobile media, challenging conventional understanding of time and space (e.g., Wajcman 2008; Wajcman, Bittman, & Brown 2008).

Thus far mostly qualitative approaches have been used to draw an overall picture of domestication process under real-life conditions (Bakardjeva & Smith 2001; Ling 2000; Taylor & Harper 2003; Tolmie et al. 2003; cf. Haddon 2006; Berker et al. 2006). These holistic approaches are realized by doing case studies and ethnographic research, mostly based on small samples. Qualitative approaches are traditionally considered as the most appropriate way to capture a holistic picture of a social phenomenon (Denzin & Lincoln 2005; Mill 1973). Some even consider qualitative approaches as practically synonymous with holistic perspectives, as opposed to "reductionist," quantitative research (Verschuren 2001). In contrast to this perspective, we suggest consideration of quantitative methods as a complementary approach for holistic analysis. Quantitative research can be holistic if it considers not only the parts but also the interrelations between them within a larger system (Ragin 1987). Such an approach enables the consideration of the wider context within which a medium is situated, be it the surrounding media "species," be it the specific user's habits, and be it the environment of domestic spaces.

Consequently, while there exists a large number of case studies, one has to note a certain lack of contextual overview, where the "careers" of different media are considered in parallel by analyzing a household's media "population" as a whole or comparing different "mediatopes" with each other. Such a study could serve as a useful complement to existing domestication studies, describing the environmental "embedding" of media technologies.

However, this type of research would require a certain level of standardization in order to manage and compare the information gathered; it would also require a firmly structured analytical logic.

In the following subsection, we develop an analytical model, which corresponds to the domestication approach but, at the same time, permits us to design (partially) standardized instruments that make it possible to analyze and compare users, media, and domestic environments. The ultimate goal of such an approach is a holistic description of the "mediatopes"—the "living" environments of the media. One must stress, though, that other prominent approaches in media studies also apply biological metaphors to analyze media evolution from a holistic perspective. They include "media ecology" (McLuhan 1964; Postman 2000) and the theory of gratification niches in "media competition" (Dimmick 2003). However, the approach used here is different because it considers groups of concrete devices instead of media types in general. Instead of asking in which situations and for which reasons people watch TV or send e-mails, we ask: When and why does a certain individual use a certain TV set or personal computer in a specific context?

The model needed for a holistic domestication perspective—which considers both individual media artifacts and the mediatope—must "transpose" the concept of the domestication approach into units that can be operationalized and observed and measured with quantitative methods. This model is presented in the next subsection.

The Triangular Model: Domestication in the Mediatopes

In an overview of existing concepts on the networked home, Venkatesh et al. (2003) propose that we consider this environment as a "living space" determined by three factors: (1) social space, (2) physical space, and (3) technological space.

We adopt this idea by taking into account (1) the users, who choose the media, place them into their households, integrate them into their daily routines, and give them meaning; (2) the household as the "physical" and social environment of the devices; and finally (3) the devices themselves. This perspective focuses on the multidimensionality of the domestication process, more than is the case in traditional domestication studies. However, it does not break with the domestication tradition because it still situates the actors' activities in the domestication rubric.

Each of these three factors contributes to the domestication process; they are closely interlinked (see Figure 1). The user characteristics influence the household characteristics on one hand and the choice, integration, and

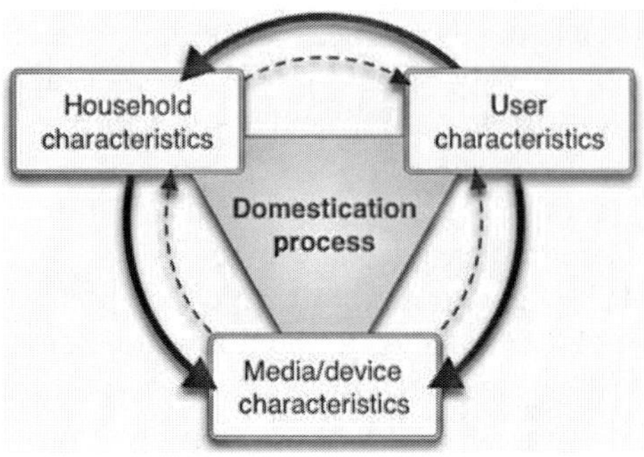

FIG. 1. The triangular model of domestication in the mediatopes.

definition of the end device on the other. The user characteristics themselves can be described using a sociodemographic profile, but also with more highly differentiated concepts such as the milieu orientation (see Bourdieu 1979) or the individual lifestyle (see Otte 2004). Different people design their living spaces (households) in different ways in order to express themselves; consequently, the overall household style reflects the socioeconomic status of its inhabitants and their general milieu orientation. However, there are probably some elements beyond the user's control that have an influence on the inhabitants (e.g., space layout and limitations of the flat or house).

In a similar vein, the media characteristics also reflect the user characteristics: Media can be considered as "extensions of man" (McLuhan 1964), not only in a purely instrumental sense as extensions of our senses, but also as symbolic additions to the user's self-definition. In this way, the device can also be seen as influencing the user characteristics. For example, the perception of others will also have an effect on the user's social life (e.g., owning a "designer" computer can influence the user's image in certain social groups). Many of the media characteristics are already "inscribed" or at least implied by the physical device, so the "reflective" influence of media on the users is beyond their control. That said, the influence of the device on the user is probably weaker than the influence of the user on the device, as media are clearly chosen in accordance with a certain use profile.

Last but not least, the household layout also defines the media characteristics. By being placed in a certain room environment, media also take a social position. For example, a device placed in the living room will be domesticated differently from a device placed in the bedroom or bathroom.

As the "triangular" model shows, domestication is a complex phenomenon, mainly because of the various interdependencies between the factors involved. In fact, the situation is even more complicated: As noted by Silverstone and Haddon (1996), domestication is a process, meaning that objectification, incorporation, and conversion do not always take place at the same time. To express the time-variant nature of domestication, we identify various phases of the domestication process and integrate them in a process model (see Figure 2).

This process has already started by the time the device enters the household. In the pre-adoption phase, the potential owners of media devices may inform themselves of the characteristics of the devices and plan a household placement in advance. After the purchase process (or other modes of entrance into the domestic environment, e.g., gifts), devices are adopted by their users, positioned in a specific (physical and social) place, and used for the first time. However, this first adoption phase does not necessarily generate a fixed meaning for devices. For example, the user's excitement over a new purchase might trigger a high degree of attentiveness toward the device during an initial "exploration" phase, which will "wear off" over time. After the initial adoption phase, the device is integrated into the social routines and time schedules of the users. At this point, a process begins that is often referred to as "continuous negotiation" (Mansell 1996, 26; Silverstone 2006). With the given model, and insights from research on the social construction of technology (cf. Pinch & Bijker 1987), this can be further differentiated into various lines of development. As described by Pinch and Bijker, the integration phase may lead to a relative "closure" (Pinch & Bijker 1987), whereby the meaning of the device stabilizes, as well as the user's routines in respect to it and its positioning in the household.

This status may last until the device "dies" or leaves the household (e.g., if it is given away as a present or

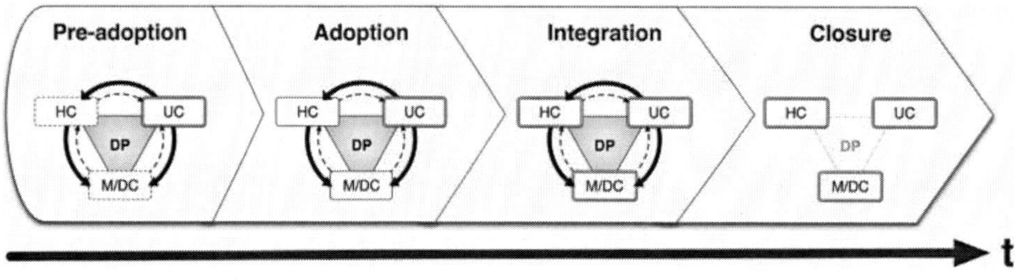

FIG. 2. Domestication as a multiphase, time-variant process.

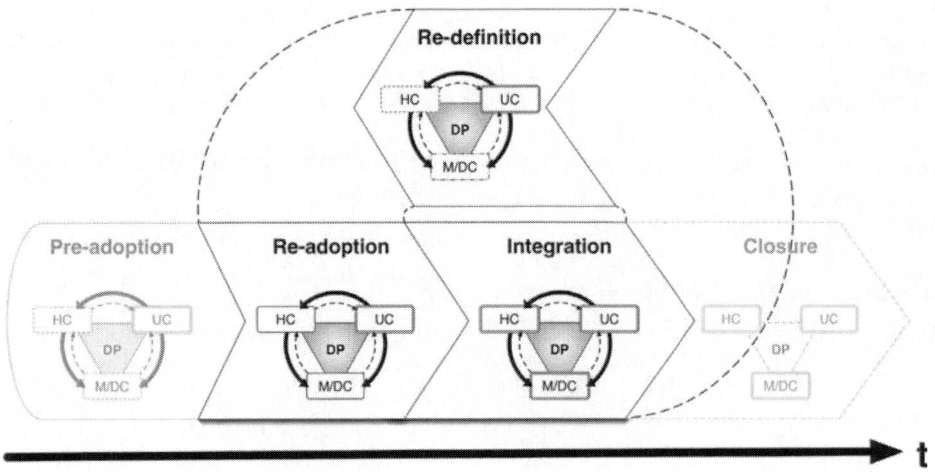

FIG. 3. Redefinition of the meaning of devices in a domestication loop.

if the device owner leaves the household); however, this is not the only way in which the domestication process might evolve; instead of a "final" closure, it may lead to a redefinition phase (see Figure 3).

The process should not be imagined as a clear-cut series of stages in reality; rather, the phases tend to overlap each other in time, and never completely correspond to the ideal types evoked. Thus, the change from pre-adoption to adoption often appears as a "series of trials" (Lehtonen 2003) leading to more and more intense use, and the stabilization is never complete, but continues to be slightly affected by changes in the user, the household, and the technology. As with any other process heuristic in social sciences, the model is not meant to be a timetable for predicting any specific device's evolution (see also Pinch 2000, 366), but as a framework that guides our observation and brings us closer to the important aspects of reality that we may otherwise overlook. For example, it guides our attention toward the aspects that remain stable in a situation of closure, while guiding it toward the aspects that change in a situation of redefinition. This model acknowledges the "organic" nature of the domestication process (as described by Mansell and Silverstone; see earlier discussion): Meaning need not always become fixed, but may change over time—e.g., a redefinition of a device can lead to a readoption and new integration (Wirth et al. 2008). An example of redefinition is the replacement of a living-room TV set with a new device, and the physical placement of the "old" TV in a different room such as the bedroom. In this case, the "old" device might be used in totally different contexts than before, while the "new" TV takes over some of the "old" TV's meaning (e.g., as the centerpiece of the family life). Obviously, such a redefinition of a device will become necessary with changes in the mediatope itself, either the household characteristics, user routines, or a new member in the media "fauna." However, the device's own characteristics are also important here: If a device becomes "old" (or even defective), it is more likely to be replaced by a new device.

The presented model thus portrays domestication as an overall process resulting from the interplay between household characteristics, media characteristics, and user characteristics over the process of domestication. The model permits consideration of domestication in different phases, starting with (a) the pre-adoption phase and the introduction into the household, (b) the integration into the social routines of the household, and (c) the long-time evolution of the device's meaning.

This process orientation sensitizes us to the differences in the mutual influences of social and technological factors in each stage of the process:

- Which aspects of a communication technology appeal to potential users at the moment of adoption?
- How do users integrate a technology into their domestic space, both physically and symbolically?
- How do the place and the social signification of the new communication technologies evolve in the long term?

While these questions are not new to domestication research, we propose to respond to them in a new way, considering the topography of media ecosystems instead of isolated case studies. This permits to compare between different technologies, users, households, and points in time in the domestication process and to account for the differences found in the field.

APPROACHING MEDIA DEVICES IN THE FIELD: DESIGN OF THE EMPIRICAL STUDY

As discussed earlier, our study focuses on the topography of media ecosystems and a relocation of the domestication process in these ecosystems; accordingly, the study can be considered to be in the reconstructive rather than hypotheses testing mode. Following the triangular domestication model, one has to take into account the characteristics of the household and the room settings, the individual user, and the specifics of each device. Furthermore, the various (possible) phases of the process must also be mirrored in the empirical analysis.

This leads to requirements that are not easily combined. A topography of media ecosystems demands that the empirical study must (a) be based on a relevant number of cases to ensure that it reflects the main "areas" of such an ecosystem; (b) be a field study that provides insight into the "real-life" conditions of the mediatopes, including all of their elements (user, household, devices); and (c) reflect on the various phases of the domestication process.

On the basis of these considerations, our research team undertook a multimethod study, including observations and interviews, with additional forms of data collection such as taking photographs, and using a relatively large sample for this type of study (100 households within our home country of Germany).

Obtaining Access to the Field: The Sample

Gaining access to the households of complete strangers for sufficient periods of time to document the entire structure of the mediatope and undertake time-consuming interviews is difficult. We dealt with this access problem by actively approaching key persons in specifically selected households. While this approach precluded a random selection of households, the households were carefully chosen using a quota scheme—i.e., we selected them based on four characteristics: household size/type, household income, and age and education of the head of the household.[1] The combination of these characteristics in the respective household had to reflect a pattern derived from a representative survey on household composition. The basis for the quota was the "Mikro Zensus" compiled by the German Bureau of Statistics (*Statistisches Bundesamt*), which is a governmental, representative study on the households and citizens in Germany. We were able to meet the goals of the given quota scheme (a $3 \times 3 \times 4 \times 2$ matrix), meaning that the 100 selected households in our study mirror the Mikro Zensus distribution for the given four factors.[2]

There were 192 people (including 18 children under the age of 14 years) living in the selected households.[3] During the observation, we coded 1,626 media in 594 rooms and took approximately 1,000 photographs. The selected households had an average of 6 rooms (including bathrooms, kitchens, and corridors) and 16 media devices. While the obtained data set is too small to warrant the use of inferential statistics in most cases and it is debatable whether quota samples actually allow for the use of inferential statistics at all (Arber 2001), it still offers a broad overview of mediatopes and many different cases that you would also find in the base population.

Tools for Working in the Field: Methods and Instruments

The general idea behind this study is comparable to that behind "milieu" and lifestyle studies; however, we consider the mediatopes rather than the general milieu of the household. In other words, the study focuses on the devices rather than the users, and analyzes these devices in their complex household context.

To get the most detailed picture of devices in these mediatopes, our multimethod study was based on the following three elements:

- First, we observed and coded the available media devices (including their type, brand, characteristics, location, and surroundings) and the entire living situation of the household using a standardized codebook (approximately 25 description criteria per media device). We also took photographs of the main living rooms in order to document the respective styles of living. This part of the study provided a comprehensive room and media profile—an observation of the mediatopes.
- Second, we gained further knowledge of the media arrangements via in-depth interviews with the heads of households. The questions posed during the interviews addressed the socioeconomic situation of the household, additional milieu-oriented household characteristics, and nonobservable media characteristics (e.g., price, purchase criteria, place of purchase). The interviews included both closed and open items and tackled both the past (how did the media get into the household?) and the future (what plans exist for future purchases/device adoptions?).
- Finally, to analyze the domestication processes and the function of the media, we undertook personal and "modular" questionnaires of all household members (aged 14 years and older), primarily using closed items. "Modular" questionnaire means that according to the observed mediatope and household settings, each household member received a personalized set of questionnaire "modules" on the specific media devices that she/he was actively using. So if somebody reported using a TV set in the living room and a computer in the study room, her/his questionnaire included two modules with questions that were specifically designed for these two devices. In the interviews, we gathered information on use habits, the perceived function of each specific device (in our example: the given TV set in the living room and

the computer in the study room), and its symbolic value to the respondents, as well as data on the social and personal situation of the household members. So the "modular" questionnaire is different from the questionnaires used in general "media use" studies, as these usually include standard questions on the general use of TV, computers etc., while our study included questions on a specific device in a specific setting.

In order to grasp various characteristics of the household and its members, the codebook and the survey followed examples of Bourdieu's (1979) empirical work and subsequent studies (Otte 2004). Questions on the uses and the symbolic value followed partially existing qualitative work on domestication (e.g. Bakardjeva & Smith 2001; Ling 2000; Taylor & Harper 2003) and partially quantitative approaches such as uses-and-gratifications (e.g., Dimmick 2003). By combining several methods and both qualitative and quantitative steps, we aimed to understand the domestication process both in the broader sense of the "topography" of media ecology described earlier and meaningful case analyses where necessary.

DOMESTICATION IN MEDIATOPES: FINDINGS OF THE MULTIMETHOD STUDY

Following our research questions, three phases of the domestication process are considered from the biological and holistic perspective in the this section: media adoption, its further integration, and its long-term evolution in the household. The findings show how the interplay of different household, user, and technological factors determines domestication during different phases of the process.

Adoption: How the Media Enter the Households

The first phase of a device's introduction to the household's ecology takes place even before the device enters the home. The decision to buy a certain device is based not only on technological and functional considerations, but also on economic and social ones; therefore, we asked users about the decision processes that led to the adoption of individual devices, as well as the adoption criteria.

A correspondence analysis of the various purchase criteria and media types clearly highlights the differences in the decision processes (see Figure 4), as it helps to identify both the degree of similarity of the different media devices and the degree of connectedness of each device by placing them in a two-dimensional correspondence map. Our analysis reveals different "families" of similar devices (that are placed in the same "area" of the correspondence map) and the fact that media are judged not only on the basis of their technological qualities but also on the social tags attached to them. For example, the analysis underlines a common understanding that mobile phones are very often purchased on the basis of their appearance ("looks") and brand image, as with a fashion item. Standard telephones are functional devices, while audio handhelds ("MP3 & Co.") are commonly purchased as the result of a buying impulse: They are cheap enough to be purchased and introduced into the domestic world with minimal advance planning. Stereos and TVs, in contrast, are usually bought on the basis of quality and price decisions, as well as brand. Given that they represent a substantial investment, people clearly plan ahead when buying a TV or stereo, and they expect these devices to become long-term members of their household.

Interestingly, according to our analysis, computers are usually bought on an impulse or based on functional considerations rather than reflections on quality and price. This is also true for portable audio systems ("ghetto blasters"). This finding is surprising given the price of computers. Our study revealed that computers are the most expensive media devices in the household (average price of €1,164), followed by video cameras (€570) and TVs (€563). Computers are clearly not expected to last long, and they are not seen as fashionable items (such as mobile phones and TVs) that represent social prestige. The exclusion of quality and price as primary decision factors is also related to the large number of "no-frills" computers in the surveyed households, many of which were built by the users from individual parts. The parts are cheap enough to be purchased as required.

In considering purchase criteria and media characteristics, the central question is, who decides on the criteria and evaluates the characteristics?[4] As our interviews included device-based questions, we received information on who decided on the purchase of each individual device under observation. Our data show that it is not always the future users who decide on the purchase of a certain device. Although men made up only 45.5% of the sample, the majority of the decision makers were male (61.8%). However, while men are still considered to be the "gatekeepers" when it comes to the introduction of new devices into the household, this trend varies very much across different media types. For example, highly "individualized" media such as mobile phones are selected by the individual users themselves, whereas "social" family media, expensive media devices, and computers are more commonly selected and purchased by men. While this reflects a somewhat stereotypical idea that men are the decision makers when it comes to media technology, it does not exclude the possibility that women may dominate other decisions critical for the domestication process, such as the purchase and arrangement of other household equipment.

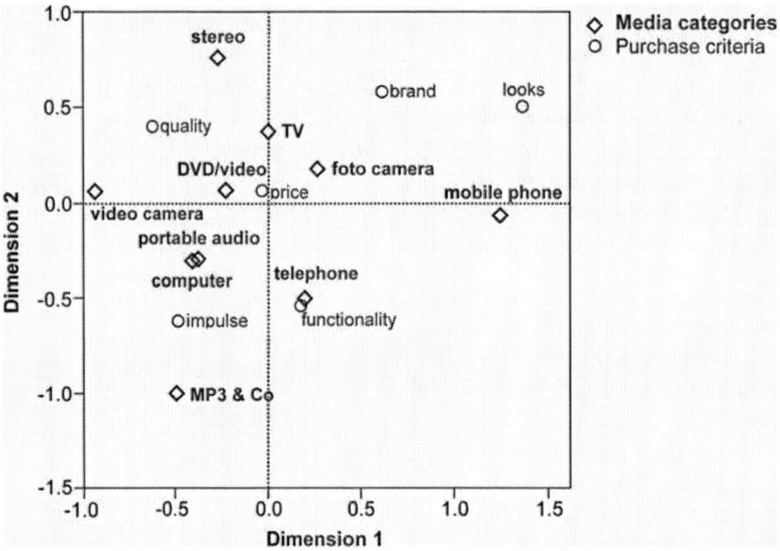

FIG. 4. Correspondence analysis: purchase criteria × media categories (symmetrical normalization; $s_1^2 = 0.074$, explaining 43.2% of variation in the data; $s_2^2 = 0.039$, explaining 23.0% of the variation).

Overall, this analysis of the pre-adoption process teaches us that the grouping of technologies and devices under the global label of "media" might represent an oversimplification, as the various species are clearly distinct when it comes to the decision and adoption processes.

Integration: The Life of Media Devices in the Domestic Space

After purchase, media devices are integrated into domestic environments, in both a space- and time-related sense. We focus on the spatial integration first (the time-based patterns follow in the next subsection). Our observation and interview material clearly supports the notion that media are consciously positioned according to their meaning for the users: Their spatial environment hints at their "place" in the social environment. So it does not come as a surprise that we could observe comparable patterns in many households, and that the basic "environmental qualities" of specific room types are also very similar across households.

A first glance at the locations of different media in the sampled households (see Table 1) itself reveals a remarkable distribution. The living room monopolizes almost half of the media present in the households. Interestingly, it is the children's bedroom that contains the second highest number of media, although children's rooms are only present in a minority of households. This finding goes in line with other studies on children's media use, underlining their role as "change agents" with respect to their families' media use (cf. Livingstone & Bovill 2001).

When considering the different media types, we find that the living room's dominance is even more pronounced in terms of the classical audiovisual home entertainment sector, being home to the majority of televisions (60.4%), DVD and VHS video devices (75.0%), and stereos (59.7%). The profile of the children's room is marked by the relatively high presence of media in general, including televisions (12.5% of all televisions), stereo systems (9.2%), computers (10.6%), and a concentration of new technologies such as hand-held audio devices (22.9%),

TABLE 1
The location of media devices

Media device's location	*n* (rooms)	*n* (devices)	Percent of all media locations
Living room	92	778	47.8
Children's bedroom	36	173	10.6
Bedroom adult	94	145	8.9
Study	31	125	7.7
Kitchen	87	93	5.7
Hybrid room work and sleep	12	63	3.9
Hybrid room living and kitchen	10	80	4.9
Entrance	63	43	2.6
Bathroom/toilet	117	27	1.7
Other room for living	26	56	3.4
Other room in the house	26	43	2.6
Overall	594	1626	100.0

and game consoles (50.0%). Overall, the children's room shows the most diverse profile of media devices.

When focusing on one device type, one can also find interesting patterns. Computers—as a relatively new addition to the mediatope—are especially interesting here. While the study is dominated by the computer and populated with telephones and mobile phones, it is not the exclusive "home" of the computer. Although 27.1% of computers are found in the study, 23.5% are located in the living room, and 24.7% are found in bedrooms and combined bedrooms/studies (mostly in very small apartments). We also found computers in the children's room (as described earlier) and every type of room except the kitchen and bathroom. So the distribution across household environments is much more diverse than one would expect, hinting at two possible interpretations: The social "meaning" of computers might not be fixed, as the experience with them is not long (in contrast to other media, like TV, where the meaning and spatial positioning is much more rigid; see later discussion); or the computer as a multifunctional device is more pliable to various home environments.

Our observation data and the additional photographic documentation reveal that most computers have one thing in common, despite their various home rooms: They are not located in the most ergonomically convenient area. One might also interpret this in the other direction: They are a source for "pollution" of the home environment. This spatial and social positioning is most obvious when examining the studies in general, in which most computers are found. These rooms are commonly poorly organized and full of materials and devices in varying arrangements. We also coded the general impression of every observed room (according to an evaluation score);[5] one-fifth of the studies were coded as being "sloppy" or even dirty, more than any other room type (see Figure 5 for some examples).[6]

In contrast to the way in which computers are scattered throughout households in rooms without clearly organized arrangements and integration rules, TV sets are usually placed in an environment that is explicitly established for watching television in a social context. Special TV furniture was found in two-thirds of all living rooms, as well as in many other rooms. In fact, the living rooms appeared to be arranged around the TV in a rather conventional way, typically with the TV housed within a large cabinet (which we informally termed the "TV shrine") and with a large sofa facing it.

These results, together with those presented in the previous section, support existing skepticism about claims of a revolutionary change toward a new "multimedia" home (as described in the introductory section and as presented in the public relations [PR] material of media companies; see Ben Allouch et al. 2006). The home arrangements described in this study are largely traditional, and the integration of computers into everyday life remains problematic; at least, they are not currently a "central" node for the social (family) life.

Media Life Cycles: Long-Term Processes of Media Integration and Redefinition

Just like young animals in the wild, new media devices compete with older ones for survival in the home environment. As long as older devices remain in working order, users are generally reluctant to spend money on the new generation of technologies unless they perceive a considerable "value added." However, new devices are desirable, not only because they often offer enhanced functionality and usability, but also for the prestige value connected with the modern and innovative in general. So "duels" for survival develop between the new and the old, and these duels also evolve over time. As our study is device based, we are able to focus on these "duels" between old and new media devices at the level of individual devices, i.e., the actual competition situation in the domestic environment.

On a very general level, our findings reveal that the domestic environments are still marked by a dominance of standard home entertainment media: Of the 950 devices we could categorize,[7] audio and video devices were the dominant types (15.2% of the devices were TV sets, 12.5% stereo systems, 11.1% portable audio systems or "ghetto blasters," 6.3% video recorders, 5.9% DVD player). Telecommunication devices (13.3% fixed and 11.4% mobile telephones) and computer devices (6.1% desktop computers and 2.8% laptops) were still common inhabitants of the mediatopes, while photo cameras (2.8% digital cameras vs. 3.9% analogue cameras), portable entertainment devices (2.4% Walkmen, 3.0% iPods and MP3 player), and other devices were much less frequent.

It is remarkable that within each of these groups, equivalent devices coexist in old (analogue) and new (digital) technological forms. Thus, we observe a number of the already mentioned substitution "duels" between rivals such as DVD players and video recorders (currently a tie), between analogue and digital cameras (with the analogue technology leading in photography and digital technology ahead in video formats), between Walkmen/Discmen and MP3 players (with the latter winning over the older technology), and finally, between fixed and mobile phones, which are in positional parity. In terms of audio consumption, there exists a three-way competition between fixed stereo systems, portable audio systems and kitchen radios, and fully mobile devices such as Walkmen and MP3 players. These duels will be won by the "new" devices—it is just a matter of time. The age distribution of media devices clearly shows that "traditional" media generally exist in the form of very "old" devices (see Table 2).

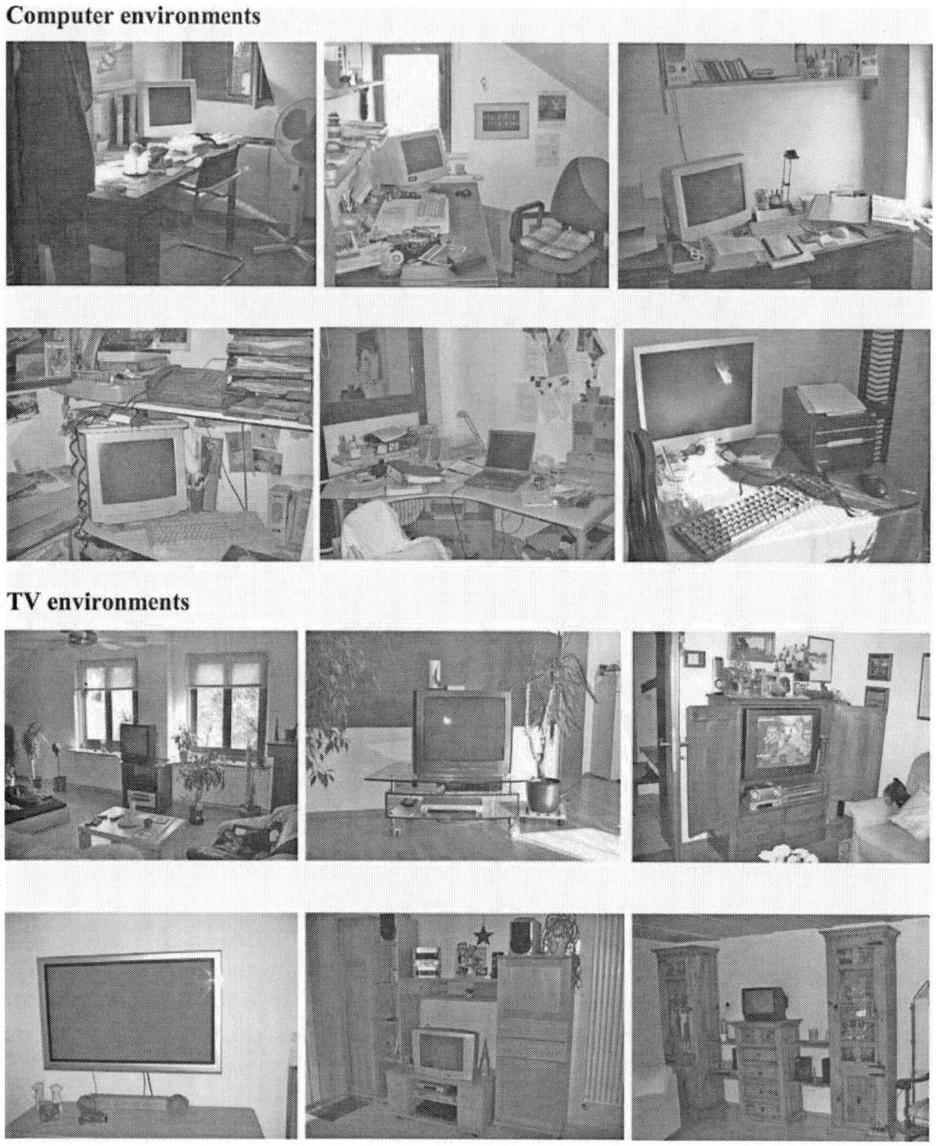

FIG. 5. Comparison of "sloppy" computer environments with prestigious TV environments (so-called "TV shrines").

One has to remember that these age groups also reflect the introduction of media technologies in some cases. While some of the "new" media can still be expected to be first-generation devices, the traditional media might well be the second, third, or fourth device of that type in the household. We therefore conclude that at least for portable audio devices, cameras, and telephones, the following years will see a general substitution throughout society of analogue equipment with digital equipment, mainly due to an inevitable generational change (based on the considerable age of the analogue devices in that category and the growing likelihood that they might simply break).

That said, some traditional media such as TVs and stereo systems appear to be seldom replaced, and are considered by consumers as long-term investments. This might also explain the industry's shift toward technologies with a more rapid generational change; however, one cannot expect equipment to be replaced unless the new technology provides an obvious advantage to the user. This effect is visible among the observed desktop computers: While the laptops found in the households were largely current models, desktop computers appeared to be older models, lagging at least one or two generations behind the current technology.

It must be remembered that the life cycle of a media device not only depends on generational changes in certain types of technological devices; it is also connected to the life of the users themselves. Thus, we find several development frames that influence the long-term process

TABLE 2
Age of media devices in the households—distribution of age groups (%, $n = 945$)

	Age of device					
Device type	< 1 year	1–2 years	2–5 years	5–10 years	>10 years	Don't know
TV	9.1	11.1	25.7	27.8	25.7	0.7
Gaming device	0.0	33.3	25.0	16.7	25.0	0.0
DVD/video	14.7	22.4	28.4	21.6	12.9	0.0
Stereo	5.9	5.0	21.8	25.2	42.0	0.0
Computer	26.2	22.6	29.8	19.0	1.2	1.2
MP3 & co.	31.2	12.5	33.3	10.4	10.4	2.1
Portable audio	4.9	7.8	17.5	20.4	49.5	0.0
Camera	40.0	30.0	25.0	5.0	0.0	0.0
Photo	25.1	21.9	25.0	15.6	12.5	0.0
PDA	66.7	0.0	33.3	0.0	0.0	0.0
Telephone	13.7	11.3	35.5	27.4	12.1	0.0
Mobile phone	30.6	38.0	26.9	4.6	0.0	0.0
Overall mean	16.4	16.9	26.8	20.0	19.6	0.3

Note. Absolute numbers have been omitted for the sake of clarity. Varying sample size (n) are due to missing answers. The "overall mean" indicates the arithmetic mean of all individual devices. As the media categories (rows of this table) sum up varying numbers of devices, the overall mean does not equal the mean of the values given for the different categories.

of domestication: One is the development of the general technology (i.e., a technology can age, like TV being a much older technology than computers, etc.), one is the individual device's own development (i.e., the device as a physical object will age), and one is the user's and the mediatope's development (i.e., the household members and competing devices will evolve and change over time as well).

This phenomenon is apparent when considering the social use of media. To get an insight into the social meaning of the media, we asked whether individual devices were used alone or in the company of others. As expected, the general distribution (see Table 3) reveals that mobile phones, computers, and laptops are to a large extent socially excluding media (in the sense already described). While portable audio devices are also mainly used alone (but to a lesser extent), stereo systems and TV sets are used in equal measures alone, with a partner and the family. Surprisingly, the social use patterns of media devices change with the age of the device, but not always in a linear fashion (see Table 4).[8]

We initially expected this trend to be primarily linked to the age of the users themselves: We imagined that very old devices would be found in the homes of the elderly, who are often widowed and living alone, thus resulting in a higher proportion of solitary use of devices. Basically, our expectation was that the media would age in tandem with their users. However, we found no clear reduction in group/partner use with increasing age; in fact, young users (under 30 years of age) appear to use media devices more often in nonsocial settings than all the older age groups.[9]

There is an explanation for this pattern, though: The trend reflects the higher number of couples, married people, and families in "middle" age groups (30 to 50 years of age), and to a lesser extent the media types used by the respective age groups (the basically "nonsocial" medium of "computer" is only used by a small percentage of those aged over 60 years, and the elderly do not use the similarly "nonsocial" mobile phones as frequently as younger age groups). These findings illustrate the importance of considering the household life cycle as a factor that is important not only for technology adoption (Brown et al. 2006), but also for its longer lasting domestication.

While the social usage of a medium is connected to its users' age, it is also linked to the device's "own" age, depending on the type of media. While portable audio devices already appear rather stable in their (non)social use in their life cycle (after the first 2 to 5 years; see Table 4), stereo sets and TVs show the aging effect that we expected: in general, the older the devices, the more often they are used alone. The reason might be the aging of the users themselves; however, as described earlier, this is not fully supported by our data. Another reason might be that the devices move from the main "social" rooms to some other environment (children's room, study, hobby room, etc.) during later phases of their lifecycle, as their place in the living room is taken by new, "next"-generation devices.

TABLE 3
Modes of social usage of media devices

	Dominant mode of social usage					
Device type	Alone	With family	With partner	With friends	Other	n
TV	29.7	28.7	39.1	2.0	0.5	202
Stereo	31.0	29.8	34.5	4.1	0.6	171
Portable audio	51.6	24.6	19.0	4.0	0.8	126
Computer	61.3	22.7	14.7	0.0	1.3	75
Laptop	81.5	7.4	7.4	3.7	0.0	27
Mobile phone	90.7	3.7	3.7	0.9	0.9	108
Overall mean	48.5	23.0	25.2	2.5	0.7	709

Note. Data are proportion of respective use type per medium, %; last column, n per media type.

Interestingly, in general, the life cycles of computers follow a much different pattern (see Table 4). New devices (up to 1 year old) are used more often in social contexts—probably because they are more commonly used as high-end gaming machines. Computers between 1 and 5 years in age are highly "unsocial" media, primarily used in work contexts and private areas. However, computers that are more than 5 years old are again used in social contexts in a much higher number of cases. Such computers seem to be used as "family machines" for surfing the Internet and acting as e-mail terminals, and they regain a somewhat more social function by losing their "workhorse" character (one selected case study illustrating this process is presented in the following subsection).

Overall, we conclude that the domestication processes do not end after the first phases of purchase and implementation into the households. The development of media in everyday settings is rather organic, and the meanings of the devices change over a long period of time, depending on the age of the device, the user's life phase, and the evolutionary process by which new devices enter the household and replace older ones.

Case Study: A Computer's Life Cycle

In this subsection, we offer a case study that exemplifies how new media technologies (in this case, a computer) can be integrated into households. It illustrates how complex this process can be. Moreover, it provides plausible explanations for the data on the social versus individual use of computers presented earlier (see previous subsection); it also shows the limitations of a purely statistical approach, supporting the call for a more integrated approach, using both qualitative and quantitative elements.

The particular computer we selected for the case analysis is located in a four-person household, with two parents (male, 38 years; female, 34 years), a daughter (15 years), and a son (12 years); both parents are working. The father is a company employee, and the mother works as a janitor; together, they have a net monthly income of approximately

TABLE 4
Change in group/partner/friends usage with age of media device

	Age of device				
Device type	<1 years	1–2 years	2–5 years	5–10 years	>10 years
TV	70.0	70.8	80.0	71.2	56.8
Stereo	71.4	92.3	65.8	73.5	62.5
Portable audio	66.7	80.0	37.5	48.3	49.2
Computer	40.0	15.4	32.0	58.8	66.7

Note. Data are percentage of media devices with the dominant use modes "with partner/family/friends," %, $n = 574$. Values represent the accumulated percentage of group/family/friends use of a given medium, based on cases with age information. The "overall mean" is not indicated here, because it equals 100% minus the use form "alone" as given in Table 3. Mobile phones and laptops have been excluded from the analysis, as they were nearly always used alone (see Table 3).

FIG. 6. Location of the family computer in the case study household.

2500 Euros. Both of them hold a secondary school qualification (Mittlere Reife). When asked about their perception of their class orientation, they both responded as regarding themselves as "working class." The family lives in a rented apartment.

We found the family's computer in a corner of the living room, which was surprising at first sight. The room also contains the usual pictures on the wall, a TV set, some books, and a stereo system (see Figure 6). The computer is clearly an "integrated" part of this typical German working class living-room arrangement, and, as it turned out, is used by the whole family, in the contexts of both individual use and groups.

When asked how the computer came into the household, the owners could only remember that it was "a gift long ago." The machine is more than 5 years old and is a brand computer. It was initially located in the study (which is the more probable location for a computer); however, when it became older and too slow for demanding uses, it was moved to the living room to become a "family" device, primarily used for surfing the Internet, listening to radio via the Internet, browsing digital photographs, and sometimes writing letters. Listening to Internet radio and browsing photographs are the uses that are most readily integrated into the living-room routines, where several persons participate in the use of the machine. While the machine is used by all household members, it is only of minor interest to them; accordingly, it receives approximately 30 minutes to 1 hour of daily use time per family member.

Now this is a typical "niche" description, and clearly shows what redefinition of machines can mean in "real life." Basically, after its "first" life as a new (and probably expensive) brand "workhorse" computer, the aging machine is given a new identity as a family machine and is completely reinterpreted in a new environment with new user profiles. The current use will inevitably end at some stage, perhaps when the machine is too slow for occasional Web surfing or Internet radio—at this stage, the domestication life cycle will come to a "natural" end.

DISCUSSION: MEDIATOPE DEVELOPMENT AND THE COMPLEXITY OF THE SOCIAL

The media industry has developed many plans to conquer the domestic space with new devices, ranging from the "smart home" to the "digital hub," focusing on links between media technology and household life. Recent proposals feature increasingly specialized, intelligent devices that fit into household contexts instead of making everyday life fit around the media. With the domestication approach, there is already a fruitful theoretical basis for analyzing how new media become part of the domestic space. Here, media technologies are not seen as solely functional "tools," but also as vehicles for the symbolic process of meaning production.

This approach so far has mostly been applied for insightful case studies of very specific environments and user activities. The perspective sheds light on domestication of individual technologies but does not allow comparison of different patterns of domestication, which vary with individual persons, media technologies, and social contexts. While every household is different as suggested by existing domestication research, one would expect to observe some common phenomena in the domestication process.

In this article, we sought to identify aspects of domestication common to various households and factors that influence different realizations of domestication processes across households. With this goal in mind, we have added new elements to the domestication approach and structured some of its elements, namely, in the form of the triangular model that permits identification of critical and in most cases measurable characteristics on household, individual user, and technology. This approach complements existing holistic approaches on media use and domestication in the household by permitting a quantitative perspective on the household and its various mediatopes.

As such, it contributes to the knowledge generated by the existing domestication research. It not only traces the theoretically postulated process during which the meaning of media is defined and redefined, sometimes even erased, but also identifies higher level trends and exceptions to the "rules" generated by domestication research, for various phases of the domestication process.

It became obvious that during the pre-adoption and adoption phases, both the perceived technological functionalities and symbolic values of devices play a central role; however, not all devices are created equal. For some devices, functional aspects are much more important, whereas others are chosen primarily on the basis of their design and social value.

Once the devices enter the household, they are physically (and socially) woven into the fabric of the domestic space. Our study shows that the spatial dimension should not be neglected here: Media capacities and profiles correspond to the social functions of their "home" rooms, and this is also reflected in the respective use patterns.

However, the meanings of the devices are not fixed: We observed long-term "media life cycles," including the theoretically postulated redefinition processes. While the meanings of some media devices approach a "closure" very soon after their introduction into the household, others keep evolving, sometimes "forced" by competition with new additions to the media ecosystem. The resulting domestication "duels" are fought both within and between various device "species": As "new" media species begin to dominate certain environments, others are moved to other niches where they are able to survive—or they disappear completely. In this way, a device's life cycle is determined by many factors in combination: the development of the "base technology" (i.e., the development of the family of devices, like "laptops in general"), the mediatope's timeframe (including household and user changes, as well as the development of competing media in the household), and its own aging process.

Overall, our study paints a picture of an evolving, "living" media world within the domestic environment of the household. However, a number of theoretical and methodological limitations remain. First, the biological metaphor applied here cannot be taken literally, and the analogies to organisms should not be stretched too far: Media devices do not have their own rationality—their social and functional logic is defined by the surrounding mediatopes, the users, and the original design of the technology and not by themselves, as they do not have agency. Second, while our study deliberately focused on devices and technologies, one should not forget that relinking these findings to the social use context is crucial in media and communication studies. We already mentioned one of these links; for example, an analysis of media environments could be related to milieu studies by analyzing in more detail the integration of media technologies in various subgroups. Third, further development of the ideas presented here should take into account the blending of spaces brought about by mobile technologies and complex media, such as personal computers, which generate their own virtual space, as predetermined by installed operating systems and user preferences (cf. Bakardieva & Smith 2001).

A "media topology," based on combined surveys and qualitative studies, is a promising project for future research—we could just scratch the surface in this article. Domestication-based approaches offer many more possibilities here, as in times of rapid development in media technologies, a closer look at the integration of these technologies into the lives of the users becomes increasingly relevant. When media environments are undergoing rapid change, the framework for connected questions such as media use and effects is also altered. Therefore, the study of mediatope evolution is not only an interesting topic but also essential for strengthening the foundations of media and communication research.

NOTES

1. The concept of "household head" may appear anachronistic in an age where households are managed in team work without hierarchy. However, it fulfilled two pragmatic functions: In first hand, it enabled us to fit our quota sample to the official data of the "Mikrozensus" which employs a definition of "household head" as the person who has the highest income within the household. Secondly, it helped identify an individual with high knowledge about the history of the household and it's media.

2. Given the nature of the sample, we mostly use simple descriptive statistics throughout this piece, as we believe that the use of inferential statistics would be somewhat misleading. The household sample has been hand picked on the basis of the quota, and its fairly small (even if it is large when compared to other observation studies). Furthermore, even if some of the results are based on a high number of cases (especially the analysis of media devices), one should not forget that these are clustered (inside households). So basically, the statistics used here are just a description of a very special data material "as it is"; any further conclusions are based on argumentation, not on mathematical inference.

3. All participants gave their consent prior to the study. Anonymity of the participants was ensured in all parts of the study.

4. The interviews on purchase criteria were only realized with the household heads. This limitation is due to the fact that it was not possible to realize in-depth interviews with all household members out of research practical reasons. Therefore, we cannot exclude that the purchase criteria of other family members (for their personally chosen devices) actually deviate from what is indicated by the household heads as the main reason.

5. Coders were trained to agree on the evaluation scores. Furthermore, anchor examples and descriptions in the code book helped them to rate in the same way, and we checked the codings based on the photographs taken in the field.

6. The reliability of such an item is debatable; however, on the basis of the photos we were able to conclude that the coding was consistent. Some of the "sloppy" rooms even contained significant amounts of trash and old food on the computer tables.

7. Storage media (like DVDs, CDs etc.)—while also being coded—were excluded from the analysis here.

8. As this is not a longitudinal study, we were unable to observe the aging of the devices themselves; however, we were able to analyze devices of a certain type during different phases of their life cycle. We are aware that these results must be viewed with caution, as they still stem from a "one-shot" sample.

9. A per-device analysis of the social or solitary use by the respective users revealed that on an average, 56.5% percent of the use by people under 30 years was solitary, while in the next age group (up to

45 years), the solitary use just reached 44.9%, in the group up to 60 years 39.2%, and in the group above 60 years 55.7%.

REFERENCES

Aldrich, F. K. 2003. Smart homes: Past, present and future. In *Inside the smart home*, ed. R. Harper, 17–39. London: Springer.

Arber, S. 2001. Designing samples. In *Researching social life*, ed. Nigel Gilbert, 58–82. Thousand Oaks, CA: Sage.

Bakardjeva, M., and R. Smith. 2001. The Internet in everyday life. Computer networking from the standpoint of the domestic user. *New Media and Society* 3(1):67–83.

Baldwin, T. F., D. S. McVoy, and C. Steinfield. 1996. *Convergence: Integrating media, information & communication*. Thousand Oaks, CA: Sage.

Ben Allouch, S., J. A. Van Dijk, and O. Peters. 2006. *Presenting the networked home: A content analysis of promotion material of ambient intelligence applications*. Paper presented at the Annual Conference of the International Communication Association (ICA). Dresden, Germany, June 19–23.

Berker, T., M. Hartmann, Y. Punie, and K. Ward, eds. 2006. *Domestication of Media and Technology.* Maidenhead, UK: Open University Press.

Bourdieu, P. 1979. *Distinction: A social critique of judgement.* London: Routledge.

Brown, S., V. Venkatesh, and H. Bala. 2006. Household technology use: Integrating household life cycle and the model of adoption of technology in households. *The Information Society* 22(4): 205–18.

Denzin, N. K., and Y. S. Lincoln. 2005. *Handbook of qualitative research.* Thousand Oaks, CA: Sage.

Dimmick, J. W. 2003. *Media competition and coexistence. The theory of the niche.* Hillsdale, NJ: Lawrence Erlbaum Associates.

Fortunati, L. 2002. The mobile phone: Towards new categories and social relations. *Information Communication & Society* 5(4):513–28.

Frissen, V. A. 2000. ICTs in the rush hour of life. *The Information Society* 16(1):65–75.

Gergen, K. J. 2002. The challenge of absent presence. In *Perpetual contact: Mobile communication, private talk, public performance*, ed. J. Katz and M. Aakhus, 227–41. Cambridge: Cambridge University Press.

Haddon, L. 1992. Explaining ICT consumption: The case of the home computer. In *Consuming technologies: Media and information in domestic spaces,* ed. R. Silverstone and E. Hirsch, 82–96. London: Routledge.

Haddon, L. 2003. Domestication and mobile telephony. In *Machines that become us: The social context of personal communication technology*, ed. J. E. Katz, 43–56. New Brunswick, NJ: Transaction.

Haddon, L. 2006. The contribution of domestication research to in-home computing and media consumption. *The Information Society* 22(4):195–203.

Haddon, L., and R. Silverstone. 1994. The careers of information and communication technologies in the home. In *Proceedings of the International Working Conference on Home Oriented Informatics, Telematics and Automation,* ed. K. Bjerg and K. Borreby, http://www.mot.chalmers.se/dept/tso/haddon/Hoit.pdf (accessed April 7, 2008).

Haddon, L., and J. Vincent. 2004. *Managing a communications repertoire: Mobile vs landline.* Fifth Wireless World Conference Managing Communications University of Surrey, 15–16 July.

Harper, R. ed. 2003. *Inside the smart home*. London: Springer UK.

Hartmann, M. 2006. The triple articulation of ICTs. Media as technological objects, symbolic environments and individual texts. In *Domestication of media and technology,* ed. T. Berker, M. Hartmann, Y. Punie, and K. Ward, 80–102. Maidenhead, UK: Open University Press.

Hirsch, E. 1992. The long term and the short term of domestic consumption: An ethnographic case study. In *Consuming Technologies*, ed. R Silverstone and E. Hirsch, 208–26. London: Routledge.

Kopytoff, I. 1986. The cultural biography of things: commoditization as a process. In *The social life of things: Commodities in cultural perspective*, ed. A. Appadurai, 64–94. Cambridge, MA: Cambridge University Press.

Latour, B., and S. Woolgar. 1979. *Laboratory life: The social construction of scientific facts.* London: Sage.

Lehtonen, T.-K. 2003. The domestication of new technologies as a set of trials. *Journal of Consumer Culture* 3(3):363–85.

Licoppe, C. 2004. 'Connected' presence: The emergence of a new repertoire for managing social relationships in a changing communication technoscape. *Environment and Planning D: Society and Space* 22(1):135–56.

Ling, R. 2000. "We will be reached": The use of mobile telephony among Norwegian youth. *Information Technology and People* 13(2):102–20.

Livingstone, S. 2007. On the material and the symbolic: Silverstone's double articulation of research traditions in new media studies. *New Media and Society* 9(1):16–24.

Livingstone, S., and M. Bovill, eds. 2001. *Children and their changing media environment: A European comparative study*. Hillsdale, NJ: Lawrence Erlbaum Associates.

MacKenzie, D.A., and J. Wajcman. 1985. *The Social Shaping of Technology: How the Refrigerator got its Hum.* Philadelphia: Open University Press.

Mansell, R. 1996. Communication by design. In *Communication by design*, ed. R. Mansell and R. Silverstone, 15–43. Oxford: Oxford University Press.

McLuhan, M. 1964. *Understanding media. The extensions of man.* New York: McGraw-Hill.

Mill, J. S. 1973. *A system of logic: Ratiocinative and inductive*. Toronto: University of Toronto Press.

Nora, S., and A. Minc. 1978. *L'informatisation de la société.* Paris: Seuils.

Otte, G. 2004. *Sozialstrukturanalyse mit Lebensstilen*. Opladen: Leske + Budrich.

Pinch, T., and W. Bijker. 1987. The social construction of facts and artefacts. Or: How the sociology of science and the sociology of technology might benefit each other. In *The social construction of technological systems,* ed. W. Bijker, T. P. Hughes, and T. Pinch, 17–50. Cambridge, MA: MIT Press.

Postman, N. 2000. The humanism of media ecology. In *Proceedings of the Media Ecology Association*, ed. J. Sternberg and M. Lipton, 10–16. http://www.media-ecology.org/publications/MEA_proceedings/v1/postman01.pdf (accessed June 10, 2010).

Ragin, C. C. 1987. *The comparative method; Moving beyond qualitative and quantitative strategies.* Berkeley: University of California Press.

Silverstone, R. 2006. Domesticating domestication. Reflections on the life of a concept. In *Domestication of media and technology,* eds. T. Berker, M. Hartmann, Y. Punie, and K. Ward, 229–48. Maidenhead, UK: Open University Press.

Silverstone, R., and L. Haddon 1996. Design and the domestication of information and communication technologies: Technical change and everyday life. In *Communication by design. The politics of information and communication technologies*, ed. R. Silverstone and R. Mansell, 44–74. Oxford: Oxford University Press.

Silverstone, R., and E. Hirsch. 1992. *Consuming Technologies.* London: Routledge.

Silverstone, R., E. Hirsch, and D. Morley. 1992. Information and communication technologies and the moral economy of the household. In *Consuming technology. Media and information in domestic spaces,* ed. R. Silverstone and E. Hirsch, 115–31. London: Routledge.

Sørensen, K. H. 2006. Domestication: The enactment of technology. In *Domestication of media and technology,* ed. T. Berker, M. Hartmann, Y. Punie, and K. Ward, 40–61. Maidenhead, UK: Open University Press.

Taylor, A., and R. Harper. 2003. Switching on to switch off. In *Inside the smart home*, ed. R. Harper, 115–26. London: Springer.

Tolmie, P., J. Pycock, T. Diggins, A. MacLean, and A. Karsenty. 2003. Towards the unremarkable computer: Making technology at home in domestic routine. In *Inside the smart home* ed. R. Harper, 183–206. London: Springer.

Venkatesh, A., E. Kruse, and E. C.-F. Shih. 2003. The networked home: An analysis of current developments and future trends. *Cognition, Technology and Work* 5(1):23–32.

Verschuren, P. J. 2001. Holism versus reductionism in modern social science research. *Quality & Quantity* 35:389–405.

Wajcman, J. 2008. Life in the fast lane? Towards a sociology of technology and time. *British Journal of Sociology* 59(1):59–79.

Wajcman, J., M. Bittman, and J. Brown. 2008. Families without borders: Mobile phones, connectedness and work–home divisions. *Sociology* 42(4):635–52.

Ward, K. 2006. The bald guy just ate an orange. Domestication, work and the home. In *Domestication of media and technologies*, ed. M. Hartmann, T. Berker, T. Y. Punie, and K. Ward, 107–123. Maidenhead, UK: Open University Press.

Weiser, M. 1993.*Ubiquitous computing*, http://www.ubiq.com/hypertext/weiser/UbiCompHotTopics.html (accessed April 7, 2008).

Williams, R., and D. Edge. 1996. The social shaping of technology. *Research Policy* 25:865–99.

Wirth, W., T. von Pape, and V. Karnowski. 2008. An integrative model of mobile phone appropriation. *Journal of Computer-Mediated Communication* 13:593–617.

Mobilising Poverty?: Mobile Phone Use and Everyday Spatial Mobility Among Low-Income Families in Santiago, Chile

Sebastian Ureta

Instituto de Sociología, Pontificia Universidad Católica de Chile, Santiago, Chile

In the last few decades physical mobility has become one of the key elements of contemporary societies. This centrality of mobility also means the development of a new kind of social exclusion caused by the problems of living in a social context in which one has to be increasingly "on the move" to access goods and services. In this article, based on fieldwork conducted with 20 low-income family inhabitants of the city of Santiago, Chile, we study the role that mobile phone usage has in relation to physical mobility in the everyday lives of these individuals. Through an analysis of the pattern of usage and mobility of these devices, we arrive at the conclusion that rather than giving rise to an experience of constant mobility and "anytime–anywhere" availability, the individuals studied face limitations and exclusions that profoundly constrict the potential "mobility" afforded by these devices.

It has been said that we live in a "mobile society" (Urry 2000). Different kinds of mobilities are at the very centre of the experience of living in contemporary society. From the availability of foreign produced clothes or food to the global adoption of concepts like citizenship or human rights, living in a modern society means having access to a vast amount of nonlocal material and immaterial products, symbols, and ideas. On the other hand, this mobile society also generates new kinds of social exclusion, mainly as a result of physical immobility (on this subject see Cass et al., 2005; Hannam et al., 2006; Kenyon et al., 2002). This is due to the fact that individuals, objects, and ideas that have problems in being mobile are less likely to participate in a social order in which constant mobility constitutes one of the main elements around which the social dynamic is structured. As Zygmunt Bauman said, "immobility is not a realistic option in a world of permanent change" (1998, p. 12). Being immobile means being left behind, and its negative consequences can be seen from the most banal aspects of everyday life to international indicators regarding social exclusion and human development.

But physical mobility is not the only way in which we can be "on the move" in contemporary society. While bearing in mind that some physical mobility is always needed (Boden & Molotch, 1994), hypothetically a certain amount of this movement can be replaced by the use of media technologies. Among them, mobile phones appear especially important in enhancing the individual's capabilities of acting-at-a-distance without the need to be physically "on the move." As the relevant literature in the field, based on research conducted mostly in developed societies, has shown, mobile phones are frequently used to overcome problems related to physical distance and mobility of people, allowing them to enlarge their area of practices and maintain connections outside the immediate space of their homes, work, and other local areas (Brown et al., 2001; Fortunati, 2001, 2002; Glotz et al., 2005; Ito et al., 2005; Katz, 2003; Katz & Aakhus, 2002; Ling, 2004; Ling & Pedersen, 2005; Nyiri, 2005).

But what happens when we shift the focus from developed to developing societies? As a growing body of research based in countries like Jamaica (Horst & Miller, 2006), Ghana (Slater & Kwami, 2005), Rwanda (Donner, 2005), and the Philippines (Pertierra et al., 2002) has shown, the meaning and usage of mobile phones among these populations do not follow the same trends as in the developed world. Such research offers consistent evidence that we cannot simply apply theoretical models produced elsewhere to the understanding of the dynamics and meanings of mobile phone usage among low-income groups. This research shows how "mediated communication takes place at a specific time and place, imbuing it with all the contingencies that it implies" (Aakhus, 2003, p. 40).

In this article we pursue one broad research question in relation to mobile phones in Chile: Can we find any relationships between mobile phone usage and the levels of spatial mobility among low-income population? We consequently analyze mobile phone use in the everyday life of a group of low-income families in the city of Santiago, Chile—the country with the highest penetration per capita of mobile phones in Latin America—focusing particularly on the relationship between this usage and their everyday physical mobility.

FIELDWORK AND METHODS

We conducted fieldwork over 10 months in 2004 in an urban location in the city of Santiago, Chile. We studied 20 low-income families, inhabitants of a social housing estate, "Tucapel Jimenez II," located on the western edge of the borough of Renca, which sits on the northwestern edge of Santiago. It has been inhabited since June 2002 and is composed of 876 flats.

Around half of these 20 families came from different shantytowns or *campamentos*[1] in the borough of Renca. The living conditions in these *campamentos* were very basic, especially in terms of the quality of housing and in terms of access to social services such as health and education. The other half of the families used to live in Renca or in other neighboring boroughs and had previously lived with their extended families (especially parents) in highly overcrowded houses, a condition known as *allegamiento* or backyard accommodation.

The families under study can be characterized mostly as young adult couples (with an average age of 35) who have on average around 2.8 children with an average age of 10. None of the parents has university or technical education and only 68% finished secondary education. For this reason, the majority work in jobs such as security personnel, taxi drivers, blue-collar workers, etc., and the levels of integration of women into the formal labor market is still very low. Only in two families did both parents have permanent jobs.

In terms of methods, the research was based primarily on in-depth interviews and observation. It mainly consisted of three stages of interviews with all the adult members of the 20 families selected, talking about their life in the housing estate, especially in terms of their adaptation to their new living space (at the moment of the fieldwork they had only been living there for a year and a half) and their use of media technologies in this process. This material was complemented with more general information about the housing estate and the living conditions of low-income population in Santiago, in order to set a general framework for the analysis.

NEW TECHNOLOGIES FOR A NEW LIFE

It is not difficult to see the movement to the housing estate as the starting point of a new life for these families. In many ways their former places of living, both shantytowns and a situation of *allegamiento*, resembled to a great degree the living conditions in rural communities rather than the kind of life associated with urban environments in contemporary societies. They lived on some sort of small and relatively isolated islands in the middle of a far bigger urban environment.

This relative isolation was worsened by their lack of the key technology of urban personal communication: the landline telephone. While they gained access relatively rapidly to other media technologies, such as television or radios, landline telephone was much slower to arrive at low-income households. As data from the Chilean Census show, in 2002 only a small proportion (4.9%) of the poorest 20% of urban households had access to a landline telephone (Larrañaga, 2004). But the slow acquisition of this technology was not only caused by their low incomes and the reluctance of telephone companies to provide telephone lines to low-income areas. There were other, more personal, reasons too.

Most of the families under study used to live in close spatial proximity with the members of their social networks, especially relatives, a situation that is quite common among low-income city dwellers in Chile (Espinoza, 1999). In these circumstances, it was not strange for them to perceive the telephone as relatively unnecessary, as some sort of luxury.

David (33 years old), Alicia (40 years old), and their three children were one of the families under study with a better financial situation. Before coming to the housing estate they used to rent a small flat in the borough of Lo Prado, located in the same building as David's parents and one brother. Alicia's parents also live nearby. They used to have a landline telephone in the flat, but it wasn't really important for them, as David said:

> We used to have a telephone in the flat we rented. I use it more now. When we had a telephone in the house we never called anyone. We paid more for keeping the service than for the calls that we made. We were reluctant to use the telephone because we saw each other regularly. Who were we going to call? We never called anyone. It wasn't important, but now it is important.

This situation was not unique to David's family. For most of the families under study, they were for the first time completely on their own—not only in terms of not having their relatives around in the neighbourhood but also in the basic experience of living in a home only with their nuclear family—after they moved to their flats in the housing estate. Some of them have found this distance to be a distressing experience; others have experienced it as liberating. In

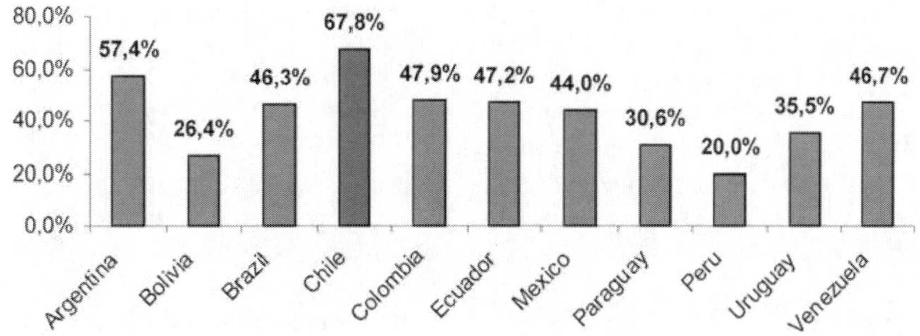

FIG. 1. Mobile phone subscribers in Latin America (2005). Source: World Telecommunications Indicators (ITU, 2005).

any case, now the management of the spatial distance with their social networks became a central issue.

But in overcoming this growing distance they have to deal with another characteristic of low-income city dwellers: their low levels of (and capabilities for) everyday physical mobility. As has been widely shown, both internationally (Church et al., 2000; Graham & Marvin, 2001; Kenyon et al., 2002) and in Chile (SECTRA, 2002; Ureta, 2006), low-income populations move less than any other group of the population. The reasons for such immobility are varied,[2] but they all produce the result that everyday movement for these individuals, especially if it is not related to work or education, is mostly limited to walking distances.

All these changes were accompanied by the growing availability and drop in prices of mobile phone handsets and services in the country. As can be seen in Figure 1, the percentage of mobile subscribers in Chile is the biggest in the Latin American context, reaching 67.8% of the population in 2005. Along with this, the country has comparatively the lowest rates for monthly mobile telephone services in the region (Barrantes et al., 2006). As a result of both high availability and lower prices, even low-income groups can access mobile telephones to the extent that in 2005, 55% of the low-income population in the city reported that they had access to a mobile phone in their homes (PNUD, 2006).

These relatively low prices, the growing distance within their social networks, and low physical mobility meant that the perception of the telephone as unimportant or too expensive changed radically in their new housing situation. While some of these families had mobile phones before moving to the housing estate, the move itself changed the status of the handsets in their minds from luxury to necessity. Now mobile phones not only represent an expensive toy or a way to be in contact when they are "on the move," but more centrally mobile phones seem to be the only reliable and affordable way through which the families can have permanent access to their now distant networks, especially the homes of their relatives. This was especially true given the refusal of telephone companies to provide private landline access to the flats of the estate, at least at the time when the fieldwork was carried out, and the relative scarcity of public pay phones in the housing estate (just 3 inside an estate of 876 flats).

The families under study were acutely aware of this situation. Ines, a married 30-year-old mother of three, used to live with her family in a shantytown in the borough of La Pintana, quite far away from the housing estate. There she used to share the same plot of land with her mother and the families of her two sisters. For this reason the movement to the housing estate was very difficult for her; it was the first time in her life that she was far away from her relatives, and she could not travel to visit them as frequently as she wanted due to their precarious financial situation. In this situation, their mobile phone was the only way for maintaining frequent contact with her relatives.

> Maybe if we had another way to communicate, if we lived closer, the mobile would be like a decoration or something not very useful, but it's useful. It's necessary. Through the mobile you know what is happening. You don't worry 'is she all right? Is she having trouble? Is my mother at home? How have things turned out?' With the mobile I have no need to be there in order to know.

For her, as for many others, the mobile phone handset generates a sensation of closeness-over-distance, even if it is not actively used. Relatives and friends are not far away if they can be reached by using mobile phones, especially if people are in a situation of need.

Although the arrival of mobile phones to these homes could imply many changes in the way home communications are managed, especially in contrast with landline phones (for a good comparison between landline and mobile telephones see Lasen 2005), here we concentrate on one particular aspect: the relationship between the use of the devices and the families' everyday spatial mobility.

MOBILE PHONE USAGE IN EVERYDAY LIFE

The perception just described, regarding the centrality of mobile phones, is not matched by a frequent use of these devices in the everyday lives of the people in this study. Our research suggests that there is, from the beginning, a significant distance between the perception of the mobile phones as important in everyday communications and the actual use that the families under study make of their mobile telephones. As Paola, a 32-year-old housewife and mother of three, told us during one conversation about her use of her mobile phone:

> I don't speak on the telephone because we do not have a [prepaid] card, but my mother calls me, sometimes. She's very bad at speaking on the telephone, especially on a mobile because it hurts her to spend her [prepaid] card. For example now she has been calling more often because my daughter is sick. She has called me three times this week, but if there's no reason she won't call me. Sometimes I have 100 pesos [U$0.20] and I call her on a public phone, but this is once a week, no more.

Paola's husband Carlos, the only source of regular income for the family, was unemployed at the time of the interviews, so they had to restrict most of the expenditures, among them telephone bills. But even in the case of families with both parents working, the situation was not different and the amount of money they could devote to mobile usage was always limited.

The payment system used by most of the families was prepaid cards. Each card cost between 3,000 (U$6) and 5,000 (U$10) Chilean pesos and the families under study tended to use one per month. However, it was not uncommon to find families whose expenditure was even less than this, just the minimum of one card every 6 months to enable them to keep receiving calls, as Chile hasa "Calling Party Pays" (CPP) system.[3]

As a result of this low expenditure, there was always a limited amount of credit available for making calls through their handsets. The interviewees, with one exception, reported that their mobile usage was always restricted because of lack of funds. They only make necessary calls with their mobiles. Even in these cases their use of mobiles is highly restricted, forcing them to develop strategies—mainly extremely short calls and the use of *pinchazos*[4] —to keep costs at the lowest possible.

In relation to the first strategy, extremely short calls, Diego (39 years old) recalled in one of the conversations that

> Every time I talk I'm quite conscious of time because of the cost, every minute is expensive. I don't relax, even on the landline, there's always something that makes you hurry, seeing the costs. If I talk for 10 minutes I know that I'm paying 300 pesos per minute, that's 3000 pesos. This is what I think, with the cost of everything we are in a hurry. As the cost of living is going up, we are under pressure when speaking on the phone. I have some minutes so I speak to my stepfather, 'Hello stepfather, how are you?' and that's it. With the phone, you have all the time here [he points to his head], you're controlling yourself, but it's difficult and then they say to you 'why are you this way? You're mean; you only give me one minute.' No, why should we talk [more]? We see each other every weekend, so knowing that he's all right is enough, that there's no problem.

Therefore for him, as for many others, the first strategy for dealing with this shortage of resources is simply to concentrate the information in the smallest amount of time possible. One consequence of this practice is that the time for communication acquires a new meaning for the users of the device. There is an internalization of time as a scarce resource, which Diego displayed by pointing to his head while talking about how conscious he is of time when talking on the mobile. Although this tendency to assign a monetary value to time is one of the defining features of contemporary societies (Adam, 1990; Nowotny, 1994), this monetization of communicative time was new for the families under study, especially in their relations with their relatives and friends, as the following extract from one of the interviews with Alicia shows (40 years old):

> [On the mobile phone] you have to talk only the necessary time, no more, enough and precise ... in fact when you have finished talking you start asking yourself 'did I spend one minute? Did I spend two minutes talking?' It is as if you become more materialistic with the mobile, as if *time becomes more visible*. In fact you lose values that you shouldn't lose, because the question should be regarding the conversation that you had with them and not the time that you spent talking; so it [mobile communication] is not good in this respect. (emphasis added)

As discussed in the previous section, in their former places of residence these families used to live in close spatial proximity to their social networks, especially relatives. Also, their low levels of integration into the labor market and low educational enrollment meant that they spent a high proportion of their time at home, commonly with their relatives around them. In these circumstances the flow of communication between members of the network was extensive and rich. This situation changed with the move to the housing estate and the increasingly telephonically mediated communication with their networks. As Alicia clearly identifies, now communication with relatives does not mean a constant interchange of messages among ever-present ones but the making of expensive phone calls to faraway places, with the result that, as Alicia sees it, communication time "becomes more visible"; it appears on the horizon of experience as a scarce resource. In most of the cases time appears as a concern as central as content, forcing them to reduce communication time to the very minimum necessary to reach a certain degree of understanding.

Along with extremely short calls, a second tactic developed by the families under study to reduce the costs related to mobile use is known as *pinchar* or *pinchazo* (literally meaning "prick"). It consists of calling a known number, waiting for a few beeps, and then hanging up and eventually waiting for the receiver to call back. Similar practices, for both mobiles and landline phones, have been found in other developing societies such as Rwanda (Donner, 2005) and Ghana (Slater & Kwami, 2005) and also in developed societies such as Australia (Carroll et al., 2002) and Finland (Kasesniemi & Rautiainen, 2002), especially among children and teenagers.

Cristina was 42 years old and single. She lived in the same flat with her daughter, her daughter's partner, and two grandchildren. At the time of the interview she had been unemployed for more than a year, with the result that her financial situation was quite critical, because only her daughter's partner had a regular income. For this reason she needed frequent financial help from her father, who lived in another area of the city. In order for her to be in constant contact with him without spending money on phone calls they have developed a system:

> With my father we always use [this system]. I call him, wait for two or three beeps and then I hang up and he said to me 'you are shameless, why don't you spend [money on the telephone]?' 'No dad, because you're not going to give me back this money' [laughs]. I use it only to receive calls. I only use it in emergencies.

But this tactic was not used solely to save money on calls. Ruth (40), who had a relatively good income, told us that she also used beeping to be in contact with her husband, but for a very different reason:

> Sometimes [the communication] is just 'pinchazos,' if he's working I beep him once in order for him to call home on the mobile.

So *pinchar* appears to be a practice motivated not only by financial matters but also for the need to be in "permanent contact," even at times when you are not supposed to be talking on the phone, like at work.

This practice, unlike text messaging, "has no content; it rarely stands on its own without some contextual cues to back it up" (Donner, 2005, p. 10). The *pinchazo* needs a previous common understanding, something that is difficult to agree on with people who are not very close. As a consequence, one cannot *pinchar* just anyone. The person with whom you use *pinchazos* has to be someone close to you, usually someone from your closest social network, such as your father as in the case of Cristina or your husband as with Alicia.

As a result of both practices, mobile communication tends to remain within the closest networks, mostly relatives living in other areas of the city, seeming to reinforce the connection with people who are known personally, as a kind of nonpresent "personalized network" (Wellman, 2001) or a "telecocoon," using the term developed by Habuchi (2005), rather than opening up the network to new connections. In this sense our findings are similar to what Horst and Miller (2005) call "link-up," a form of communication through mobile phones, characteristic of low-income populations, in which "the most important element is not the content of conversations but their use to maintain connections over time" (p. 760). This form of communication is similar to what the Russian linguist Roman Jakobson (1984) identified as the "phatic" function of language that only serves to establish or maintain contact between the speakers, regardless of its particular content. In many cases this way of communication not only complements direct or face-to-face communication, but almost completely replaces it, as seen in the study with relatives and friends who lived in other cities or in other areas of Santiago. Mobile phones frequently constitute not only a tool for managing faraway social networks, but also the vehicle permitting its existence.

This movement from face-to-face to "mobile" mediated communication is not without costs. In practice this change from extended conversation to "link-up" is experienced as a loss of frequency and quality in their communication with their social networks. For example, Rosa, a 32-year-old mother of two, told us:

> Sadly as it's pre-paid, I have to be conscious of the time passing. I have to speak very fast otherwise it would be too expensive. This mobile eats up the minutes too fast. . . . I'm always very conscious to just say the necessary and I can't take any liberties. . . . This affects communication, because it is frivolous, too cold, 'Hello, how are you? That's good, bye!,' too fast, too tough and as it's expensive so you are in a hurry. On the landline you can have the luxury of talking longer because it's cheaper. What I say on a normal telephone I have to say in less than half the time on the mobile.

As Rosa clearly recognizes, the very limited use of the mobile phones means that communication becomes more strategically and explicitly goal-oriented; it becomes, in Rosa's words, "frivolous, too cold . . . too fast, too tough."

This perception is not limited to their extended families. When their relationships with their intimate networks became telephonically mediated, people also perceived an impoverishment in the communication:

> I call him [her partner] very little, only for urgent stuff, if the mobile rings and it's me he gets worried, the first thing he says is 'what happened?'; so I cannot call him to say 'I love you' or 'have a nice day,' I cannot call him for that. (Alejandra, 36 years)

From a phenomenological standpoint, we can say that in the case under study the mobile systemizes the real world, "replacing meanings with messages, consensus with instructions and insight with information" (Myerson, 2001, quoted in McGuigan, 2005, p. 55). In effect, mobile communications, in comparison with their former situation, impoverish the connections between the families under study and their nonpresent social networks.

MOBILE PHONES AND SPATIAL MOBILITY

In addition to cost constraints that limit use, we see very limited physical mobility of the handsets. This limited mobility can be partially explained by the fact that, as we saw earlier, mobile phones were the only phones present in the homes and often these households had only one handset. Thus, in contrast to developed countries where mobile telephones are the ultimate personal technology (Ito et al., 2005; Ling, 2004), for these households their mobile phones were essentially a family device, not mainly the property of one private individual but a collective good, as Cristian (age 38) clearly recognizes:

> The mobile belongs to all of us . . . We bought this mobile when Marcos was at the hospital. When Marcos left the hospital we left it here. Everyone uses it, for example if Paula needs to give a phone number, she gives this number, and I do the same, all of us.

In terms of spatial mobility this collective nature of the mobile means that it cannot move if the family, or at least its central node, does not move with it. In the cases under study this central node was commonly the mother. The mothers are the ones who interface with distant social networks:

> Thanks to the mobile I'm in contact with the rest of the world, because my mother now lives in Lo Barnechea [at the other end of Santiago], but thanks to the mobile I can find her and know how she is and if something is happening to her. [The mobile] shortens the spaces, the times, everything. (Patricia, 30 years)

They are also the communication link within a family, especially between a parent absent at work and the children:

> It is important, especially here [in the housing estate], the mobile is fundamental, because if I haven't got one I would be completely isolated . . . without a landline I'm already isolated, without a mobile it would be terrible . . . I spent some time without the mobile, because it failed, and it was a complete chaos! Because I needed it urgently sometimes and my children needed me and there was no place to call me, only by intuition I called them sometimes and they were looking for me desperately! (Rosa, 34 years)

Mobiles are their main form of connection to the world beyond the housing estate, at least during the working week, as Pepa (36 years) told us: "With the mobile I feel connected to the world, without it I feel isolated."

Beyond the typical association between males and technology, especially new technology (Faulkner, 2001; Wajcman, 2000), the primacy of mothers' use in relation to mobile phones was even acknowledged by their partners:

> When my wife is at home [the mobile phone] is always there, and when she goes out she takes it, it's always with her. I've never carried the mobile [laughs] . . . only when I go out with her, then I carry it . . . but only in order to answer it, because they are always calling her. (Jonathan, 34 years)

The possession of mobile telephones by mothers does not imply necessarily immobility. Based on previous research (Green, 2002; Ito et al., 2005; Kenyon et al., 2002, 2003; Ling & Haddon, 2001) we could hypothesize that family members, especially mothers in this case, can use mobile phones to enhance their physical mobility outside the home by using the technology to virtually be "at home" while moving about the city.

However, none of the family members interviewed affirmed that they were more "on the move" due to the possession and use of a mobile phone. As Alicia said, "The mobile hasn't changed my routine, because I'm not very good at going out, from one place to the other [laughs]" (Alicia, 40 years old). In practice the family members, and obviously their mobile phones, stay at home. For instance, when asked why they don't use the mobile phone outside the home, Diego, a married 39-year-old father of four, answered:

> [Our mobile phone] is here in the house. It doesn't move. It's as if it was here, fixed. . . . It is the telephone of the house. The telephone does not move from here. We never move it around anyway, because we don't go out.

As Diego said, they don't use the device as a mobile for the simple reason that they "don't go out." We thus see that the causes of spatial immobility (low income, the location of the housing estate on the outskirts of the city, low participation of both women and men in the labor market and in formal education, etc.) are not easily affected by the availability of mobile technologies (Ureta, 2006). Since the causes of limited mobility are structural, simple availability of mobile technology is unlikely to change them. Mobile phones could probably play a role in the alleviation of mobility-related social exclusion, but only as part of major socioeconomic and cultural changes.

Therefore in this specific social context the opposite phenomenon occurs. It is not the device that changes the patterns of mobility due to its "mobile" nature, as could be interpreted from a technological determinist position. On the contrary, it is the constant interactions between social and technical elements, among them the technical characteristics of the devices, which constitute the use and meaning of mobile phones for the users and the relationship of this usage to their physical mobility. In this particular case study, these interactions mean that mobile phones are not used in a "mobile" way. In its everyday practice the device is "translated" (Callon, 1986) into a different technology, a much more common one: a fixed landline telephone.

Cristian, for example, was a married 38-year-old father of four children, whose ages range from 10 to 20 years old. He worked as a receptionist in a military complex near the city center, one hour away by bus from the housing estate, where he has to travel every day. His wife, Andrea, worked as a seamstress in a knitting factory in the west side of the city. For this reason their only mobile phone was very important for managing their family communications, especially with their two youngest children, who arrived home from school earlier than the rest of the family. As a result of this situation, when asked about the mobility of the device, he answered:

> [We use mobile phones] not for what they are, because the mobile is the one that can be located wherever it is. For us the mobile is here, like a fixed line. It does not move from the house. We would not use it otherwise. The mobile is here and if I want to call home, I know it will be always here, even when sometimes we all go out we commonly forget it, and leave it here. One good thing about the mobile phone is that you can call anytime and if I'm out you will still be able to contact me, but we don't use it this way. It is not like a mobile phone for us.

For Cristian, as for many others, in their everyday practice the handset "is not like a mobile phone"; it has become something different: a landline telephone. Even though he recognized the advantages of the mobile phone in terms of mobility ("you can call me anytime and if I'm out you will still contact me") he did not use it this way. At this stage of their family, he and his wife had little need to be reachable while "on the move"; they just needed a fast and reliable way to know that their children had arrived home safely.

The relationship between mobile phones and physical mobility is not very different from that observed when landline telephones reached homes in the first half of the twentieth century (De Sola Pool, 1977; Fischer, 1992; Marvin, 1988). As it happened then, in most of the cases, what we found was only a partial replacement of some physical mobility by the use of the phone, both at micro and macro level.

On the one hand, in the case of the micro-movements, or journeys in local areas mainly by foot, the possession of mobile telephones diminishes the need to go out of the flats to use public pay phones.

> Before [mobile telephones] communication was not so fast, so direct. Then you had to take time, for example if you did not have a telephone, the [public] telephone was to 2 or 3 blocks away and I had to go there. It was a waste of time as going to call and coming back here takes at least 10 or 15 minutes. Not now, now you use the mobile phone. How much does it take?—2 or 3 seconds to look for the number, to dial [the number] and already you are in communication with another person. (Jonathan, 34 years old)

On the other hand, the use of mobile telephones allows them to save some macro-movements, or movements outside the local areas, commonly involving the use of motorized means of transport, especially avoidance of trips that would have been unnecessary, through the communication and coordination with nonpresent peers.

> [With mobile telephones] I do not have to go to all the places. For example, this morning a friend called me and it saved me a trip! [laughs]. I didn't go and I saved time, because if I had gone there, I wouldn't have found her. It would have been a problem because going there and coming back [takes time], I would have got here late. (Johanna, 50 years)

But this particular translation of the device is not necessarily fixed. As Marianne de Laet and Annemarie Mol demonstrated in their study of the Zimbabwe Bush Pump (2000), technology, especially when it is moved from one environment to another, is fluid, "its boundaries are vague and moving rather than being clear or fixed" (p. 225). Mobile phones were fluid in their translation as landline telephones in the housing estate at the time of this study, and they can be fluid again in the future if the environment changes, especially if there is an increasing integration of these groups into a kind of urban life that requires higher degrees of physical mobility.

This situation can be observed in the case of Ramon, married 39-year-old father of four who worked as a taxi driver. Due to the nature of his work, which obviously required constant physical mobility, he was "on the move" most of the day in different areas of Santiago, especially in the city center. This situation made communication with his family difficult, especially with his wife, who did not work and stayed at home most of the day. He therefore bought a mobile phone in order to be always reachable in case of need.

> They can reach me. To reach me is to have me present at the minute I am needed; this is what is important. My work [forces me] to go to many places, [but if my family need me] they do 'pum' [he mimics someone calling and talking through mobile phone] and there I am. That is to say that, if Alejandra [his wife] solves the problem she says to me 'listen Ramon, you know, things are going well' or when things go wrong 'listen to me, you know, you must come back to us now.'

One interesting point in Ramon's case was that his family had one handset. So when he took the mobile phone within him, his wife and kids had to call from one of the public phones in the housing estate. Here the constant physical mobility of one member provided a good reason to use the mobile phone as it was designed, as a mobile device, even if this use precluded its use as a fixed telephone for the household.

Both examples show us how mobile phones are fluid devices, technologies that "originally born to be mobile may change, when the need arises, in fixed technologies" (Fortunati, 2001, p. 87) and the other way around. It is the practical use of the device as mobile or fixed that establishes its degree of mobility. Only when the phone is needed as mobile does it become one; otherwise, it is translated only as a landline phone, as Ruben recognizes:

> [The mobility of the device] it's not so important. For people who use them, who work with them, for them it is important. [If] he has a job and he needs to have a telephone, so they can localize him wherever they are. They need to know where he is, [but] not for me. The telephone we bought is the telephone we leave here, in the house. [For me] it is not important to be mobile, to be [always] findable, no. (Ruben, 36 years old)

In summary, we can see that mobility depends on much more complex circumstances and characteristics than the mere disposition of certain mobile technologies. Therefore, the influences and effects that the use of devices has on physical mobility have to be seen in a much wider context that includes not only the aspects directly related to mobile use, but the diversity of elements related to the everyday life of individuals in urban societies.

CONCLUSIONS

There appear to be no important relationships between the use of mobile phones by the members of families studied and their everyday physical mobility. This lack of a strong relationship can be explained, at least partially, by two key factors: the very limited use of the mobile devices by the households studied, and the structural constraints that limit their everyday spatial mobility.

On the one hand, even though that they recognized mobile phones as a key resource for management of communications in their new living environment, this perception was not matched by a frequent use of their handsets. Given the relatively high costs of service, they were forced to develop certain strategies to keep the phone in use without expending too much on it. These strategies helped them to "win the fierce battle to keep a mobile in permanent operation" (Slater & Kwami, 2005, p. 10), but at the cost of reduced quality and depth of their communications. Mobile communication for them was not the natural replacement of their former face-to-face communication, but a poor succedaneum for situations of specific need. In order to properly communicate, they still had to have face-to-face conversations.

On the other hand, everyday mobility of these families cannot be easily affected by the mere availability of a mobile technology, even if hypothetically these families could use them more freely. To ease the structural constraints, and subsequently to increase their everyday mobility, general improvements in the conditions of life of these families are needed, especially greater inclusion in Santiago's urban society (higher incomes, higher educational enrolment, greater integration of women in the labor market, better access to means of transport and urban infrastructure, etc.).

In this context it seems right to ask, what is the need for mobile phones if they are not used in a "mobile" way? What we found here, and in accordance with other studies (Fortunati, 2001; Lasen, 2005), is that above all mobile phones create accessibility over distance, especially in a time of need. This connectivity is not between increasingly mobile "urban nomads," but between people who live their lives in a more or less limited number of fixed localities and need a fast and dependable way to be in contact with each other. As shown in the previous section, this situation makes them practically and symbolically translate their mobile phones into landline telephones, because this is the communication technology that they need at this stage in their development.

Although our analysis cannot claim to be representative of any general population, and more research on the subject is needed, we can conclude from the analysis presented here that the use of the mobile phone by the members of these families clearly shows a new face of their still incomplete integration within contemporary Santiago's society. For these families, mobile phone space is not the space of mobile freedom that advertising images and marketing campaigns present. It is a contested space, a space of inequalities and exclusions, as much as other spaces of the city can be. It is an unequal space where these families are situated, but over which they have little control or autonomy. Their immobility and exclusion in concrete urban space have a parallel in the space of mobile phone communications. They are there—on the housing estate, with their mobile telephone handsets—but their capabilities to move both in physical and/or communicational ways appear limited and constrained: always waiting for someone to come or, in this case, call.

NOTES

1. Like Brazilian *favelas* or Argentinean *villas miseria*, *campamentos* are neighborhoods made of low-quality housing, characterized by an illegal occupancy of land, and commonly located, but not always, in the outskirts of cities.

2. Such as less available money to spend on public transport, little access to car and other means of private mobility, a location in areas with little access to the networks of transport, little integration of women to the labor market, etc.

3. That means that the mobile subscriber does not pay for incoming calls, just for the ones that he/she made.

4. One interesting point to make here is the almost inexistence of text messaging in the communicative practices of the individuals under study. Only two people mentioned text messaging as something that they usually do, while most of the people didn't even mention this practice when they were asked about how they deal with the costs involved in using the telephone. There are many possible causes for this lack of use (literacy limitations, antiquity of the devices, etc.), but it is interesting to note the difference with more developed societies or other developing societies, like the Philippines (Pertierra et al., 2002),

in which text messaging is by far the most popular option to avoid the high expenses of using mobile phones.

REFERENCES

Aakhus, M. 2003. Understanding information and communication infrastructure in everyday life: Struggling with communication-at-a-distance. In *Machines that become us, The social context of personal communications technology*, eds. J. Katz and M. Aakhus, pp. 27–42. New Brunswick, NJ, and London: Transaction.

Adam, B. 1990. *Time and social theory*. Cambridge: Polity Press.

Barrantes, R., Galperin, H., Agüero, A., and Molinari, A. 2006. *Asequibilidad de los servicios de telefonía móvil en América Latina*: Montevideo: Dialogo Regional sobre Sociedad de la Información (DIRSI)—International Development Research Centre (IDRC).

Bauman, Z. 1998. *Globalization, The human consequences*. New York: Columbia University Press.

Boden, D., and Molotch, L. 1994. The compulsion to proximity. In *NowHere: Space, time and modernity*, eds. R. Friedland, and D. Boden, pp. 257–334. Berkeley: Unversity of California Press.

Brown, N., Green, N., and Harper, R. 2001. *Wireless world, Social and interactional aspects of the mobile age*. London: Springer.

Callon, M. 1986. Some elements of a sociology of translation: Domestication of the scallops and the fishermen of St Brieuc Bay. In *Power, action and belief: A new sociology of knowledge?*, ed. J. Law, pp. 196–223. London: Routledge.

Carroll, J., Howard, S., Peck, J., and Murphy, J. 2002. 'No' to a free mobile: When adoption is not enough. *Proceedings of the 13th Australasian Conference on Information Systems*, Melbourne, Australia, Victoria University.

Cass, N., Shove, E., and Urry, J. 2005. Social exclusion, mobility and access. *Sociological Review* 53(3):539–555.

Church, A., Frost, M., and Sullivan, K. 2000. Transport and social exclusion in London. *Transport Policy* 7:195–205.

De Laet, M., and Mol, A. 2000. The Zimbabwe Bush Pump: Mechanics of a fluid technology. *Social Studies of Science* 30(2):225–263.

De Sola Pool, I., ed. 1977. *The social impact of the telephone*. Cambridge, MA: MIT Press.

Donner, J. 2005. The rules of beeping: Exchanging messages using missed calls on mobile phones in sub-Saharan Africa. *55th Annual Conference of the International Communication Association*, May 26–30, New York.

Espinoza, V. 1999. Social networks among the urban poor: Inequality and integration in a Latin American city. In *Networks in the global village*, ed. B. Wellman, pp. 147–184. Boulder, CO: Westview Press.

Faulkner, W. 2001. The technology question in feminism: A view from feminist technology studies. *Women's Studies International Forum* 24(1):79–95.

Fischer, C. 1992. *America calling, A social history of the telephone to 1940*. Berkeley: University of California Press.

Fortunati, L. 2001. The mobile phone: An identity on the move. *Personal and Ubiquitous Technology* 5(2):85–98.

Fortunati, L. 2002. The mobile phone: Towards new categories of social relations. *Information, Communication and Society* 5(4):513–528.

Glotz, P., Berschi, S., and Locke, C., eds. 2005. *Thumb culture. The meaning of mobile phones for society*. Bielefeld: Transcript Verlag.

Graham, S., and Marvin, S. 2001. *Splintering urbanism. Networked infrastructures, technological mobilities and the urban condition*. New York: Routledge.

Green, N. 2002. On the move: Technology, mobility, and the mediation of social time and space. *The Information Society* 18: 281–292.

Habuchi, I. 2005. Accelerating reflexivity. In *Personal, portable, pedestrian: Mobile phones in Japanese life*, eds. M. Ito, D. Okade, and M. Matsuda, pp. 163–182. Cambridge, MA: MIT Press.

Hannam, K., Sheller, M., and Urry, J. 2006. Editorial: Mobilities, immobilities and moorings. *Mobilities* 1(1):1–22.

Horst, H., and Miller, D. 2006. *The cell phone, An anthroplogy of communication*. London: Berg.

Ito, M., Okabe, D., and Matsuda, M., eds. 2005. *Personal, portable, pedestrian: mobile phones in Japanese life*. Cambridge, MA: MIT Press.

ITU. 2005. *World telecommunications indicators 2005*. Geneva: International Telecommunications Union.

Jakobson, R. 1984. *Ensayos de Lingüística General*. Barcelona: Ariel.

Kasesniemi, E., and Rautiainen, P. 2002. Mobile culture of children and teenagres in Finland. In *Perpetual contact: Mobile Communication, private talk and public performance*, eds. J. Katz and M. Aakhus, pp. 170–192. Cambridge: Cambridge University Press.

Katz, J., ed. 2003. *Machines that become us: The social context of personal communications technologies*. New Brunswick, NJ: Transaction.

Katz, J., and Aakhus, M., eds. 2002. *Perpetual contact. Mobile communication, Private talk, Public performance*. Cambridge: Cambridge University Press.

Kenyon, S., Rafferty, J., and Lyons, G. 2002. Transport and social exclusion: Investigating the possibility of promoting inclusion through virtual mobility. *Journal of Transport Geography* 10(3):207–219.

Kenyon, S., Rafferty, J., and Lyons, G. 2003. Social exclusion and transport in the UK: A role for virtual accesibility in the alleviation of mobility-related exclusion? *Journal of Social Policy* 32(3):317–338.

Larrañaga, O. 2004. Poblacion vulnerable, vivienda patrimonio y vecindario. In *Como ha cambiado la vida de los Chilenos. Analisis comparativo de las condiciones de vida de los hogares con menor bienestar economico (Censos 1992 y 2002)*, eds. J. Ramos, E. Valenzuela, O. Larranaga, P. Medrano, and V. Gubbins, pp. 45–56. Santiago, Chile: Insituto Nacional de Estadisticas (INE) publicaciones.

Lasen, A. 2005. History repeating? A comparison of the launch and uses of fixed and mobile phones. In *Mobile world. Past, present, future*, eds. L. Hammill, and A. Lasen, pp. 29–60. New York: Springer.

Ling, R. 2004. *The mobile connection. The cell phone's impact on society*. London: Elsevier/Morgan Kaufman.

Ling, R., and Haddon, L. 2001. Mobile telephony, mobility and the coordination of everyday life. In *Machines that become us*, eds. J. Katz and M. Aakhus, pp. 245–266. New Brunswick, NJ: Transaction.

Ling, R., and Pedersen, E., ed. 2005. *Mobile communication. Renegotiation of the social sphere*. New York: Springer.

Marvin, C. 1988. *When old technologies were new, Thinking about electric communication in the late nineteenth century*. Oxford: Oxford University Press.

McGuigan, J. 2005. Towards a sociology of the mobile phone. *Human Technology* 1(1):45–57.

Nowotny, H. 1994. *Time. The modern and postmodern experience*. Cambridge: Polity Press.

Nyiri, K. ed. 2005. *A sense of place: The global and the local in mobile communication*. Vienna: Passagen Verlang.

Pertierra, R., Ugarte, E., Pingol, A., Hernandez, J., and Decanay, N. 2002. *TXT-ING selves: Cellphones and Philippine modernity*. Manila: De La Salle University Press.

PNUD. 2006. *Informe de Desarrollo Humano en Chile 2006—Las Nuevas Tecnologías: ¿Un salto al futuro?* Santiago: Programa de las Naciones Unidas para el Desarrollo.

SECTRA. 2002. *Encuesta Origen Destino de Viajes, Santiago 2001—Informe de difusión.* Santiago, Chile: Secretaria de Transportes (SECTRA), Gobierno de Chile.

Slater, D., and Kwami, J. 2005. Embeddedness and escape: Internet and mobile use as poverty reduction strategies in Ghana. In *Working Paper 4,* eds. A. Skuse, and J. Tacchi, pp. 1–16. Adelaide: Information Society Research Group (ISRG).

Ureta, S. 2006. *Machines for living in. Communication technologies and everyday life in times of urban transformation,* PhD thesis. London: London School of Economics.

Urry, J. 2000. *Sociology beyond societies: Mobilities for the twenty-first century.* London: Routledge.

Wajcman, J. 2000. Reflections on gender and technology studies: In what state is the art? *Social Studies of Science* 30(3):447–464.

Wellman, B. 2001. Physical place and cyberspace: The rise of personalized networking. *International Journal of Urban and Regional Research* 25(2):227–252.

Index

Page numbers in *Italics* represent tables.
Page numbers in **Bold** represent figures.